SENTENCED TO DEATH
Saved from the Gallows

SENTENCED TO DEATH

Saved from the Gallows

COLM WALLACE

Waterford City and County
Libraries

SOMERVILLE PRESS

Somerville Press Ltd,
Dromore, Bantry,
Co. Cork, Ireland

First published 2016

Designed by Jane Stark
Typeset in Adobe Garamond Pro
seamistgraphics@gmail.com

ISBN: 978 0 9927364 91

Printed and bound in Spain
by GraphyCems, Villatuerta, Navarra

This book is dedicated to Harry Gleeson,
an innocent man hanged by his own country.
It is also in memory of the
innocent victims mentioned within.

CONTENTS

ACKNOWLEDGEMENTS. 9

INTRODUCTION 11

1. John Hogan. 16

2. Charles Molloy 23

3. William Devereux 30

4. Hannah Flynn. 36

5. Patrick Aylward. 44

6. Denis Leen 52

7. James Murray 62

8. Hannah O'Leary. 71

9. Martin Joyce & Annie Walsh. 78

10. Jane O'Brien 88

11. Elizabeth & Rose Edwards 94

12. Thomas Kelly 101

13. James Tierney (O'Neill). 110

14. Patrick Boylan. 120

15. Mary Somerville 129

16.   Martin Griffin 136

17.   Stephen Murphy 143

18.   Agnes McAdam 150

19.   Daniel Duff 157

20.   John Fanning 164

21.   Mary Agnes Daly 172

22.   Frances Cox 178

23.   Patrick Heffernan 187

24.   William Hopkins 194

25.   Robert Stevenson 200

26.   Denis Foy 209

27.   Thomas O'Rourke 216

28.   James Kelly 222

29.   Shan Mohangi 230

30.   Noel Callan & Michael McHugh 239

AFTERWORD 246

SOURCES 247

ACKNOWLEDGEMENTS

This book has been a long time coming, but it was worth every second. I could not have finished, or even started, without the care and support of my family and friends.

First and foremost, I would like to thank Rebecca for her unlimited patience in putting up with me while I was writing this book. I could not have undertaken this project without her endless support and belief that I could do it.

A heartfelt thanks to Kathleen who kindly proofread this book several times, making it what it is today with positivity and patience.

To Kerry-Anne, Siobhán and Mark, thank you all for the education you gave me growing up and still give me today.

I wish to thank Dónal and Diarmaid who were there when it all started. The two most knowledgeable men I know.

I am indebted to all the teachers who inspired in me a love of knowledge. May O'Neill, Michael O'Neill, Paul Gannon and countless others.

To Teresa and my colleagues, an incredible group with a profound love of learning and education.

I am thankful also to Declan, Philip, Andrew, Alice, Gerrard, Michael, William, Darragh, Paul, Gerard, Marie, Peter, Frank, James, Harry, John, Wes, Dermot, the Sheridans, the Griffins (my second family!), Michelle, Claire, Brendan and many others. Whenever I have needed them, they have been there.

To all the Wallaces and Fitzgeralds in Ireland and further afield, and to everyone in beautiful Renvyle by the sea.

A special thank you to the staff of the National Archives who provided invaluable help with my research.

The photos in this book were supplied by the National Library of Ireland and by author, Patrick Kelleher. A sincere thank you to both for their kindness.

I would like to express my sincere gratitude to Andrew Russell and the Somerville Press for immediately seeing the potential in this project and working tirelessly to make it a success.

Finally, I would like to thank my mother and father for their unending love, support and encouragement. Without their selfless dedication to my education, I would not be writing these words.

INTRODUCTION

"Although I have always objected to the death penalty, there is no other way that I know of that ordered conditions can be restored in this country."

W.T. COSGRAVE, Taoiseach, 1922

"The fruit of my experience has this bitter aftertaste: that I do not now believe that any one of the hundreds of executions I carried out has in any way acted as a deterrent against future murder. Capital punishment, in my view, achieved nothing except revenge."

ALBERT PIERREPOINT, Irish state executioner, 1974

There can be few more chilling phrases to hear than "I sentence you to death". In the last century many Irish prisoners, found guilty of the crime of murder, saw a judge place a black cap on his head and heard those immortal words being uttered. For some of those prisoners, the sentence was carried out and they were brought to the gallows and hanged. More often than not, however, the condemned prisoner received word that their sentence had been commuted to one of life imprisonment. Sometimes the reprieve came shortly after the sentence. In many cases, however, the prisoner languished in a condemned cell and lived with the reality of the death penalty until days, or even hours, before the execution was due to be carried out. These reprieves were decided by the government and given for a multitude of different reasons. It is hard to think of a more important decision.

Ireland has had a long and bitter history of capital punishment. In the centuries before we became a nation, the British had used the death penalty as a weapon to quell the dissent of the restless Irish population. Pádraig Pearse, Roger Casement, Fr John Murphy and Robert Emmet are amongst the Irish rebels who were hanged, shot and beheaded. The last man publicly hanged in England was also an Irishman. Michael Barrett, a member of the Fenian movement from Fermanagh, was hanged in 1868 for his part in planting a bomb that killed twelve Londoners in an attempt to free IRA prisoners. His execution was observed by thousands of British civilians cheering jubilantly while singing "Rule, Britannia!"

It is therefore not surprising that the Irish rebels responsible for the independence of the country had originally planned that they would do away with the hangman altogether, when their time came to write the laws of the state. The original draft of the Irish Constitution did not actually enact the death penalty, an unusual position in an era when it was used in almost every corner of the earth. However, the impending Civil War soon changed minds. The newly-formed Irish Government decided that hanging should be kept on the statute books in the case of the most serious of crimes so as to preserve law and order. Many Irish citizens still viewed the punishment with distaste, however.

It may have been because of this attitude that an Irish hangman was never employed. The government relied instead on a succession of English executioners to arrive to our shores and perform the grim task. The Pierrepoints were the most prominent of the executioners used and they often found themselves being met off the boat by large crowds of Irish people jeering and hissing. Albert Pierrepoint himself later remarked that he carried a gun in his pocket on his Irish missions, such was the level of hostility he faced from the native population. The IRA even plotted to kidnap the notorious hangman at one stage, and would have done so if they had been able to intercept him on his way to the execution chamber in Mountjoy. The sight of an Englishman being paid by the Irish Government to kill Irish citizens was unpalatable to many, it seems, even if most of these citizens were known to have committed unspeakable crimes.

The Cumann na nGaedheal government, having decided to implement capital punishment, used it freely during the Civil War. They showed little mercy to captured republicans, with Minister for Home Affairs Kevin O'Higgins remarking that it was not "going to be a draw with a replay in the autumn". Eighty-one republicans in total were executed by Irish firing squads in the years 1922 and 1923. Incredibly, this is more than three times the number executed by the British during the War of Independence. The Irish executions included such leading republicans as Joe McKelvey, Liam Mellows and Rory O'Connor. The executions came at the point of a gun in a firing squad and occurred in places as varied as Tralee, Tuam, Waterford and Ennis. This was to maximise the impact on local republicans and act as a warning against supporting the anti-Treaty IRA. Six IRA men were also executed by the government during the Second World War. Between the years of 1923 and 1954, twenty-nine people were also executed by the state for "common murder".

Out of the twenty-nine individuals hanged in Mountjoy, all but one was at the hand of a member of the famous Pierrepoint family. The unfortunate individual was held in the condemned cell where the executioner viewed them through a small hole in the wall, carefully calculating their measurements so as to ensure the rope would be the desired length. When it was done properly, the prisoner's neck would be broken and their death instantaneous. If the rope was too short, however, the prisoner would endure prolonged strangulation. If it was too long, there was a chance of decapitation. It was generally a rapid demise, apart from a couple of distressing exceptions. In 1901, when Ireland remained under British rule, Timothy Cadogan was sentenced to death for the shooting dead of land agent William Bird in Bantry, Co. Cork. Due to a lack of care by the hangman, James Billington, the rope was not of the desired length. Instead of his neck being broken, Cadogan suffered a long, agonising death by strangulation, leaving the spectators deeply distressed.

The majority of men and women sentenced to death were more fortunate, however, receiving an eleventh-hour reprieve instead of the noose. What was it that made the state decide in some cases to let justice run its course, while in other instances to alter the sentence to penal servitude for life? Far from being a lifetime, these sentences generally ran for between three and twelve years and the prisoner was then released back into society. So who got reprieved, and why? The answers are complex and illogical in many cases. Women almost exclusively received a reprieve, the execution of a member of the fairer sex considered to be distasteful, regardless of the crime. The one exception to this rule is Annie Walsh of Fedamore, Co. Limerick. Walsh was hanged in 1925 for conspiring with Michael Talbot to murder her husband. This book will describe crimes committed by other women which were pre-meditated and violent. Annie Walsh's crime does not stand out and leads one to wonder why exactly she was judged more harshly than the rest.

Another anomaly is the case of Waterford man William O'Shea. In 1943 he and his friend, Tommy White, conspired to murder O'Shea's wife, Maureen. White duly shot and killed the unfortunate woman on the roadway. When arrested, White immediately told the Gardaí of the plot the two men had formed. He was undoubtedly responsible for the shooting but found unfit to plead by reason of insanity. William O'Shea had certainly known about the killing in advance but pleaded not guilty as he had not fired any shot. It was not enough to save him, however, and he was hanged for his part in plotting the murder. In the same year, Martin Griffin of Galway also murdered his wife. He viciously attacked her with a hatchet in a drunken rage after an apparent argument over inheritance. Griffin admitted the crime but pleaded not guilty due to intoxication. He was also found guilty and sentenced to death, before being granted a last-minute reprieve. Based on those two cases from the same era, it is difficult to know why the state felt O'Shea deserved the ultimate penalty while Griffin's case warranted mercy.

Perhaps there is the greatest injustice involved in capital punishment, the frailty in the legal system where two people are punished differently for an almost identical crime. The execution of Harry Gleeson leaves an even bitterer aftertaste. Gleeson was hanged in 1941 for the murder of his neighbour, Moll McCarthy in New Inn, Co. Tipperary. The trial was unsatisfactory and subsequent examination of the case shows a conspiracy of sorts against the unfortunate Gleeson. The real perpetrators were said to be powerful members of the local community who used Gleeson as an easy scapegoat. Gleeson went to his death despite being completely innocent of the despicable crime. After many years of pressure, Gleeson was finally exonerated in 2015, the only person executed who ever received a pardon by the Irish state. Cold comfort indeed.

Conversely, there are many arguments in favour of the death penalty in the most extreme cases of murder. Like any country, Ireland has been home to some extremely evil individuals over the years whose crimes sickened the nation and made many feel that they deserved no better than the gallows. The thirty-one victims in this book were all innocent individuals, ranging in age from a few minutes old to 83 years, who were shown no mercy. They were beaten, strangled, poisoned, shot, drowned, burned, stabbed, tortured or even decapitated by their murderers, many in assaults which their killer planned and afterwards went to great lengths to conceal. In 1951, when the threat of the death penalty hung over the heads of convicted killers, the homicide rate in Ireland was a mere seven. In 2011, just sixty years later, capital punishment had become a distant memory and the homicide rate had exploded to fifty-two. Did the hangman's noose also act as a deterrent to many contemplating a murder?

One hundred and sixty-four men and women were executed in the Republic of Ireland in the twentieth century. There is no question that many of them were deeply violent individuals who committed horrendous crimes against innocent people. An eye for an eye can be an attractive prospect. The question remains however; do you trust the government to decide who should live, and who should die?

JOHN HOGAN

"Christ, you have me shot."

1922 will go down as one of the most violent and tragic years in Irish history. The Civil War was a conflict amongst Irish men and women that caused neighbour to turn against neighbour and created divisions in many rural communities that would take generations to heal. James Cullinan was one victim of the bloody conflict. He was shot dead on Hallowe'en night 1922. It was one of three murders in the country to occur on that single day, further evidence of the widespread and mindless violence that was sweeping the newly-formed nation. The British forces had pulled out of Ireland just months before, leaving a heavily-armed Irish population with precious little law and order to oversee them. This turbulent period saw an explosion in the crime rate and was exploited by some to settle old scores. The shooting dead of James Cullinan over a trivial quarrel showed the chaotic nature of the times and the lengths some people were prepared to go to defend their family's honour. Like many of the murders that occurred in 1922, however, the authorities would not catch up with the killer for over a year due to the lack of law enforcement. In more peaceful times, however, the perpetrator would be caught, tried and sentenced to death for the crime.

James Cullinan was about 40 years of age and from the village of Kilnamona, just outside Ennis, Co. Clare. His father had died just weeks before Hallowe'en 1922, leaving James to work on the farm with his two brothers. The three remaining Cullinans were hard workers, keeping livestock and growing crops. They also owned a nearby bog, from which they cut turf to heat their small cottage. James was described as a strong and proud man, known to be a good athlete and hurler who did not suffer fools gladly. In the years leading up to 1921, the Irish justice system had almost collapsed. This left local Sinn Féin courts as the only arbitrators of the law in rural areas, although they were not recognised by many. Early in 1922, James Cullinan, an ex-IRA man himself, had been summoned to a Sinn Féin court to answer questions about an argument he had been having with his uncle about inheritance. Shots had been fired outside his uncle's house and the local community was bitterly divided about the matter. The Hogan family, who lived in the nearby townland of Tullassa, had taken the side of Cullinan's uncle in the dispute. James Cullinan had attacked one of the Hogans in Ennis for this reason. The Hogans were well connected within the IRA, however, and this caused Cullinan to be summoned to court. He completely ignored the order and did not turn up for the appointed sitting. This bold act marked him out as an enemy to some within the republican forces.

On 31 October 1922, Cullinan went to his bog and gathered turf for the long winter ahead. He put the turf on his horse and set off home at about 4 p.m. He walked towards home alongside the animal and was almost at his destination when he met John Hogan. Hogan, alternatively called Seán or Jack, was a 22-year-old captain in the "Irregulars" or the anti-Treaty IRA and a son of the man who had been attacked by James Cullinan. He was in charge of the IRA's active service unit, who at this time were still fighting the elected government of the country. It was therefore unsurprising that John Hogan had a rifle on his person. Cullinan and Hogan had a less than harmonious relationship and a confrontation quickly ensued between the two men.

Mary O'Donnell, a neighbour of Cullinan, was outside her uncle's home when she heard from the road what sounded like a gunshot, not uncommon in Ireland at the time. She did not move until she heard a second gunshot, at which point she ran out to investigate. O'Donnell saw John Hogan, whom she knew well, standing at her gate. He said to her, "Mary, come down to Seamus Cullinan. I'm after shooting him and I do not know if he's badly injured or not." Mary did as requested and was met with the sight of James Cullinan lying critically injured on the road. He was bleeding heavily and appeared to have been shot at close range with a rifle. John Hogan was standing nearby, holding a firearm and pacing anxiously. He opened Cullinan's vest and showed Mary O'Donnell the wound in the right side of the chest. He then asked her to say an Act of Contrition in Cullinan's ear, which she did after some hesitation. Cullinan was, at this point, haemorrhaging blood but still alive. The injured man said to Hogan "Jack, why did you do it?" Hogan did not answer him directly but told Mrs O'Donnell that he and Cullinan had got into an argument and he had shot Cullinan when he had attempted to take his rifle from him. Mary then asked Cullinan himself what had happened, but he only answered that he was dying. Hogan seemed upset and asked Mrs O'Donnell to fetch her neighbour, Michael Hickey. Hogan himself ran to a neighbouring house belonging to the McMahon family. He told them to get their horse and cart ready to bring Cullinan to hospital, as he was seriously injured.

Michael Hickey arrived quickly on the scene when told the news. Cullinan still lay on the road but Hogan had at this point fled and was nowhere to be seen. As was the norm at the time, a priest was the first man sent for as it was felt that spiritual needs came before medical ones. Fr Patrick Murphy, the curate of the neighbouring village of Kilmayley, arrived on the scene. He must have been a man ahead of his time as he arrived on a motorbike, a rare luxury in the Ireland of the early 1920s. Cullinan was carried to the house of Mary O'Donnell's uncle, William Hickey, where he was given the Last Rites by Fr Murphy. Murphy then took a deposition from him. Murphy would later say that the bed Cullinan lay on was saturated with blood but the injured man was perfectly conscious. Cullinan complained of having cold feet and begged the priest to fetch him a hot-water bottle. When he returned, the victim told him that the bullet had gone "right through him", and identified Hogan as being the shooter.

Murphy asked if there had been a row between the two men. Cullinan answered that there had not. He stated "As I was coming along the road with a horse and creel of turf, Jack Hogan appeared behind a fence with a rifle. (He said) Put them up and I'll make you let my father pass the next time you meet him. I put the horse on the road and I faced the fence where Hogan was standing." At this point, Hogan told his neighbour twice to "put them up and advance", but Cullinan refused. Hogan then called Cullinan "some ugly names" before attempting to get over the fence. When he could not do so, Hogan aimed his rifle at Cullinan and fired it twice without warning. One shot missed its intended target. The second went through the right side of Cullinan's chest, causing him to immediately fall on the road. After this statement, the priest called an ambulance. Cullinan begged those present "leave me as I am. Leave me die in the bed." They refused, moving him to the ambulance although blood was pumping out of the wound. Their hopes of saving Cullinan's life were in vain however, and he died on his way to the hospital "in the arms of Fr Murphy".

Cullinan's inquest was held in Ennis District Hospital three days after his murder. His brothers, Martin and Lot, identified the dead man. They added that their brother had no political involvement whatsoever, although their family had become embroiled in a disagreement with their uncle over inheritance recently which had since turned nasty. Dr John MacClancy of Ennis also appeared, telling the court that Cullinan had died due to shock caused by loss of blood. He stated that the bullet had entered Cullinan's chest, leaving a small wound. It had not lacerated but had exited through a larger jagged hole in his back. His condition had been hopeless and he had succumbed to his injuries about an hour later.

The jury also listened to the evidence of Mary O'Donnell, Fr Murphy and Michael Hickey and found that Cullinan had been murdered unlawfully. John Hogan, however, had absconded after the attack and was nowhere to be found to face the charges. He would remain on the loose for two months. He was finally apprehended by the authorities on 31 December 1922, and held in custody until the Civil War was over. His trial, along with a plethora of other Civil War murders, finally began at the Dublin County Commission in November 1923.

John Hogan appeared on the stand and told the court that he was the son of a small farmer from just outside Kilnamona. He worked as a railway fitter but was also a seasoned IRA activist and had been well known to the authorities before this trial. His account of the tragedy differed slightly from that given by James Cullinan. Hogan, described as being of respectable appearance, claimed that on that Hallowe'en he had been drinking tea in his father's house with some of his comrades for about an hour. He collected his rifle and ammunition and left to go across the fields to visit some other IRA volunteers. When he got to the road he saw James Cullinan coming along with a horse. When Cullinan was twenty-five yards away, Hogan stood in front of him and shouted "Halt, put your hands up." Cullinan refused, asking, "What is this for?" The accused then apparently told Cullinan that from that point on when he met Hogan's father, Thomas (69), on the road he must let him alone about his business as he was "an inoffensive and delicate man". Cullinan, despite having a rifle pointed at him, allegedly responded that he didn't care about Hogan and his father and he would do what he liked to them. Hogan told him angrily that he would not. Cullinan began moving towards Hogan, getting within six yards. Hogan said, "For God's sake stand, or I will fire." Cullinan told him to shoot away and Hogan shot up in the air. Hogan then took a step back before Cullinan sprang towards him. Cullinan then grabbed the top of the rifle and pulled it down. John Hogan claimed he then attempted to shoot Cullinan in the leg for his own protection but hit his chest instead. Cullinan fell and gasped, "Christ, you have me shot." Hogan answered, "I could not help it, why did you try to grab my rifle?"

Hogan apologised to the court for the killing and said that he had no intention of meeting Cullinan with the gun. He claimed to have been afraid that Cullinan, a bigger man than he, would take the gun and shoot him with it. His counsel pleaded with the court that Hogan had been in fear of his life, and the shooting was "entirely unintentional". Despite the fact that Hogan had halted Cullinan and pointed a shotgun at him, they asked the jury to find him guilty of homicide in self-defence. The jury seemed to have some sympathy with this version of events as they returned after fifty minutes with a verdict of guilty, but without malice aforethought. They strongly recommended the prisoner to mercy. The judge was unimpressed. He refused to accept the verdict, reminding the jury that an armed Hogan had admitted to halting Cullinan and trying to shoot him in the leg, showing his intention of committing violence against him. The jury again retired and this time returned with a straightforward guilty verdict. Hogan was asked if there was any reason the death penalty should not be pronounced. He replied, "An IRA officer (like him) could have better evidence but my superior officers are in prison. As regards Father Murphy's statement, I could prove that he has an old prejudice against me." It was to no avail. The judge donned the black cap, sentencing Hogan to be hanged on 30 November.

It was reported in the newspapers that week that the government had a problem. Ireland had no official hangman to execute their first condemned prisoners, John Hogan amongst them. John Ellis, the English hangman, was contacted and offered £15 per execution as his fee. He travelled over on 29 November 1922, to officiate in the first hanging in the new state, that of William Downes. Downes was a Dubliner who had shot policeman Thomas Fitzgerald during a robbery. Justice was mercilessly swift, the execution occurring just over a month after the murder. Ellis' services would not be required in the case of John Hogan, however. Hogan, who was due to die the day after William Downes, was instead reprieved just over a week before the execution was fixed. He was given a sentence of penal servitude for life instead.

Hogan spent a turbulent time in jail. He was transferred to Portlaoise Prison in February 1924, where he immediately hatched an escape plan. He and fourteen other convicts attempted to get four civilians to aid them in absconding. Their plan was foiled but the prisoner then went on hunger strike for two weeks. He was generally found to have an uncooperative and sullen demeanour towards prison officers. He refused for long periods to wear prison clothes and was confined to his cell for five months solitary confinement until he agreed to do so. His health also suffered, causing him to spend several months in the infirmary. Throughout the 1920s, several attempts were made on Hogan's behalf to secure his release, but each was met with refusal. Finally, after nine year in prison, John Hogan was released from custody in October 1932.

CHARLES MOLLOY

"We struggled for a second or two and then a shot went off."

In 1923, a crime was committed in broad daylight on a busy Irish road with several eyewitnesses. Despite the overwhelming evidence about the identity of the culprits, the case took nearly three years to come before the courts. Ireland's justice system was in its infancy and stretched beyond its capabilities. The newly-formed Civic Guard were struggling under the weight of a lawless society in the aftermath of the bloody Civil War. Added to that was the fact that a substantial number of Irish people still refused to recognise the authority of the Gardaí in the early 1920s. When this case did come before the courts, the public would be shocked and appalled at the senseless nature of the crime.

After the handover of power, "King's County" was renamed Offaly. The west of this county is synonymous with rich peatland and the quiet road from Ballycumber to Ferbane is no different. In February 1923, however, it would be the scene of a fatal confrontation.

Charles Molloy was 19 years old and a labourer from Derrynagun, a small townland on the outskirts of Ballycumber. His father had also been a labourer but had died some years before, leaving his wife to raise her family of seven children in their three-room cottage. Molloy and his brother Peter (16) had grown up in troubled times with no father figure. The brothers had republican sympathies but they were also involved in common criminality in what was a lawless period of Irish history. The

Molloys were friendly with an older man, Michael Coyne, who was from the neighbouring townland of Pollagh. The trio came up with a plan to make what they thought would be easy money. They picked Monday 12 February 1923, as the day where they would carry out a robbery on local delivery driver John Finlay. They planned to seize Finlay's consignment of alcohol and any other valuables. They did not foresee any resistance, assuming in the most dangerous of times that the sight of a gun would be enough for the driver. The three conspirators borrowed a rifle from a friend the night before and hid it in some bushes. They were well aware of where Finlay's route would take him and they picked a disused stable overlooking the "High Road" at Leabeg, two miles from Ballycumber, to wait for the delivery to pass that way. The would-be raiders assembled at 11.30 a.m. They all wore trench coats and caps, a common attire for IRA members at the time. Charles Molloy was also armed with the rifle.

At about 1 p.m. that afternoon, John McCormack was fencing in Leabeg. He was a farm labourer employed by a local man named Boland. McCormack saw three men waiting in the stable, which was situated in one of Boland's fields. He was surprised at their presence but greeted the men. Both Molloys and Coyne returned the salute. Instead of trying to conceal their criminal plans, however, the raiders openly boasted to McCormack that it was their intention to rob a D.E. Williams' van, which they knew would be passing that way in the afternoon. They said they were going to rob it to get alcohol. McCormack, shocked at this admission, simply replied that it was a soft day. He then returned to his work, unsure if the men had been telling the truth or idly boasting. The three young men waited in the stable for about an hour. At that point, McCormack spotted a van coming around the corner on the main road. He then saw all three men leave the stable and jog down in the direction of the road. He was eighty yards away and had a clear view of the unfolding incident.

John (Jack) Finlay was aged 26 and from a large family in Killeenmore, four miles south of Tullamore. The powerfully-built Gaelic footballer had spent much of his youth in the IRA and had been arrested by the British during the War of Independence, spending a considerable amount of time in prison. With freedom won, Finlay had avoided taken sides in the bitter Civil War, instead gaining honest employment as a delivery man for Mister D.E. Williams. D.E. Williams Ltd was a popular distillery company in Offaly's largest town Tullamore, twelve miles east of Leabeg. The company manufactured whiskey and distributed it throughout Ireland and beyond. Finlay had set off that morning as usual with his consignment, which also included bread, in the cart behind his horse.

As Finlay rounded the corner beside Boland's farm just after 2 p.m., the three men watched his approach. When he came nearer their vantage point they rushed down, approaching the van and holding up their hands to indicate that they wanted him to stop. Finlay had little choice but to do so. Charles Molloy then produced a rifle from under his coat and pointed it at Finlay, commanding that he hand over any valuables from within the van. The strongly-built ex-soldier did not meekly accede to their request as expected, however. Instead he refused to give the highwaymen any of the goods, disembarking and standing bravely in front of them on the road. A "general wrangle" ensued and Finlay pushed one of the men. At this point, a horrified McCormack witnessed Charles Molloy level the rifle at Finlay and shoot him through the heart at point-blank range. Finlay managed to turn around and take a couple of steps towards the cart before falling down. He was dead within seconds. The three men panicked and forgot about the cargo. They left empty-handed, running across the bog in the direction of Derrynagun.

Just before the shot had rung out, a man named Patrick Guinan had driven around the corner and was just a couple of yards from the incident. He saw John Finlay attempting to push back the aggressors before Charles Molloy raised the rifle and shot at the unfortunate van driver. Guinan, from the neighbouring townland of Lemanaghan, was able to recognise all three of the assailants. Edward Cornelly, who had been working on a nearby bog, also heard the shots and rushed to the scene to find Finlay lying dead by the side of his van. Just after 3 p.m., a number of schoolchildren came upon the horrific scene and ran away in tears. They informed the local postman, Martin Brett, who was well known to Finlay. Brett arrived on the scene and called his friend by name but there was no response. John Finlay was taken directly to hospital. He was dead on arrival, however. Death was due to shock and haemorrhage caused by a bullet wound to the chest which struck his heart.

The death of the hard-working and well-liked Jack Finlay caused much revulsion and anger in the Offaly area and his funeral was quickly organised by his IRA ex-colleagues. Astonishingly, despite several eyewitnesses able to connect the three men with the shooting, the conspirators were only apprehended two and a half years later. In September 1925, Charles Molloy was finally arrested at his sister's house. He was brought to the station in Ferbane where he told the Gardaí that his recollection of 12 February 1923, was that he had been at home until the evening. His mother had been in bed and there was no one else present. At 6 p.m. he had gone into his local village of Ballycumber, staying until around 8 p.m. Molloy claimed that he had then gone home and immediately retired to bed. He said he had never used a rifle and that he did not know John Finlay. He also insisted that he had not seen Michael Coyne on that day or any day since. Michael Coyne's version of events differed, however. He told the guards that he and the Molloys had organised the hold-up to steal money and drink. Coyne admitted to being present when Charles Molloy shot the delivery man.

The case eventually came to trial in Dublin Central Criminal Court on 25 January 1926. The delay in the court case can be partially explained by the court having seventeen murder cases pending in that particular month, most going back a year or more. The defendant, Charles Molloy, was now 22 years of age. As he was the man who held and shot the rifle, it was he who was indicted on a murder charge. He pleaded not guilty to the charge. Peter Molloy and Michael Coyne, the other two men who had attempted to rob Finlay, had a *"Nolle Prosequi"* entered against them by the state on the charge of murder, instead pleading guilty to the lesser charge of attempted robbery.

Since his arrest, Charles Molloy had changed his story. Faced with Coyne's incriminating statement, Molloy now admitted that he had been in Leabeg at the time of the incident with his brother and Coyne. He asserted that the men's initial plan had been to rob the van but they had decided against it at the last minute. They walked down to the road, standing in front of the horse and cart. Molloy raised his hand and asked "Have you any cigarettes?" Finlay answered in the negative. Molloy claimed that he responded with "I will take your word" and said it was all right. Finlay allegedly replied "Let it be all right." Molloy stated that he then turned to walk away. He was ten yards away when Finlay rushed at him and attempted to take the rifle. "We struggled for a second or two and then a shot went off. I did not level the rifle to shoot Finlay, nor did I fire it."

Molloy was cross-examined and asked why he had brought a loaded rifle to Boland's farm if he had not meant to use it. He said that it was for protection and that the shooting was an accident. He thought the sight of the rifle would be enough for the driver and that he would not have to use it. Molloy further said that he had lied about his movements on the day in his initial statement to the Gardaí as he did not think that they had the authority to arrest him, even if some of them were in uniform. Peter Molloy corroborated his brother's evidence saying that the two men had been in holds and a shot had rang out which struck Finlay. The prosecution disagreed, describing the case as one of cold-blooded murder, a premeditated attack on a working man for selfish gain. They also pointed to two eyewitness accounts of Charles Molloy deliberately raising the gun and aiming it at the unfortunate delivery man. Charles Molloy's defence team told the court that Michael Coyne was the real villain of the piece and that Molloy, a naive teenager, had been led into the situation by the older man. Previous to this incident they alleged that Charles had never held a rifle before. They pleaded with the jury to accept that the gun had gone off accidentally when Molloy panicked after being tackled by Finlay.

Whether or not the jury believed the story, they had no recourse but to convict a man who brought a loaded rifle to rob a delivery man "for drink" and ended up shooting him dead. They took just thirty-five minutes to find Charles Molloy guilty of murder, although they added a strong recommendation to mercy on account of his youth and "the unsettled state of the country at the time". Molloy was asked if there was any reason why the sentence of death should not be passed on him, to which he replied, "No." Justice Sullivan thus sentenced Molloy to death for the crime, scheduled for 24 February.

Molloy's counsel applied for leave to appeal the sentence on the grounds that Molloy had abandoned his intention of robbery and was walking away when he was tackled by Finlay. They argued that this was a case of manslaughter and the jury had not been given the option to give that verdict. The leave was refused and the sentence upheld. On 19 February, however, the sentence was commuted, the order being signed by Timothy Healy, the first Governor-General of the Free State. Michael Coyne received five-years' penal servitude for attempted robbery. Peter Molloy, a minor at the time of the offence, received just a six-month prison sentence. Charles Molloy could consider himself extremely fortunate to receive a commutation. The 1920s were a bloody time and the government would execute fifteen civilians in that decade, over half the state's eventual total of twenty-nine. Molloy served just over six years in prison and was released in June 1932, in the general amnesty granted due to the Eucharistic Congress which was taking place in Dublin that year.

Interestingly Molloy was pardoned on the same day as another condemned man, Patrick Fagan. A National Army Private, Fagan had shot his superior, Lieutenant Patrick Moran, in August 1922, killing him instantly. Fagan was swiftly captured but his murder trial took over three years to come to court. It was finally heard in February 1926, just after Charles Molloy's case. Fagan pleaded not guilty, claiming that it had been an accidental shooting. He received the death penalty regardless. Like Molloy however, the jury recommended him to mercy due to "the unsettled state of the country at the time". Both Fagan and Molloy would be reprieved and sentenced to penal servitude for life instead. The government had chosen at this time to show some leniency to republicans convicted of murder in the troubled days of the Civil War, a leniency that had been absent in the years before.

WILLIAM DEVEREUX

"We had a little dispute."

The overwhelming majority of all Irish people executed, or indeed sentenced to death, had committed the crime of murder against one person. Waterford native William Devereux is an exception to this rule. In February 1923, he murdered his sister-in-law Anne Devereux in the home they shared in an unspeakably brutal attack. He then turned his attention to his niece, Anne Devereux's infant daughter Kathleen, striking her with a hatchet. She, too, passed away from her injuries some days after the horrific attack. She was just ten months old.

William Devereux was born in the townland of Rochestown, Co. Kilkenny but had lived almost all his life at Number 28 Slievekeale Road, near the centre of Waterford City. He was 56 years of age but was described in contemporary newspaper reports as a "peculiar, poor-looking man of middle age". Devereux was an unmarried coach maker who lived as a tenant in the home of his brother James, despite being almost twenty years older than him. James and his 33-year-old wife Anne had married in 1910 and by 1923 had six young children under the age of twelve in the crowded dwelling. Relations between William and his sister-in-law were strained and they were known to quarrel occasionally. James later said that sometimes his wife and William were "on good terms, and sometimes nothing would pass between them". William was supposed to pay £1 weekly to his sister-in-law who acted as housekeeper, and this was often a bone of contention between the pair. On 12 February 1923, James Devereux went to work in the village of Kilmacthomas, eighteen miles outside the city. His wife, brother and children were thus left together in the house. When James returned three days later, his wife would be dead and his daughter dying.

At about 1.40 p.m. on 15 February, William Devereux Jnr ran screaming out of his home. He was the son of James and Anne and just five years of age. He rushed to a house two doors down and attracted the attention of some neighbours, Margaret Lacy and her son Edward. William "was in a terrible condition and crying", but the Lacys could not understand what he was saying. They accompanied the hysterical child the short distance back to his house. When Margaret got to the door, which was ajar, she called in, "Mrs Devereux, leave in the child out of the rain." She got no answer so pushed the door open slightly. The Lacys were met with a horrifying sight. Ten-month-old Kathleen Devereux was lying in a pool of blood just inside the door. She was still alive but mortally wounded. The infant was lying at the feet of her mother. Anne Devereux was also face down and motionless on the floor. She was dead, having been nearly decapitated with a hatchet. The two neighbours did not enter the home but ran to summon help. By the time they returned with a doctor a large group of shocked local people had already gathered around the gruesome crime scene. The two victims of the callous attack were taken to Waterford City Infirmary. Anne was dead on arrival but Kathleen was alive, although in a critical condition. Her brain was partially protruding through her skull and she did not survive, succumbing to her injuries five days later.

William Devereux Snr was immediately suspected of having committed the crime, having been seen by neighbours running away from the area shortly before the Lacy's horrific discovery. The military arrived and made enquiries, ascertaining that the coach maker had come home from work for his lunch hour just before 1.30 p.m. His dinner had just been eaten before the merciless attack on his sister-in-law and little niece. After a further search, the authorities discovered a bloodstained hatchet three hundred yards from the house in a tillage field. It appeared to have been thrown from the road and was identified by Edward Lacy as belonging to the Devereux family. The hatchet had been sharpened three months before and was identified as the murder weapon. Devereux was eventually apprehended just outside Waterford City at 4 p.m. the next day. When charged and cautioned by Sergeant Finn, he answered, "All right." Later, on being brought to the barracks, the prisoner commented "I have no statement to make. We had a little dispute, and she fired the poker at me but it did not hit me. I then struck her with the hatchet I had in my hand twice."

Dr Philip Purcell examined Anne Devereux's body after the attack. The results were disturbing and showed a sustained and brutal attack. A deep wound to the back of the neck had practically severed her head from her body. She also had a gaping two-inch gash on her scalp. The doctor also opined that she had been lying on the floor when the savage blows had been struck. William Devereux had gone on to hit his ten-month-old niece several times with the hatchet. Kathleen Devereux had severe scalp wounds and had died due to haemorrhaging of the brain.

The trial began at Dublin County Commission, the precursor to the Central Criminal Court, which was also located on Green Street. The case was not heard until 22 November 1923. Ten months was a long time in those days when the Irish justice system was mercilessly swift. Like many murder cases at the time, however, it had been delayed by the ongoing Civil War. A jury was chosen, although "all women called as jurors were asked to stand by", possibly due to the disturbing details of the case. Devereux pleaded not guilty, despite being faced with many witnesses, his own confession and irrefutable circumstantial evidence.

James Devereux, brother of the accused, took the stand. The recently widowed father was a train driver, employed by Waterford County Council. He identified the hatchet as belonging to his household. He described William as "sometimes moody and sometimes all right" but added that his brother had never before injured or threatened any of his family members in any way. John Connery, of Durrant's coachbuilding factory, also gave interesting evidence about the character of the accused. He told the court that he had worked with

William Devereux for nearly forty years and was his manager at the time of the murder. On Valentine's Day 1923, the day before the attack, William Devereux came into work appearing agitated. He told Connery that he had rowed with his sister-in-law and she had given him no breakfast. Connery sent him to the dining hall to get some food, suggesting to him that he should consider having his meals outside the house from then on. Devereux made no reply. Devereux was again at work the next morning at 8.30 a.m., working until 1 p.m. Connery accompanied him up the road at lunchtime, enquiring as to whether he wanted to eat in the dining hall again. Devereux replied that he would not as "things are all right at home", a chilling statement in light of events that were about to unfold. Devereux did not return to work after lunch, which was uncharacteristic of him. Connery was also probed about the personality of his employee. He replied that Devereux was occasionally moody, but never seemed violent in any way. He was "a quiet and harmless man, always attentive to his work. He would be moody for a minute and then clasp his hands as if in prayer. During that time he would be thinking to himself and would not mind anybody talking to him."

No evidence was presented by the defence, and Devereux did not take the stand to explain his violent actions. His defending Counsel, Mr Lennon, asked the jury to find that "Devereux was insane at the time of the commission of the crime." Mr Carrigan, prosecuting, pointed to the fact that Devereux had absconded shortly after striking the fatal blows, which showed that he understood the gravity of the terrible act he had just committed. He referred to the case as a terrible double tragedy, pulling no punches in illustrating the fatal injuries of the two murder victims. "The child had been brained by a blow, and the mother was almost decapitated, the head being nearly hanging off. The injuries had been caused (by Devereux) by blows of a hatchet." Dr Hackett, medical officer of Mountjoy Prison, was thus an important witness to determine Devereux's state of mind at the time he had ended the lives of his sister-in-law and niece. Like all those being tried for murder or manslaughter, Devereux had been placed under observation by a psychiatrist after his arrest. Dr Hackett had observed the accused since October and he suggested to the court that the defendant was in no way mentally abnormal although he considered him "sullen and silent". He agreed that Devereux could fully distinguish right from wrong.

In light of the overwhelming evidence, the jury found William Devereux guilty of murder. The judge, as was customary, asked him if he had anything to say in reply to the charge. According to one report Devereux "made no reply but continued in the lethargic state which characterised him throughout the trial." He was duly sentenced to death, scheduled to take place on Saturday 22 December 1923, just three days before Christmas. This was the sixth death sentence passed by the Dublin Commission in the space of two weeks. Another incredible and tragic incident happened at this juncture. On hearing the sentence of death, a minor witness in the trial, Mary Hanrahan from Waterford, dropped dead from shock.

The judge had announced before passing the death sentence that Devereux "presented an appearance of real sorrow" and he would be satisfied if mercy was exercised. Devereux was duly reprieved on 19 December, just four days before he was due to climb the scaffold. The Minister for Home Affairs announced his sentence would be reduced to one of penal servitude for life. It is impossible to know why the Cumann na nGaedheal government of the day saw fit to commute Devereux over the other three men executed in that month. His murder was more gruesome and he had killed twice, an innocent woman and vulnerable infant. There were certain question marks over the mental state of a man who would commit such a senseless and unprovoked attack against a woman and child, and the judge's merciful words were undoubtedly crucial. Penal servitude for life did not mean any such thing, however. William Devereux served nine years in prison, being released in June 1932. He returned to live in a lodging house in Mayor's Walk in Waterford City. After less than a year of freedom, however,

William Devereux was walking down Lady Lane in the city on 10 April when he was hit by a sudden seizure. He collapsed on the ground and was dead minutes later. No inquest into his death was considered necessary as Devereux had been known to suffer from a weak heart.

William Devereux narrowly avoided becoming the second Waterford native to be hanged in the twentieth century. The first was Patrick Dunphy, who had also murdered two members of his family. Dunphy was 74 years of age but had two young sons, John (11) and Eddie (9). The elderly man decided that the small boys were more trouble than they were worth, however, and that the money he could recoup from his insurance on their death would be more valuable to him. He poisoned Eddie with strychnine in September 1899. The boy's death was attributed to natural causes. In December of the same year, Dunphy also gave John a glass of strychnine. He died within minutes, although this time the death was considered suspicious. The organs of the two children were examined and found to contain large amounts of poison. Dunphy was found guilty and sentenced to death for the callous double-murder. There was some hope that he would be reprieved due to his advanced age but it was not to be. Patrick Dunphy was hanged in April 1900, making him the first, and the oldest, person to be executed in Ireland in the twentieth century. William Devereux would receive more leniency for his actions.

HANNAH FLYNN

"I would have your life!"

Margaret O'Sullivan and her husband Daniel owned a decent-sized farm in the townland of Culleenymore, Co. Kerry. This picturesque hamlet lies in the shadow of Ireland's largest mountain range, MacGillycuddy's Reeks, and is about four miles from the town of Killorglin. The two-storey house had been bought for Margaret by a former employer, a clergyman, and was described as a "very comfortable residence". The couple had been married for eleven years but had no children of their own. Ireland's rural west coast in 1923 would have been an impoverished place, recovering from the bloody and divisive Civil War and haemorrhaging young people through emigration to every corner of the world. The O'Sullivans however, had bucked this trend and were doing relatively well. Well enough, in fact, that they were able to employ several farm hands to help with their daily labours. In April 1922, they also decided that they needed an extra pair of hands to help Margaret around the house. For this reason they chose to hire Hannah Flynn.

Flynn was born in 1896 in the townland of Anglont, just over a mile outside Killorglin. She was from a family of nine children and grew up in a small cottage in the locality. Her father was an agricultural labourer and Hannah, described as a sullen and rather dull woman, would have had precious few opportunities other than domestic servitude. She had been well known to the O'Sullivans for the past five or six years, however, and seemed a good fit for the job. The 28-year-old was tasked with helping the couple in their household duties and would spend most of her day working in close proximity to Margaret. The couple soon found the young girl an unsatisfactory employee, however, listing theft and disobedience amongst her transgressions. Dan O'Sullivan described Flynn as "too much of a thief around the place." She also did not get on well with Margaret O'Sullivan. Eventually the couple had enough and Hannah Flynn was dismissed from her post in June after just two months. She did not take her dismissal with good grace. She returned to the home of her former employers on several occasions at night-time over the next three or four weeks. She shouted abuse at the O'Sullivans and attacked Dan with a sweeping brush as he came in from the bog one day, telling him she "would have his life". In a separate incident, Flynn also beat Dan with a stick until it broke in the presence of several members of her own family. She only relented when her brother pulled her away. After this incident, the terrified O'Sullivans sent a young boy, Sheahan, out to get turf for them instead. Hannah Flynn saw Sheahan coming along with a cart. She first attacked him before breaking the cart. On another occasion, she had thrown stones at Mrs O'Sullivan when she had driven past on a pony and trap. Finally she had taken the turf from another servant boy of the O'Sullivans and commandeered it for herself, shouting that she was keeping it as the couple owed her money.

Hannah Flynn's grievance, apart from her sudden dismissal, was that her former employers owed her unpaid wages from her time with them, claiming it was around 50s. Although the couple were adamant that she had been paid the wages she was owed, Margaret went to the Flynn household and gave Hannah 45s. to keep the peace in the hope that she would desist from her campaign of intimidation. The O'Sullivans were now satisfied that they had appeased their tormentor and believed that they could get back to life as normal. Hannah Flynn was not placated, however. She still harboured an inexplicable burning resentment towards her former employers and she was prepared to go to extreme lengths to exact her revenge.

At 10 a.m. on Easter Sunday 1923 (1 April), Dan O'Sullivan left his house in the direction of the village of Listry. The round trip was a long one, taking over two hours on foot, but Dan intended to travel there to attend Mass. Margaret would usually have accompanied him but on this day she waited at home alone. This was so she could make preparations for the Easter Sunday dinner, always a special occasion in Irish family homes. When Dan returned just after 1 p.m., he was surprised to find the front door locked from the inside. He walked around to the back door and entered the kitchen where he was met with a grotesque sight. His wife was lying dead on her back on the floor of the kitchen, having been mangled with a hatchet to the point that he could not definitively identify her face at the time. Her brains partially protruded from her battered skull and her body also had several violent gashes. The floor, the stairs and the walls of the house were all splattered in blood and the place was in complete disarray. The O'Sullivan home had been thoroughly ransacked, both upstairs and downstairs. All the money and securities, valued at £600, had been taken from the house, as well as some items of women's clothing. Sixteen guineas that had been left in the parlour had also been stolen. Outside the house lay a bucket of bloody water, indicating that whoever had committed this violent crime had nonchalantly washed their hands and clothes in a bid to conceal their gruesome crime. They had then absconded with the money and valuables, leaving Margaret O'Sullivan dead on her kitchen floor.

Daniel O'Sullivan quickly informed his neighbours, one of whom was sent to inform a priest and a doctor. Another neighbour, who had arrived at the scene after hearing about the grisly incident, discovered a hatchet belonging to the household lying under the stairs beside the blood-stained wall. Both the handle and the iron were covered with blood and hair. These were subsequently proven to belong to the victim of the barbarous attack. The hatchet had been kept hidden in a press so it was believed that the killer must have had intimate knowledge of the house. It was ascertained that Margaret's preparations for dinner had not even begun when the intruder had struck as there was a joint of meat still in the larder. A lamb that she fed every morning had also not been released from its pen. These facts indicated that the attack had happened just minutes after Daniel O'Sullivan had departed for Mass and that the attacker may have lain in wait until his departure. A hammer was also discovered in the vicinity. It had not been used in the butchery but to break open a trunk upstairs which had contained the couple's valuables.

The army arrived on the scene initially, coming from the local village of Beaufort. They picked up the deceased woman, covered her head and laid her maimed body on the table. The newly-formed civic guards came afterwards. By this stage, almost the entire population of the area had turned out to aid in the search for the murderer. Suspicions abounded in the area that a local person had been responsible and a young man was arrested shortly after the crime. He was released soon afterwards. Although many felt that a male must have been guilty of the frenzied attack, Hannah Flynn's previous resentful behaviour towards the victim made her a prime suspect too. She was arrested the day after the murder in the town of Tralee, eighteen miles distant. Inspector Ryan said she made no comment when charged with murder and seemed indifferent to her arrest and subsequent incarceration.

Hannah Flynn's trial did not begin until 27 February 1924, due to the large accumulation of cases caused by the Civil War. She was originally to have faced justice in her home county of Kerry, but her defence applied for a change of venue as they maintained she would have been unable to get a fair trial in the locality, where the details of the ghastly murder were well known and widely discussed. This application was granted and Flynn was finally brought before the Dublin City Commission, charged with wilful murder. She pleaded not guilty despite the large amount of incriminating circumstantial evidence to link her to the murder.

Dan O'Sullivan took the stand early in the trial and described the morning of his wife's murder. He told the jury of his trip to Mass and his surprise at finding the front door locked. He went on to detail the awful discovery he made at the back entrance. Unsurprisingly, he seemed deeply affected by the evidence and was overcome with emotion, rendering him unable to answer questions about the dreadful scene that had greeted him on his arrival home. This led the judge to say that "those harrowing details might be got from another witness." Hannah Flynn listened to her former employer's tearful testimony with casual indifference.

Flynn lived in a labourer's cottage in Dungeel, about a mile outside the town of Killorglin. The cottage had been immediately examined after her arrest and leading away from it, across a potato field, were a series of remarkable footprints. These same footprints were discovered in a field leading to Mrs O'Sullivan's cottage. One of the boots Flynn wore when arrested was larger than the other, and they were not of the one pair. This was exactly like the footprints discovered in both fields. Hannah Flynn denied that she had been in the Culleenymore area at all, instead insisting that she had walked to Tralee on the night before the murder. She claimed to have left Killorglin between 6 and 7 p.m. and walked the eighteen miles to Tralee. She had then slept in a house in the town. Flynn was unable to locate this house or anyone who saw her in the town. She said that while in Tralee she had been offered a job but had refused it as the wages were too low. The person who was alleged to have made this overture could not be traced. She asserted that she left the town at 7 a.m. the following morning and had not returned to Killorglin until the afternoon of Easter Sunday.

Several witnesses were discovered who could refute Flynn's version of events, however. Two men vowed in court that they had seen her in the Culleenymore area on 31 March, the night before the murder. One of these witnesses was John O'Sullivan from nearby Ballymalis. He told the court that he was walking home from Killorglin at 10 p.m. when he met Hannah Flynn walking in the opposite direction. She had a shawl on her head which she pulled across her face, as if to avoid detection, as she passed him. She was walking in the direction of Margaret O'Sullivan's house and was about half a mile from there. She was three miles from her own house. Unsurprisingly, the vast majority of local people had been at Easter Sunday Mass at the time of the actual murder. The Gardaí did find five witnesses willing to testify that they had seen Flynn around 11 a.m. on that morning, One of these, a local fisherman, stated that Flynn was walking in the direction of her own home from Culleenymore. She appeared to be concealing something under her shawl. The prosecution also reminded the court that the hatchet and valuables had been well hidden in the house and could only have been discovered by someone well-acquainted with the O'Sullivan home. A brown shawl, belonging to the deceased and missing since the day of the murder, was also being worn by Flynn when arrested, although she had cut some tassels off it.

Mr Lennon, defending, assured the jury that Hannah Flynn could not be linked with the crime scene, despite the evidence they had heard to the contrary. He also intimated that she would not have been strong enough to inflict such savage wounds on Mrs O'Sullivan. She was just 5'4" and the hatchet was too large for her to wield. Dr Sheehan, a medical officer of Milltown, Co. Kerry, refuted Lennon's claim. He told the jury that, in his opinion, any person with moderate strength armed with the hatchet could cause the wounds seen on the deceased. The doctor also said that since the first wound came from behind, Mrs O'Sullivan was likely to have been knocked unconscious. This meant the accused would have had free reign to continue the savagery unabated.

The jury believed the conclusive evidence against Hannah Flynn and she was found guilty of murder. The jury did also recommend mercy for the prisoner however on account of her "low mentality", an unusual reason. Mr Justice Pim gave Flynn the mandatory death sentence and set the execution date for 27 March 1924. The judge did promise that he too would personally strongly recommend the condemned prisoner to mercy. Up to this point in the trial, Hannah Flynn had shown no emotion and maintained a sullen and disinterested demeanour. On hearing these words, however, she cried out for the first time. She had to be helped from the dock in tears by warders.

Hannah Flynn came within three weeks of becoming the first

woman executed by the state. The Governor-General saw fit, however, to commute her sentence to penal servitude for life. There can be no doubt that her premeditated crime was as violent and vicious as any committed in this country. The jury's unusual use of the words "low mentality" to describe the accused may well have worked in her favour as the government would not want to be seen to execute a woman of subnormal intelligence. The state was well aware of the danger she posed to society, however. Her actions leading up the murder, as well as the killing itself, showed a woman who was capable of unspeakable violence. She also seemed untroubled by remorse. The prison authorities would describe Flynn as "not quite normal" during her time behind bars and no family member was willing to take her when the time for release came. The government thus kept Hannah Flynn in jail for a lengthy eighteen years until November 1942, when she was admitted into the care of the Good Shepherd Nuns.

It was widely thought that Hannah Flynn's gender rescued her from the gallows and that if a man had committed such a despicable murder he would have been hanged. The following year, however, an Irish woman's gender would not be enough to save her from the noose. Annie Walsh (née Barrett) married Ned Walsh in 1916 and moved to Fedamore, Co. Limerick. Ned was thirty years her senior and the couple lived in abject poverty in a small cottage outside the village. It was an unhappy marriage and Annie Walsh began an affair with her husband's nephew, Michael Talbot. The lovers eventually decided to murder Ned Walsh. They hoped that Annie would receive compensation for his death and they could use it to elope together. Ned Walsh was killed in his own home with a hatchet on the night of 25 October 1924. Annie did not stick to their story about an intruder, however, immediately telling the Gardaí that Michael Talbot had murdered her husband. Talbot, realising that he had been double-crossed, pointed the finger at Annie Walsh for the murder. Both defendants pleaded not guilty in court, with each placing the blame squarely on the other. It would not prove to be a clever strategy. Both prisoners were found guilty and hanged in August 1925. Annie Walsh had 'hoped until the end that her sentence would be commuted.' Looking at the history of condemned women in Ireland, it was a reasonable aspiration. For reasons known only to the Irish Government of the time, however, Annie Walsh would not be as fortunate as Hannah Flynn, becoming the only woman in the history of the state to be hanged.

PATRICK AYLWARD

"Don't tell your mother or I'll kill you."

The Dublin Commission was set up after the Civil War in 1923. In the absence of a functioning court system, it dealt with the long backlog of serious crimes which had not been tried during the conflict. It had a busy few months and imposed the death penalty on many occasions. One of the most shocking crimes to come before the makeshift court involved Kilkenny native Patrick Aylward. The killing of defenceless children is an especially repugnant crime. It is impossible to fathom why someone would commit such an act. Unbelievably, Aylward's motivation was said to have been a long-running feud with his neighbours. The question remains, a century after this strange trial, however. Did Patrick Aylward murder an infant to exact revenge on a family he despised?

Patrick Aylward was a farmer from the townland of Rochestown, a mile and a half from Mullinavat in South Kilkenny. Like many defendants at the time, contemporary records did not state his age, merely describing him as "middle-aged". In a lot of cases in the early part of the last century, the people themselves were unsure how old they were as many had no birth certificate at all. Instead they often described themselves as "middle-aged", "elderly", "about 35 or 36" and so on. Aylward, it transpired from later prison records, was born in 1860, making him about 63 years old at the time of the murder. He had spent nearly forty years in America, spending most of his time in Connecticut where he made plated cutlery. He decided to return to Kilkenny in 1922 to take care of his two elderly brothers, both of whom still lived on the family farm. One brother, William, had since died leaving Patrick to earn a living on their twenty-five acre farm for himself and John, his remaining sibling. Fifty yards away from the Aylward homestead lived their neighbours, the Holden family. The family included Patrick, his wife Mary and their eight children. Relations between the two households were not good.

Patrick Aylward had complained many times about the alleged trespassing on his land by fowl and goats which belonged to the Holden family. On one occasion, Aylward set his dog on a goat belonging to Mrs Holden which had wandered onto his land. After this incident a dead fowl belonging to the Holdens was found in the haggard of Aylward. Mary Holden described her neighbour as violent and said that he had twice struck her with his stick. Aylward would deny this accusation, later telling the authorities that Mary Holden was "of the tramp class" and that the Holden family had a campaign of intimidation against him, even involving their children. He asserted that the mother of the Holden household had attacked him on more than one occasion while her sons constantly annoyed his animals and had used his well as a toilet. What started out as a minor disagreement was about to take a far more sinister turn.

On the evening of Saturday 21 April 1923, Patrick Holden was out at work while his wife was minding the children. At 5 p.m., Mary put her eighteen-month-old baby William to bed. She then left for the nearby townland of Lisronan where she was planning to buy an outfit for her eldest son's confirmation scheduled for the following week. 1923 was a particularly dangerous time with the Civil War still ongoing and crime rampant. Despite this, the Holdens saw fit to put eight-year-old Patrick in charge of the house. They told him to lock the door from the inside and stay there. He was left with his brother Michael, his sister Mary and the infant, William. William, the second youngest of the Holden family, was a "very feeble child, barely able to move hand or foot." He suffered from rickets and was not able to crawl or walk. His mother said "he would stay (in bed) for a month without leaving it." That is where he was, sleeping peacefully, when his mother left.

45

Some minutes afterwards, Patrick Aylward allegedly walked the short distance over and rapped at the door of the Holden house, demanding admittance. Patrick, Michael and William were all in the kitchen at this point. After some deliberation, they opened the door to their neighbour. When Aylward entered the room he turned around to the door and twisted the key, re-locking it from the inside. He next extracted the key and put it in his pocket before allegedly telling the children that he "would put an end to the trespassing." William was still lying down asleep in a bed near the fire wrapped in swaddling clothes.

Aylward lifted the small boy and walked over to the fire in which sticks were burning. He then allegedly held the infant down over the burning grate. Patrick Holden endeavoured to intervene but he was powerless against the strength of the older man. Aylward stayed watching the crying infant as he burned on the fire, all the while using a stick to hold off the other children making sure they could not aid their infant brother. Just as William's clothes caught fire, Aylward said, "Don't let them goats into my haggard anymore", before dropping the key and striding out the door. The other children quickly removed their infant brother down from the burning-hot grate and put him in a bucket of water to try and quench the flames. They then put the severely-burned baby back into his bed and locked the door.

Patrick Holden Snr arrived home within the next few minutes to be met with several hysterical children and a baby suffering from life-threatening burns. There were no Gardaí in the area at that turbulent point in Irish history, so Holden instead sent for a local GP. The doctor had to come from Waterford, a journey of over ten miles, and consequently he did not arrive until the next morning. Meanwhile the Holdens wrapped the baby in cotton wool and waited. When Dr Coghlan finally called he knocked at the back door of the house. Mary Holden, unsure of who it was, did not answer the door as she was too afraid. Coghlan then saw Patrick Aylward walking by and asked him if that was the Holden's house. Aylward told him that it was before adding "they're all mad over there." When the doctor was eventually admitted to the Holden house, he described the baby's condition as follows: "He was in a state of collapse…charred black all over the back and over the lungs. There were burns on both the arms towards the elbows." William Holden was subsequently brought to hospital but died within twenty-four hours of the incident. His death was attributed to toxaemia, a type of blood poisoning caused by the heat he was subjected to.

Early on the morning after the tragedy, Patrick Holden went to Aylward's house and accused him of roasting his son. Patrick Aylward strenuously denied it, implying that the Holdens had told their children to tell lies about him. The coroner's inquest took place just days after the murder. Aylward appeared and denied having any part in the burning, claiming that he had no grudge against the Holden family. Nevertheless, the jury recommended that the Gardaí pursue the matter further. The coroner called the case a sad and regrettable occurrence. He had harsh words for the Holdens as well, however, telling them that he did not know whether to sympathise with them because they "left this little infant and three other little children and went away a quarter of a mile from home". Aylward was arrested on 8 May. He replied, "I did not do it."

Patrick Aylward's murder trial began on 26 November, just days after William Devereux's death sentence was pronounced. The evidence of the Holden children was critical to the case against Aylward. Mr Carrigan, prosecutor, described the prisoner as "charged with a crime which, if proved against him, was as terrible and hideous a crime as any one described as a human being could commit." Aylward himself, permitted by the court to sit for the duration of the trial, maintained a "cool demeanour" throughout, despite the gravity of the charges against him. He pleaded not guilty to the charge.

The prosecution characterised Aylward as a strange and immoral creature. They described his house as "not fit for human habitation. He kept cattle on the ground floor…and lived in his loft. The place was a veritable cesspool and manure heap." When Dr Matthew Coghlan took the stand, he was asked about the condition of the young boy and whether the other children could have accidently inflicted such wounds on him if they had taken him out of the bed to play with him. The doctor stated that he did not believe that William Holden's injuries could have occurred accidently as they were too severe. He added that as the boy had been suffering from rickets, a disease usually caused by malnutrition, his bones were seriously underdeveloped. For this reason the doctor replied that the infant could not, in his opinion, have got out of bed and burned himself on the fire. He was further questioned about the character of the accused, Aylward. Coughlan described him as a "degenerate" and said that when he met him he "made up his mind that he was mentally abnormal." He opined that the accused was responsible for his actions, however, and capable of distinguishing right from wrong.

The next witness was 9-year-old Patrick Holden. Holden was described as an intelligent witness, although he had never gone to school and was unable to write his name. He gave his account of the tragic day. He described letting Aylward into the house. Aylward asked him, "What do you want to leave the goats in the haggard for?" He then broke a mug and searched under the bed for something. After getting up he fell along the bed. Finally he grabbed William and put him across the fire, holding his back against the burning grate. Patrick described trying to take William off the fire and how Aylward would not let him near his brother. Another younger son in the house, Michael, also appeared on the stand to recount the events of the day. He described Aylward had raised a stick at them as they attempted to rescue their infant brother. As he left the house, Aylward said, "Don't tell your mother or I'll kill you."

Aylward admitted to the court that he had been around the Holden house with goats earlier in the day but had not burned the child, adding "Don't you think I have a soul to save as well as everyone else, or what do you think I am?" He also said "I could not bear to look at a child burning on the fire, not to mind do it myself." He told the court that he was "thunderstruck" at the accusation that he had harmed William Holden and that when Mr Holden had accused him he thought his neighbour "was getting out of his mind". Patrick Aylward told the court that he did not know why the Holden children would be telling lies about him but he thought they had been put up to it by their parents.

A local farmer, James O'Keeffe, spoke for the defence. He stated that he had arrived at the Aylward house at 4.45 p.m., around the time the burning was supposed to have taken place. He had stayed until night-time having tea with Aylward and his brother. John Aylward, 75-year-old brother of the accused, also gave the accused man an alibi. He stated that he and Patrick had been tending a sick cow all day and were in the house from the early evening until 9.15 p.m. and that his brother had not left at any stage. Patrick Aylward told the court that the last time he had been inside the Holden household was five months before the tragedy when he had gone over to tell Mrs Holden to stop her sons from chasing his sow. He claims that on this occasion Mrs Holden hit him with a scrubbing brush and he had hit her back with his walking stick. The defence also reminded the jury that Mrs Holden had not mentioned Aylward in her initial evidence to the authorities, merely stating that the child had been burnt.

The trial took just one day and despite the contentious and contradictory evidence the all-male jury needed just ten minutes deliberation before passing a guilty verdict. A majority of the jury did, however, give a recommendation to mercy on Patrick Aylward for the wilful murder of William Holden. The judge commented that he agreed wholeheartedly with the verdict before passing the sentence of death on the prisoner. On hearing the sentence, Aylward remarked "I am not guilty at all. I have not been in that house for five months. May God forgive the woman who put the lie on me and God forgive the jury." The judge said he would pass on the recommendation to mercy to the appropriate quarters but went on to say that he "could not hold out any hope of mitigation of the sentence he was about to impose." Aylward was sentenced to death, to be carried out two days after Christmas on 27 December. He was sent to Mountjoy to await his fate.

Five executions were scheduled for the month of December 1923, due to the backlog caused by the Civil War. It would be the busiest ever time at the gallows of the Irish State. Thomas Delaney and Thomas

McDonagh were executed within half an hour of each other. Delaney had attacked and killed 74-year-old Patrick Horan with a pair of tongs and a slasher in the course of a robbery. Horan was an elderly shopkeeper from Banagher, Co. Offaly and Delaney was disturbed in the act by locals. His guilt was not in question and he would pay the ultimate penalty for the crime. McDonagh had killed his neighbour, Ellen Rogers, in Loughglynn, Co. Roscommon. The two had fallen out years before and had an argument about money. McDonagh went home, retrieved his shotgun and shot Rogers dead. Unusually, McDonagh had asked not to be visited by his wife in the lead up to the execution. Peter Hynes also faced the hangman. A native of Drogheda, Hynes had killed a soldier named Thomas Grimstone in Co. Meath. Hynes claimed he believed Grimstone was a "Black and Tan". He had beaten him to death in the middle of the night with an iron bar and then concealed his body underneath straw and hay in a loft. He too was convicted and hanged. William Devereux (see Chapter 3) was more fortunate than any of the above. He received a last-minute reprieve, possibly due to question marks over his mental condition.

Patrick Aylward, who had attracted national attention for his unspeakable brutality against a helpless child, could not have been too hopeful of a commutation in light of the frequent use of the death penalty at the time. However numerous local people, including the Bishop of Ossory, petitioned government minister Kevin O'Higgins, questioning the guilt of the elderly man. They also mentioned the Holden family's "bad moral character", and alluded to a previous incident when another Holden child had been burned to death in suspicious circumstances. This tragedy was said to have occurred in Piltown in 1910 but whether there was any substance to this allegation is not known. Either way, it was announced just hours before the execution that the death sentence was to be commuted to one of penal servitude for life. The minister was not obligated to give a reason for this sudden commutation but one can only wonder as to whether it was linked to the fact that a man was being put to death solely on the evidence of children. There also seems to have been a reasonable doubt present. Patrick Aylward served just under ten years in prison, being released under the general amnesty in 1932 in honour of the Eucharistic Congress. His brother had died shortly after the trial so Patrick resided in an old persons' home in Kilkenny after his release. He died there three years later in November 1935. To the end, he maintained that the Holden family had framed him and strenuously denied having any part in the burning of William Holden.

DENIS LEEN

"Never let on boys about the creasing of that fellow."

By December 1923, the Civil War had been officially over for some six months. However, sporadic skirmishes still occurred. The situation in the south-west of Ireland was particularly difficult to control, especially in Counties Kerry, Limerick and Cork, part of the so called "Munster Republic". Kerry had a huge republican contingent and the National Army struggled to gain popular support there, often having to bring in men from outside the county to maintain an uneasy peace. These transfers of troops often occurred by sea as the area was too dangerous to access by land. More than seventy state soldiers had been killed in Co. Kerry alone during the conflict, which led to a significant number of reprisals by the army. The National Army were not popular in the county and their credibility had been badly damaged by the Ballyseedy massacre when they deliberately blew up a landmine, killing eight republican prisoners nine months before. The murder of Thomas Brosnan in Scartaglen in late 1923 would cause similar outrage in the district.

Scartaglen is a small village in East Kerry and was a strong republican heartland in the aftermath of the Civil War, like most of the county at the time. One army captain described it as "an independent zone, a small republic of its own." On Monday 3 December 1923, a group of anti-Treaty IRA men entered the Scartaglen Garda station brandishing rifles, despite the fact that a truce had been called in the

Civil War. Sergeant Woods was in charge of the station and was told by the armed men to go up the stairs. The sergeant turned and was on the first step when he was shot in the back of the head, killing him instantly. The IRA raiders then ransacked the station, stealing arms and any valuables present before absconding. The government viewed this murder as an attack on the newly-formed Free State. The Kerry army command immediately moved troops from Tralee and Castleisland into the area in an attempt to capture the offenders. An army lieutenant named Jeremiah Gaffney was placed in charge of one group of soldiers sent to the district.

Jeremiah Gaffney was 23 years old and a native of Kingstown (later Dún Laoghaire), Co. Dublin. Typical of lieutenants in the fledgling army, Gaffney was a young man with experience of fighting the British. He had been in the Old IRA and during the War of Independence he had seen plenty of action, including the burning of the Custom House in Dublin. He had taken the pro-Treaty side in the Civil War, joining the National Army on its formation. He rose quickly through the ranks and in 1922 he was sent to Kerry to try to put order on the troubled region. Gaffney had been stationed at Scartaglen until the Civil War was over and had become well known to the locals. As he had lived and worked in the village previously, Gaffney was given orders to lead a group of soldiers to discover the identity of the killers of Sergeant Woods. It was hoped that his local knowledge would work to his advantage. What his superiors did not know about Gaffney was that he had a festering hatred of one family in the area and he was willing to go to extraordinary lengths to gain retribution.

The story of Gaffney's feud began in Scartaglen in 1919. A man from the village named John Brosnan went against the wishes of his family and married his neighbour, Miss Ellen Keane. His family did not approve of the match and it did not last. About three months after the nuptials, Brosnan abandoned his new bride. He left the country and emigrated to America, never to return. The newly married Mrs Brosnan, known locally as Nurse Keane, now found herself abandoned and alone at the age of 22. After her husband's departure, she went to live with her father in Scartaglen. She resided there for a couple of years until the contingent of Free State soldiers were posted to the village, Gaffney being their lieutenant. He became friendly with the nurse and by July 1922, they were sharing a house in the area. Many people in the area began referring to Nurse Keane as "Mrs Gaffney" despite the fact that she was married to another man.

This behaviour must have seemed scandalous to small-town Ireland in the 1920s. Keane's in-laws, the Brosnan family, complained bitterly about the behaviour of the married woman and the soldier, despite the fact that her husband had departed the country without her. Cornelius Brosnan and his family were amongst those unhappy about the conduct of their cousin's wife. Cornelius was aged about 50, his wife Johanna being ten years his senior. The pair owned a small pub in Scartaglen while Cornelius also worked as a blacksmith. They had one son, Thomas, who was 18 years old. The family publicly berated Mrs Keane for her behaviour, which they considered immoral. Keane refused to listen to her in-laws and continued the affair. She was angry at the gossip and the moralising of the Brosnans, however. So angry, in fact, that she plotted revenge against the family, poisoning the Brosnan's well. She did this by sneaking onto their property and pouring toxic Jeyes' Fluid into the spring water. The Brosnans later publicly accused her of the act and she eventually admitted it, even going to the Brosnan house to apologise. The apology was not accepted, however, and the two parties were not on speaking terms coming up to Christmas 1923. Gaffney, Keane's lover, had also borne the brunt of the Brosnans' ire. The Brosnans told anyone who'd listen that he was an adulterer. On another occasion Cornelius referred to the lieutenant as "the limb of the devil". This snub rankled with Gaffney and he was determined to seek vengeance.

On 6 December 1923, three days after Woods' murder, Gaffney and several of his troops left their barracks in Castleisland after 4 a.m. They drove in an army truck towards Scartaglen. Instead of making enquiries about the murder, however, the soldiers went into one of the local pubs, drinking their first pint at 5.30 a.m. They performed no official business in the village that day, instead drinking in several local establishments and walking around aimlessly. They came back to Castleisland drunk at around 2.30 p.m. and continued their carousing. At around 5 p.m. that evening, an intoxicated Lieutenant Gaffney told his driver, Volunteer McNeill, to get the truck ready. McNeill did so, although his superior did not tell him where the men were going. The soldiers started the four-ton vehicle with a push and drove off, with Gaffney in the cab along with Sergeant Michael O'Shea and four volunteers: Denis Leen, Michael O'Shea, Daniel Brosnan and McCusker. All the men except the driver wore civilian clothes and carried firearms. McNeill drove the men out to the crossroads near Scartaglen where they got out. Lieutenant Gaffney told his driver to park up a side road and stay in the truck. In a chilling indicator of what was about to occur, he also remarked "Don't be alarmed if you hear shots." It was 5.30 p.m.

The soldiers then walked the short distance to Scartaglen. When they arrived in the village, Gaffney directed them to Brosnan's pub. The commanding officer then gave Leen his revolver and told him to go into the pub, fetch Tom Brosnan and bring him outside. Tom's father Cornelius was serving, and on seeing Leen he went in behind the counter, assuming that the man wanted a drink. Instead of asking for alcohol, however, Denis Leen enquired if Brosnan's son was around. Brosnan was surprised, although not alarmed, at the question from the armed soldier. Leen was not disguised and Brosnan had never seen him before. Cornelius would later say that he "had no suspicion of him." He willingly brought the men down to his mother's pub where Thomas was playing cards with some neighbours, including a local Garda. Thomas accompanied the men back to the pub. Leen asked Thomas if he had any drink and Thomas replied that he had plenty. The soldier then asked for whiskey, which Brosnan said he would get outside. Leen answered that it didn't matter, before adding "Never mind. Come on, you will be back in a few minutes." Cornelius offered to join the men on the walk but Leen told him that he wanted to talk to Tom privately. Thomas Brosnan then trustingly joined Volunteer Leen and walked outside, leaving his father behind. Cornelius Brosnan would never see his teenage son alive again.

Cornelius grew worried about an hour after Thomas had left the house on the cold winter's night. He walked up to the Chapel Cross and stayed there for ten minutes to see if he could hear anything. He then went to two houses in the village to see if his son had been seen. Finally, he went to the Garda station and enlisted the help of Guard Boylan, who had a lamp, and the two men searched the immediate area by bicycle. Six hundred yards from Brosnan's house, just out the Castleisland Road, the two men discovered the body of Thomas Brosnan, Cornelius's only child. He had been shot several times, including twice in the thigh and once in the lower back. He was dead. Meanwhile, the drunken party of soldiers had returned to the truck within an hour, arriving back in Castleisland at 7 p.m. As they neared the town Gaffney told his charges "Never let on boys about the creasing of that fellow."

Much of County Kerry was horrified by the murder of young Thomas Brosnan. Although the population had grown accustomed to violence and murder, Thomas Brosnan was popular locally and not thought to be involved in political activity. Lieutenant Gaffney was arrested on the morning of 12 December and brought to Tralee Garda station. The other men in the party to Scartaglen were also detained, although 27-year-old Tralee native Denis Leen had gone on the run in the meantime. Gaffney was unrepentant, complaining to the arresting Gardaí that they would not have made as much of the matter if it had been someone from the Free State army who was shot. He also threatened the arresting officers that they would be sorry if he was interfered with. Despite these warnings, Gaffney was detained in the general office. By 6.30 p.m., however, two of Gaffney's National Army colleagues had helped the prisoner to escape from custody. The local Kerry people were outraged. A soldier had callously murdered an innocent young man and had then been helped to flee before he could face justice. It did not look good for the army, who made every effort to recapture the fugitive.

Gaffney was eventually apprehended nearly a month later on 9 January in North Richmond Street in Dublin. He had a Smith and Wesson .45 revolver and six rounds of ammunition in his possession but offered no resistance when arrested. He was transferred to Tralee on remand, where he was met by a large hostile crowd booing and jeering him. Cornelius Brosnan even emerged from the crowd and attempted to hit the prisoner, who was hurriedly brought into the courthouse. One week before this, on Thursday 3 January, Denis Leen had also been located by the Liverpool police. He had wired to his wife to send him money from Castleisland, which she did. He was arrested in the post office by the Liverpool police while awaiting the delivery. The Gardaí travelled over and brought Leen back to Ireland where they arrested him and charged him with murder. He answered his arrest with the statement. "It was not I shot him, it was Gaffney. And only for Gaffney I would not be here tonight and if I knew where he was I would soon tell." Five soldiers in all, the two O'Sheas, Daniel Brosnan, Denis Leen and Jeremiah Gaffney were charged with murder. All five pleaded not guilty. The two O'Sheas were acquitted, on the grounds that they had fired no shots. Daniel Brosnan, the other soldier present, offered to give evidence for the prosecution against Leen and Gaffney. This left just the two men who were accused of firing the shots to face the court for their role in the death of Thomas Brosnan.

Jeremiah Gaffney's trial was scheduled first. It began on 13 February 1924, in the Dublin City Commission on Green Street. A defiant Gaffney wore civilian clothing and pleaded not guilty to the charge, refusing to take the stand in his own defence. Ellen Brosnan (Nurse Keane), Gaffney's former lover, was called to the stand. Keane, who had written to one of the national newspapers announcing her horror at the murder of Thomas Brosnan, testified that she had been nursing a patient a mile from Castleisland when the attack was occurring. She also told the court that she had heard the army truck passing the house earlier in the evening but denied vehemently knowing anything else about the circumstances of the shooting.

Volunteer Daniel Brosnan, who had been in the truck on that fateful night, gave evidence of the night of the tragedy and would prove to be a crucial part of the evidence against Gaffney. After Leen had brought Thomas Brosnan back to his own house, the witness explained that they had proceeded to the Chapel Cross. At the crossroads, he and Sergeant Michael O'Shea met Lieutenant Gaffney and Volunteer Michael O'Shea while Leen and Thomas Brosnan walked ahead in the direction of Castleisland. As they stood talking at the crossroads, Brosnan said he heard six shots coming from the Castleisland direction. Gaffney then told the other members of the party to go back to the lorry. They set off walking, passing the body of Thomas Brosnan lying still on the road. Leen, who was carrying a "Peter the Painter" rifle, accompanied them. Gaffney waited behind. They continued walking until he heard two gunshots and a loud whistle behind them. Gaffney caught up with the men and said to Leen "You did not shoot him right at all, I had to put two charges in him." Gaffney was asked by the other men on the way to the truck why he had shot Thomas Brosnan. Gaffney claimed that Nurse Keane had told him that Brosnan was involved in the murder of Sergeant Woods, although Brosnan's father had described Thomas and Woods as the "best of friends." Daniel Brosnan admitted that he had heard before the operation that Thomas Brosnan was going to be "creased", but he told the court that he did not know what this word meant, presuming that Brosnan would get a beating in order to get information.

The defence team brought forward evidence that Gaffney had been severely injured in an accident which led to him undergoing surgery in 1915 for a skull fracture. Surgeon McArdle deposed that he had little hope of recovery at the time. He had taken away a piece of skull the size of half a crown from Gaffney, whose eye was protruding from its socket. McArdle opined that due to this serious surgery, Gaffney would be unable to deal with any sudden excitement, especially when under the influence of drink. The judge scoffed at this eight-year-old event having a bearing on the mind of the accused, who had led a perfectly ordinary life thereafter. The defence counsel also complained that Gaffney had been condemned to die in the media before he entered the court. He had been portrayed as a member of the National Army who took it upon himself to gain personal vengeance on an enemy. They asserted that Leen had fired the fatal shots and the testimony by fellow officers against Gaffney was to save their own skins. They described Daniel Brosnan as not caring "whether he put the guilt on Leen or Gaffney so long as he himself went free." Mr Carrigan for the prosecution disagreed, describing the crime as one that "could only be committed by the most evil anarchist."

On 15 February, after a two-day trial, the judge summed up, concluding at 7.30 p.m. The jury was then discharged to consider the evidence. They returned after fifty minutes having failed to agree on a verdict. Judge Pim was unhappy with their indecision, complaining that a jury should be able to make up its minds after two full days of evidence. The foreman said that there was no possible hope of a verdict but Judge Pim replied angrily that he would see them again at 11 p.m. They eventually returned after 10.30 p.m. that night with a verdict of guilty, with the standard recommendation to mercy. The judge described the murder as "premeditated, cold-blooded and horrible." He told the court that the prisoner deserved no mercy and sentenced Gaffney to hang on 13 March.

Denis Leen's trial was next, beginning on 20 February. Leen was aware that Gaffney had been sentenced to death and must have been anxious, considering it was he that had fired the first shots into Brosnan's body. The defence gave no evidence except the solicitor's closing statement. Leen's counsel told the jury that his client had obeyed the order of a senior officer and only shot Brosnan once in the lower body. Gaffney had planned and prepared the murder and Leen had no idea what was about to happen. Jeremiah Gaffney had finished off Brosnan with two shots himself. Surprisingly, the jury had less trouble with the verdict in this case than Gaffney's. They found Denis Leen guilty after one hour of deliberation. When asked if he had anything to say, Leen merely thanked his counsel. His death sentence was fixed for a week after Gaffney's, on 20 March.

Jeremiah Gaffney went to his death in Mountjoy Prison at 8 a.m. on 13 March. A small crowd had gathered outside but none of his relatives chose to be present, oddly. Shortly before the execution had been due to take place, a warder opened a side door to enter the prison. When he did this, a young girl with tears in her eyes tried to run in behind him but was repelled. Her identity was never disclosed. It was said that Gaffney had been resigned to his fate and that he showed no reluctance to accept his punishment. The ex-lieutenant had, however, done a decent thing before his execution. Gaffney had written a note, to be released after his death, completely exonerating his colleague, Denis Leen. In it, he took complete responsibility for Thomas Brosnan's death, stating that he had threatened to shoot Leen if he did not follow his orders to shoot the young man. He also added that Leen's shots had not critically injured Thomas Brosnan and Gaffney had spotted him attempting to jump over a fence. Gaffney had then fired two shots into Brosnan, killing him instantly.

The Leen family had grown increasingly desperate in the days leading up to the executions, even writing to the British government imploring them to petition the Irish government for mercy on account of Leen's service in the First World War. It became immaterial when Gaffney's confession was forwarded to the Minister for Home Affairs, however. In light of the new testimony Denis Leen was reprieved on 21 March, his death sentence being commuted to one of penal servitude for life. This was later altered to three years penal servitude. Leen served just over two of them, being released from Portlaoise Prison in June 1926. He was fortunate to have been partially exonerated due to the honesty of his doomed colleague. If Gaffney's confession had never come to light, he may well have faced a grimmer prospect.

Did Jeremiah Gaffney deserve to die for his crime? He undoubtedly used the power he had as an army official to condemn and murder a young man without trial. There was very little evidence to suggest that Thomas Brosnan had been involved in any illegal organisation, so it seems the killing stemmed from Gaffney's personal vendetta. In the year of 1923, however, many extrajudicial killings had been carried out by the National Army (including one you will read about in the next chapter), the Ballyseedy massacre being just one example. The army, frustrated by the murder of their own colleagues, frequently took the law into their own hands. They often killed enemies without trial as retribution for murders committed by the IRA. Gaffney may not deserve much sympathy for what was undoubtedly a horrific crime motivated by revenge. That being said, he was executed by the state while countless men who had committed similar acts would go completely unpunished. The murderers of Sergeant Woods, incidentally, were never found.

JAMES MURRAY

"Goodbye, now; I may not see you again."

Joseph Bergin was a native of Mountrath, Co. Laois. As a young man he had left a job as a shop assistant to follow the well-trodden path of the time into the Free State army. By the age of 23 he was employed as a military policeman and stationed in the Curragh Camp in Co. Kildare. Bergin was not scheduled to work on Thursday 13 December 1923, but despite this he woke up early and dressed in civilian clothes, leaving the camp on a friend's bicycle at 7 a.m. He told his comrades that he was on his way to buy himself a motorbike, which was to cost £35. It was thought, however, that Bergin had a far larger sum than this in his possession. Oddly, as he left he shouted to a companion, "Goodbye, now; I may not see you again." Bergin spent the day in Dublin city but later that evening he was back in Kildare town, being seen at 8.15 p.m. at the Railway Hotel. He was in the company of a tall man. After this, Bergin visited a young acquaintance of his in the town, arriving at Miss Peggy Daly's house at 8.30 p.m. He came alone, stayed for about twenty minutes, and left afterwards on a bicycle. Bergin was later seen in a motor car being driven away from Kildare town in the direction of Rathangan. He would never be seen alive again.

A group of schoolchildren were walking along the banks of the Grand Canal in Milltown, Co. Kildare the day after Joseph Bergin's trip to Dublin. The canal is eight miles from the Curragh and connects the capital city with the River Shannon. The children noticed what looked like pools of blood in the water. They inspected the area closer only to be met with the horrific sight of a young man's bullet-ridden body floating in the reeds. He wore no boots or socks and his hands were tied over his head. A belt from a trench coat was also tied around his neck. The horrified children went for the nearest adult, publican Laurence Kelly. Kelly ran the short distance to the canal and also spotted the man's body floating below the bridge. The Civic Guard in Newbridge were informed immediately and they arrived and removed the corpse to a store nearby, holding an inquest the following day. Joseph Bergin's brother, William, identified the badly disfigured corpse as that of his brother. Evidence was found that the body had been thrown over the parapet of the bridge. The doctor conducting the post-mortem deposed that Bergin had flesh wounds to the scalp, ear and face and had been tortured before being shot six times in total, including four bullets into the head. Death had occurred before the body was placed in the water. There was no sign of the money in Bergin's pockets but there were two military passes, one of them signed by a Mr J. Murray.

On the day after the inquest, two Gardaí were cycling at Guidenstown, a townland not far from Milltown Bridge. As they passed a disused house, known locally as "Ennis's house", they noticed the track of a motor-car going up the avenue. Ennis's house was used frequently by the republican subversives and had been raided on numerous occasions. Consequently, it was well known to the Gardaí. The two officers entered the house and found a blood-stained table as well as blood on the floor and on a pair of scissors. There was also a bullet jammed in a door. A broken whiskey bottle was at the scene and there was a strong smell of alcohol. In the fire lay a tie covered in blood and soot. It was later shown to belong to Joseph Bergin. After further examination, Gardaí came to the conclusion that Bergin had been kidnapped, gagged and tied-up before being brought to the empty house in a car. While he was in the house he had been interrogated, tortured and shot several times, before his corpse was unceremoniously thrown from the bridge into the canal by his drunken murderers. The Gardaí had found the crime scene and their next priority was to trace the "J. Murray" whose signature had been on the note in Bergin's pocket.

James Murray was a 23-year-old native of Dún Laoghaire, Co. Dublin. He was an ex-captain in the Free State army but by December 1923 had worked in the intelligence-gathering department headquarters in Dublin for eight months. The Free State and republican forces both had spies in their ranks who gave sensitive information to the other side. Murray's job was to identify and interrogate suspected informers in the ranks of the National Army. Michael Costello was Director of Intelligence for the Free State army and James Murray's superior. On 8 December, a week before Bergin went missing, Costello ordered that Bergin be put under surveillance by the army. Murray was put in charge of the suspected informer's case and several days later he confirmed that Bergin was covertly meeting members of the anti-Treaty IRA. The military policeman was allegedly getting sensitive information from republican prisoners in Tintown Camp, the Curragh, where he was employed. He was then communicating it to the IRA outside. It was ascertained that Bergin was due to meet the intelligence director of the republicans on 13 December.

Costello ordered Murray to travel the thirty miles to the Curragh Camp and intercept Bergin on his way from the meeting, informing him that the army knew of his treachery. He ordered Murray to get an admission from the suspect and investigate what information had been passed to the IRA. Murray agreed and Costello brought him downstairs and provided him with a Ford Touring Car. Murray was afterwards seen driving down the Infirmary Road with two unidentified men. It was 5 p.m.

At 7 a.m. the next morning Murray came into the barracks and woke Costello, telling him that he "had got on very well" and that he had obtained a number of important documents from Bergin. He also told his superior officer that the suspect had confessed during the interrogation that he had passed information to the IRA. Murray mentioned nothing about injuring the suspect although he did add that he had not brought the car back to the headquarters, instead leaving it at Crown Alley, several streets away. When asked by

Costello why he had done this, Murray replied that he "did not want the fellows in it to be seen in the barracks", making no explanation as to why he had not just dropped them off somewhere on the way. An army employee was subsequently sent out to collect the car. He noticed that it was very dirty and that there were bloodstains on the mat and upholstery. The employee attempted to clean the car that day but was unable to do so.

The Gardaí already had Murray in their sights and they took possession of the car the next day, discovering the bloodstains. Costello quickly requested a meeting with Murray. He told him not to give any statement to the Gardaí. Before the Gardaí had the opportunity to interview him, James Murray was sent to Liverpool, and subsequently Scotland "on important government business". While there, Colonel Costello arranged that James' brother Michael would go over. The two Murrays then absconded to Argentina. James would later testify that he had been told by Costello to emigrate for a year and wait for the heat to die down. He did not follow this advice, however, returning to Ireland within eight months. James Murray was arrested at his home on the Convent Road in the Dublin suburb of Dún Laoghaire just over a year after Bergin's murder on Christmas Eve 1924. He had been wanted in connection with the killing since he had left the country and was detained within hours of arriving back.

The murder trial began on 9 June 1925 in the Dublin Central Criminal Court. Dr William O'Kelly, State Pathologist, gave evidence of the human blood found in the Ford car. The tyre tracks at the disused house were also conclusively linked to the army car that Murray had been seen driving that day. A witness also reported a sighting of Murray with another man outside the Railway Hotel in Kildare, close to the area where Bergin had last been seen.

Director of Intelligence of the National Army, Michael Costello, was asked some probing questions in relation to his role in the sordid affair on the stand. He denied any knowledge of ordering or covering up the murder.

Did you pay any money to (James Murray) after the crime?
None whatever.
Did you endorse any cheques for the prisoner after the murder?
No.
If the prisoner states on oath that he went abroad on your suggestion
and that you actually paid his expenses, would you deny it?
It is absolutely false.
Was there any sanction by you that Bergin was to be shot?
Absolutely not.

Costello was asked numerous questions which he refused to answer due to "privilege" and the importance of secrecy in the security forces. A number of letters, supposedly written by Costello, were produced. These begged Murray to emigrate and wait for the heat to die down. Justice Hanna then asked Gleeson, defending, whether he was implying that Costello was in league with Murray to conceal the murderers. Gleeson replied that he believed Costello was. He told the jury that none of the corporal's evidence should be believed.

Murray himself took the stand on the third day. Sensationally, the accused told the trial that he had not gone to Kildare on 13 December at all. He admitted getting into the car with the two men in civilian clothes, neither of whom he knew by name. As they were driving, Murray said the men mentioned that their journey was to do with the Bergin case. Murray had become nervous and refused to accompany them further. He got out of the car and went back to Costello in the barracks, explaining that he would not be going to the Curragh. He spent the evening in Dublin instead, going to the Theatre Royal and the Winter Gardens. He afterwards met his brother Michael, also a soldier, and accompanied him home to Dún Laoghaire. He had given the two men in the car his address and the next morning they arrived at his house. They handed Murray a packet of papers for Costello. The men revealed that Bergin had admitted to meeting the IRA head of intelligence the previous day but they did not mention using any violence against him. They merely told Murray to inform the corporal that they got on all right. Murray dropped the two men to Crown Alley before going to wake Costello. That evening Costello told him the body of Joseph Bergin had been found. He also told Murray to keep quiet about the whole affair. Murray said that he met Costello again the next day, Costello seemed nervous and told him that the Gardaí were getting hot. Murray swore that at this stage Costello gave him £50 "for expenses", a huge sum of money at the time, before urging him to leave the country.

Murray denied going abroad as a fugitive, insisting that he had been ordered to leave. He had returned early "to have the whole thing cleaned up". The prosecution at this stage produced a confession allegedly written and signed by Murray in the presence of his brother just before he had fled abroad. The statement described Bergin's capture by Murray and two other men. It stated that they arrested Bergin and brought him to an empty house where they tortured and interrogated him. While they were searching Bergin's clothes, they found dispatches from meetings he had been having with the IRA. He was immediately shot dead and his body thrown over the Milltown Bridge into the Canal. Murray said in the statement that when he told Costello of the shooting, Costello answered that Bergin's death would be referred to as "one of the usual unofficial executions". Murray denied point blank in court writing or signing the statement and his counsel, Mr Gleeson, complained bitterly about it, as it had not previously been referred to in the trial. A handwriting expert agreed that the handwriting belonged to Murray, however.

Michael Murray, brother of the accused corroborated his brother's evidence. He stated that he had met him on the night of Bergin's murder and that they had spent the night in Dublin before going home. He claimed that Costello had given him money to give to James and asked him to convince his brother to go to South America. Michael Murray had accompanied his brother to Argentina, staying for several months before returning to clear James's name. Finally, Michael Murray revealed that the writing on the confession was not that of his brother but that of Costello who, he said, had "perjured himself in the trial."

Corporal Michael Costello was recalled to the stand to answer the fresh accusations against him. He flatly denied them all.

The defence counsel addressed the jury at the end of the four-day trial. Their case was that Murray got into the car with the two men, with whom he was not acquainted. When he realised the violent nature of the work being undertaken, he immediately left the car and only met the men again in the morning. Murray knew nothing of what happened to Bergin and had taken no part in his death. He had gone abroad under instruction but had come back voluntarily to clear his name. The defence asked, "Where were the other two men from the car and why were they not on trial?" The defence added that Corporal Costello knew that Bergin was to be murdered and that Murray provided a convenient scapegoat. He derided the confession as being false and stated that the state would have brought it forward immediately in the trial if they felt it was legitimate. Gleeson also complained about the Ministry for Defence, which he claimed had withheld important information which would have exonerated his client. He urged the jury to acquit.

The prosecution, conversely, stated that Murray had chosen to live the life of a hunted man. Mr Carrigan, prosecuting, asked the jury if they "were prepared to believe the government were capable of endeavouring to shield a guilty man?" He also stated that he had not read aloud the confession made by Murray in mercy to the prisoner, as it showed that Murray "had gone down to the place to kill a man like a dog." Judge Hanna, in summing up, stated, "I never knew a case like it, by reason of the way people in high authority in the state were involved." The jury needed just one hour and twenty five minutes to find James Murray guilty, despite a lack of hard evidence linking him with the crime scene. When asked if there was any reason why he should not be given the death penalty, Murray made a heartfelt plea.

"I merely wish to state that I am innocent, I have been made the scapegoat for this crime of which I am innocent. I only hope that the officers who have sold my life away will be prepared to meet their

God when they meet Him, as I hope to be prepared to meet Him. I have nothing more to say."

It was to no avail. Justice Hanna gave the only sentence he could in the circumstances and sentenced Murray to be hanged. The defence applied for leave to appeal on eighteen grounds, chief amongst them the confession, which they claimed was inadmissible. They also stated that the prosecution had no evidence of what happened between the time Murray got into the car and his conversation with Costello the next morning. Fingerprints were found on several items in the house in Kildare but none matched the condemned man. The leave to appeal was unanimously rejected by the Court of Criminal Appeal.

However, on 19 July the Governor-General commuted the death sentence to one of penal servitude for life. The evidence against Murray was flimsy but it is quite possible that he was involved in the murder. In the midst of the brutal Civil War, the Free State army frequently executed rank and file members of the IRA without trial. Rumour abounded in republican circles that Joseph Bergin had been tortured and mutilated, before being tied with a rope to a car and dragged along the roads. Murray almost paid with his life for the vicious incident, even though there were countless similar killings of spies where the participants went wholly unpunished. Murray, very similar to Jeremiah Gaffney before him, was made an example of by the state. Unlike Gaffney, however, he narrowly escaped the gallows. If he was present, he was certainly not the only participant in Joseph Bergin's brutal murder and the cover-up may well have gone into the upper echelons of the Irish Army. The other men in the car were never officially identified. James Murray was an uncooperative inmate and he went on hunger strike in prison on more than one occasion. His health deteriorated and he eventually died four years after his conviction, succumbing to tuberculosis in the isolation ward of Portlaoise Prison in September 1929.

The lawless National Army was plagued by cases like those of Gaffney and Murray in the early 1920s. W.T. Cosgrave had remarked during the

Civil War that "I am not going to hesitate if the country is to live, and if we have to exterminate ten thousand republicans, the three million of our people is greater than this ten thousand." Many soldiers took him at his word. Noel Lemass, brother of subsequent Taoiseach Seán, was one of many republicans to receive such an unofficial execution. He was kidnapped in broad daylight in Dublin in July 1923. His dismembered body, which had been riddled with bullets, was found some months later in the Dublin Mountains. James Murray's name had also been linked to this case. One witness asserted that Murray admitted to shooting Lemass and throwing his body into the River Liffey. Nevertheless, no one was ever prosecuted for this murder.

Captain James Murray may have been a bloodthirsty murderer responsible for two gruesome executions without trial. It is also possible that he acted as a convenient scapegoat for the hugely undisciplined National Army. A large amount of inexperienced recruits had been gratefully welcomed into the army to fight the anti-Treaty forces as the Civil War raged on. After the unrest had been quelled, there were thousands of trigger-happy young soldiers with access to ammunition who were most unsuited to a career with the armed forces. Shortly after the Murray and Gaffney incidents, the Minister for Defence Richard Mulcahy decided to reduce the size of the army from 55,000 soldiers down to just 18,000.

HANNAH O'LEARY

"My hands are clean anyway."

The murder of a family member causes major suffering and devastation to the remaining relatives. Unless, of course, it was they who were jointly responsible for it. On 10 March 1924 a farmer named Michael Walsh, from Kilkerran in West Cork, was using a local field as a shortcut to check on some cows when he made a shocking discovery under a bush. It was a sack which appeared to be full of parts of a dismembered human corpse. A severed head lay fourteen yards away from the sack. According to newspaper reports of the time, Walsh was so badly affected by the horrific sight that he spent time in a mental hospital afterwards. The arms and torso of the male corpse lay scattered around the field. His skull had been beaten so badly that fragments of bone were lodged in his brain. The body, which had lay unconcealed in the open, was found in eight pieces altogether, some dumped in a nearby river.

Gardaí arrived quickly in the area after receiving a telegram informing them of the disturbing find. They were soon made aware of a farmer from the locality, Patrick O'Leary (40), who had last been seen ten days before at 10 p.m. on the night of 25 February. In light of this development, they went directly to a pub in the village of Milltown where they found Cornelius O'Leary (about 37), brother of the missing man. Guard Reynolds and Sergeant Devoy accompanied him to the field and showed him the remains, before asking him if it was the body of his brother Patrick. Cornelius seemed surprisingly unperturbed by the grisly find but identified it as his brother, "Yes, this is Pat." A few minutes later, he looked again and said "I do not know whose head it is." The Gardaí reminded him that he had just identified the head as his brother's. Con replied "Oh, I am innocent. My hands are clean." He also told the police that he had not taken part in any murder. The Gardaí had not accused him of anything of the sort and their suspicions were immediately aroused at this unusual reaction to seeing a murdered loved one.

If they thought that more clarity would come from the other members of the O'Leary family then they would be proven wrong. Hannah and Mary-Anne, Cornelius' two sisters, were also asked to identify the head of their brother. The Gardaí laid the head out on the table in front of them. Incredibly, both women seemed disinterested and claimed never to have laid eyes on that person before saying, "Paddy was not so thin in the poll." One of the Gardaí present was casually acquainted with Patrick and he was able to quickly identify the head as belonging to him. The sisters then looked again for several minutes until Mary-Anne (41) eventually admitted it was her brother. Some time later Hannah (38) followed suit. None of the three siblings seemed surprised by the horrendous sight before them. Furthermore, none of them expressed any regret or sorrow at the butchery of their brother.

At the wake on the following day, a large crowd of mourners came to pay their respects. They were appalled, however, to see various body parts from Patrick's dismembered corpse strewn around in an open coffin on the kitchen table. One mourner informed Con at the wake that "suspicions are strong against you". Con replied that he was "freed" of the crime, and so were all the people of Kilkerran. He also said, "I'll go to heaven, anyway." One Garda remarked to Hannah, who was known locally as a surly and bad-tempered woman, that it was a terrible case. She replied coolly, "Wisha, it can't be helped." A day later, the O'Leary's dog was seen running past the house holding a human arm stripped of flesh in its mouth. The total lack of grief shown by the family was a cause of shock in the area and the Gardaí quickly started to look into the background of the eccentric O'Leary household. It was soon discovered that it had not been a happy home.

The father of the family, Patrick, had died in 1921 at the ripe age of 80. He had eight children, one of whom had died. Three others had moved away and lived outside the Kilkerran area leaving Con and Patrick on the farm with their two sisters. Unsurprisingly Patrick Snr chose to give the farm to his widow on his death, instructing that it would next pass to Patrick, the elder son. The forty-acre farm included several cows and two horses and was situated on good land outside the village of Kilkerran. Unusually Con, the younger brother, chose not to work at home, labouring instead for local farmer William Travers. Patrick was not happy with this situation, thinking that Con should help out on his own farm. He was so displeased with his brother's employment that twice in August 1922 he went to Travers and complained about it. Travers told Con about this confrontation but Con replied that he would not work for his brother as he would not get paid.

The two brothers did not have a good relationship and had not spoken for several years, the animosity even preceding the death of their father. Mary-Anne, considered the friendliest of the family, also worked and lodged away from home in another local farm. This left Patrick to run the farm, with Hannah and his mother in charge of minding the house. The apparent unwillingness of two of the siblings to work with Pat perhaps show how the relationship between him and the rest of the family had broken down some time before. Patrick, considered locally to be an awkward man, did not even sleep in the house with the rest of the family as this would have meant sharing a bed with Con. Instead he made his sleeping quarters out in the hayloft. Things had come to a head shortly before Patrick's disappearance, when his three siblings had visited the parish priest, Revd Kearney, and consulted him about their brother. They told the priest that Pat had sold cattle at a local fair and had not informed the family about the transaction. The O'Learys believed he was not giving them any money in an attempt to squeeze them out. The priest came back the next day, offering to mediate between the two parties. This overture was declined by Mary-Anne, just days before Pat's disappearance. By late February 1924, relations within the family were toxic.

Patrick was missing for nearly ten days before the body parts were discovered yet no member of the family had contacted the authorities, nor expressed concern about his whereabouts. On 27 February, presumably the day after Patrick was murdered, a strange thing had happened. Con had arrived at Travers farm at 5 a.m. as they were leaving early to get to the fair in Rosscarbery, a fifty-mile round trip. Con appeared to be in a confused state and told his employer that he had seen "A man on the road." When asked to elaborate, Con told him it was "one of the little people...from the other world." He had then taken a horse and cart and gone to Rosscarbery via a longer road that he had never used before. This route allowed him to avoid passing his own house. When Travers questioned him about this unusual behaviour, Con told him that he thought this road was shorter, even though both men knew that this was not the case. It may have been that Con's guilty conscience was causing him to act bizarrely.

When the Garda questioned the family as to why they hadn't reported their brother missing, Con replied that Patrick was in the habit of going away and he didn't take any notice as he was expecting him home any day. Mary-Anne said that she expected him to write any day, although she was forced to admit later that her brother was illiterate and would not have been able to pen a letter. The O'Learys' neighbours had enquired of Pat's whereabouts at one stage but the family told them he had gone to Bandon fair on 27 February and had not returned since. After the discovery of the dismembered body, the Gardaí searched the hayloft and found that Patrick's bed had been freshly made with new bedclothes. Notwithstanding this, a bloodstained fork was unearthed underneath the bed and Patrick's sleeping quarters also appeared to have been the scene of a violent row, with traces of blood visible in several places, including on the walls and the potatoes in the loft. The Gardaí believed they had sufficient evidence to be confident that a murder had occurred and that it had been committed by a member of the O'Leary family. None of the O'Learys would admit to anything, however, insisting that they knew nothing of his disappearance. For this reason, all four members of the household were arrested, including the elderly mother, Hannah O'Leary. The four O'Learys were charged with having murdered Patrick O'Leary at some point between 26 February and 7 March. This family quarrel turned vicious murder became easily the most closely-followed murder trial in the history of the new state. The public gallery in the courthouse "was filled to its utmost extent every day."

The trial was fixed for Green Street, Dublin on 23 June 1925. Mary-Anne O'Leary had died of natural causes while in custody. The state's charge against their mother was also withdrawn due to lack of evidence. This left just Con and Hannah to face the court for the murder of their brother. They were tried jointly with Con showing keen interest in the proceedings while Hannah mostly sat bowed with a shawl around her head and did not look up. Both of the accused pleaded not guilty to the charge. The defence argued that there was no evidence and no bloodstains found on any clothing belonging to the accused pair. They added that there was no way the court could know which member of the O'Leary family committed the crime, if any, and that the real perpetrator may not even be in the courtroom. The defence counsel also asked, "Might it not be Mary-Anne?", a convenient defence for the two defendants with her death having occurred in the weeks coming up to the trial. Neither defendant took the stand. Their defence team also refused to call witnesses for the defence, saying that there was no need due to the total lack of evidence that a murder had been committed by either defendant.

Mr Campion, prosecuting, said the murder had "transcended in horror the many crimes which had been tried in that ancient courthouse." He emphasised the horrific nature of the death and dismemberment of Patrick O'Leary. He called the two accused monsters for attempting to blame their deceased sister for the crime and reminded the court of their total lack of interest in the horror that had been inflicted on their brother. The jury deliberated and were deadlocked. A hasty second trial was convened hearing the same evidence. This jury had no such hesitation and needed only thirty minutes to produce a guilty verdict for both defendants. A recommendation to mercy was given to Hannah, presumably on account of her gender. Con received no such comfort. Hannah and Con O'Leary were thus sentenced to death by Mr Justice Hanna. Both O'Learys maintained their innocence of the charge, Con saying "I had not hand, act nor part in the murder…I am going to die an innocent man." Hannah answered, "I did not kill my brother." The two siblings appealed the conviction but after a four-day hearing their appeal was refused.

On 27 July 1925, just before the sentence was to be carried out, Hannah O'Leary received a last-minute reprieve from the Governor-General and her sentence was commuted to one of penal servitude for life. The governments of the day never gave a reason for such commutations, but it was speculated afterwards that it was down to her gender. Leniency for Con O'Leary was not forthcoming, however. He went to the scaffold at Mountjoy Prison on 28 July at 8 a.m. The records state his demeanour was "calm", although the same was said for all condemned prisoners. Another newspaper report describes how a warder, who had helped Cornelius O'Leary to the scaffold, fainted after witnessing the hanging. No Irish execution had been conducted publicly since 1868 and the standard line was that it had proceeded without incident. Whether Con O'Leary or any of the other condemned prisoners really went peacefully to their deaths will never be known, although Albert Pierrepoint would later comment "I love hanging Irishmen. They always go quietly and without trouble. They're Christian men and they believe they're going to a better place." Hannah O'Leary Jnr was finally released from prison in September 1942. Like Hannah Flynn before her, O'Leary was considered mentally subnormal and had no family member willing to accept her on her release. She was thus sent to live out her days with a community of Good Shepherd Nuns.

In February 1924, Hannah O'Leary Snr shared her home with four of her children. Barely a year later three of them were dead, one of natural causes, one murdered and a third hanged. The fourth was imprisoned in Mountjoy Prison. By 1927, she was in her mid-seventies and living alone in Kilkerran. She had little choice but to sell on the farm. The new owners wasted little time in destroying the house and sheds, the scenes of the unimaginable horror. Hannah O' Leary Snr died in the County Home in Clonakilty in January 1928, thus completing the eradication of the entire O'Leary family in West Cork. The hearse carrying her remains drove through Clonakility where it was reported that "the only person in attendance was the undertaker." A fittingly tragic end to a truly horrific case.

MARTIN JOYCE & ANNIE WALSH

"What can they say to me when they did not see me do it?"

"Everyone will be relieved when the curtain is at last rung down on this year old tragedy, which reads more like a Russian play than a story of life in the west of Ireland." So read one editorial on the lengthy saga that occurred in the South-Western Connemara village of Rosmuc in May 1928. Rosmuc was a world away from the affluent streets of Dublin, where the court case would eventually conclude. The scenic fishing and farming village was strongly Irish-speaking and maintained many of Ireland's most ancient cultural traditions. Economically, however, Rosmuc, like much of the west coast, was impoverished and ravaged by emigration. Most of its residents eked out a living on the stony soil and stormy seas in the beautiful yet barren area. Admiring the stunning landscape, it is easy to understand why Pádraig Pearse, leader of the 1916 Easter Rising, had chosen the tranquil peninsula to build his cottage. It was a place where he felt at home and could get inspiration to write some of his most important works. The peaceful area's experience of crime rarely extended beyond the illegal distillation of poitín. Murders in the quiet rural area were almost unheard of until May 1928.

Annie Joyce was from Lettermore (Leitir Mór), a small village situated in South Connemara. It lies just across the bay from Rosmuc by boat, which would have been the preferred method of transport at the time, although it is nearly twenty miles by road through the winding peninsulas.

In 1912, Annie followed the well-travelled path from Connemara to Boston, America aged just 19. While there, she met and married Colman Kelly, who was from the Aran Islands. They had three children together but he died of influenza after just five years of marriage. Annie returned to Lettermore shortly after her husband's untimely death. Within three months she was married again, this time to Daniel "Sonny" Walsh, whom she had met just four weeks before the ceremony. They wed in 1919, the year after the First World War and three years before Ireland would gain its independence. Sonny was about 52 years old and from Turloghbeg, Rosmuc. He brought his new bride and her three children to live in his labourer's cottage situated on thirty-five acres beside Camus Bay. Sonny was known to be a kind, hard-working and industrious man, but also a heavy drinker. He was a carter and farmer and worked hard, giving most of his earnings to his new wife.

Annie was not particularly happy with her new lodgings, however. She had lived in good conditions in Boston and her new house was small and damp while she described her new husband as "queer" and "strange". His sister Kate, a former matron of the workhouse in Oughterard, lived with the newly-weds for the first year of their marriage, but Annie's relationship with her new sister-in-law was also strained. After the year had passed, Kate emigrated to America leaving Annie and Sonny together in the house. The couple quickly had three children of their own, bringing the number of people in the small cottage to eight. Sonny was indeed a gentle soul, described by others as "quiet and simple" and perhaps somewhat of a pushover, tolerating things that would be quick to anger others. He had also been involved in a serious accident when he was a child which may have affected his mentality. The lower portion of his face was scarred and burned when he was just three years of age and the event had a major effect on him, according to his sister Kate. Within a couple of years of being married Sonny had resorted to sleeping in a small back room with just two beds. Some of the children also shared this room. Sonny's wife occupied her own room at the front of the house. Martin Joyce then arrived on the scene.

Martin Joyce was a second cousin of Annie Walsh and was about 26 years of age, well over a decade younger than Annie. He lived at South Shore, just under a mile from the Walsh cottage. At some point in the mid-1920s he started to spend a large amount of time in the Walsh household, although he had no particular business in the house, nor did he do any work on the farm. Eventually, Joyce started sleeping over in Annie Walsh's room while her husband slept next door. Sometimes this happened once a week, other times much more frequently. Sonny apparently raised no objections but unsurprisingly the illicit liaison became big news in the rural area. At the bog a neighbour named Martin Conroy warned Sonny, "Take care of yourself, Martin Joyce is going to your home." Sonny returned to Annie and complained bitterly about the situation to her. She was furious and demanded to know who had said it to him. He would not tell her at first, but eventually gave her Conroy's name. When he did she put her on her boots and started walking out the door. Sonny asked where she was going and she replied "to choke Martin Conroy." Annie was a woman with a violent temper.

On 30 May 1928, Martin Joyce sent Mary, one of Annie's daughters from her first marriage, to a local island to purchase a bottle of poitín. It cost 6s. When the child returned, Martin waited with Annie in the house for Sonny to come back from working in the fields, where he was moulding potatoes. When he arrived back that evening, Martin suggested to him that he and Sonny should walk to Oughterard, a town twenty miles to the north-east. He proposed that they could collect a crib for the cart from Sonny's first cousin, who lived there. He also reminded Sonny that he needed to pay interest on a loan to the bank. Sonny agreed, despite the lateness of the hour, as he had grown accustomed to doing these long walks at night. Sonny and Martin shared the poitín. By the time the three departed the house, Sonny Walsh was well under the influence of drink. Martin Joyce had consumed only "two glassfuls and was fairly sober". Annie had not drunk any alcohol. The children later deposed that the three figures left via the backdoor of the house and tramped a path towards the main road by Sonny's brother John Walsh's house, but did not enter. The occupants of that house spotted them walking by but did not converse with them. Sonny Walsh would not be seen alive again.

At 7 a.m. on the morning of 31 May, Marcus Conneely was cutting turf two miles from Walsh's house when he saw a man's body face down in the Mill Stream. Conneely did not recognise him but some men who were passing subsequently identified him as Sonny Walsh. The matter was immediately reported to the Guards in Rosmuc who arrived on the scene. Sonny had drowned in just three or four inches of water in the stream just over two miles from his home. Sergeant Gallagher described a wound to the side of Sonny's head and "blue blotches on his face". When Dr J.J. Gibbon examined the corpse on the same day, he found clay on the inside of the teeth and some minor injuries to the scalp. Gibbon attributed death to asphyxia caused by drowning. When Sonny left the house, his wife said she had given him 30s. which he had put it in his pocket to purchase the crib in Oughterard. When he was discovered his pockets contained a stone, a stud, bread, butter and string. There was no money.

The first of the Walshs to hear the news was Annie's daughter, Mary. She came to her mother to tell her that Sonny was drowned. Soon afterwards, an inquest was held by the Galway coroner into the death of Sonny Walsh. Annie gave evidence that her husband had left home alone before midnight to go to Oughterard. She had bolted the door and went to bed and she did not find out until the next day that she been widowed for the second time. Her deposition was not questioned and a verdict of "found drowned" was returned. That appeared to be the end of the tragic episode. The wake was held the day after Sonny's death and lasted two nights. Martin Joyce attended briefly the second night but did not return to the house for a month. Sonny was buried and very little happened for several months.

Locals had been well aware of the relationship between Martin Joyce and Annie Walsh, however, and many suspected foul play. It was felt locally that it was strange that seasoned drinker Sonny could have drowned in a shallow puddle. Rumours became more intense as Joyce was described as being in Annie's house night and day within a month of the funeral. Tongues quickly began to wag again and someone in the locality contacted a relative of Sonny's in America, who in turn put pressure on the Irish authorities to re-open the case. Sonny's brothers were also suspicious from the off of the strange circumstances of their brother's death. They even enquired about the possibility of taking custody of his three youngest children from Annie, an application which was refused. By late 1928, however, the Gardaí had begun to look into the case again. When they interviewed Martin Joyce on 27 October in Rosmuc Barracks he told them that he had been drunk on 30 May. He had gone to Camus looking for work, before going to a wake on the local island of Illaunmore. He had drank two bottles of poitín while there before sleeping that night on the side of a mountain, not waking until morning. Joyce denied staying in the Walsh household that night. He said he was rowed back to the mainland where he met a neighbour, Maggie Canavan, who was the first to inform him of the death of Sonny Walsh. Unfortunately for Joyce, no one at the wake could vouch for him having been there. Sonny's body was exhumed in November, with Gardaí were now treating foul play as a real possibility. Martin Joyce and Annie Walsh were the most likely suspects and locals were not surprised when they were arrested and charged with murder shortly afterwards.

The trial began in Dublin Central Criminal Court on Monday 17 June 1929, just over a year after Sonny's death. The accused were tried together, the judge denying requests for separate trials. Both pleaded not guilty to the murder charge. An interpreter was required for many of the witnesses who were only proficient in Irish, making this a far longer trial than was normal at the time.

Early in the trial, Catherine Kelly, eldest daughter of Annie Walsh and stepdaughter of Sonny, was called to the stand. She asserted that Martin Joyce had asked her if she would like Sonny to die and she had answered that she would. He had then told her that if Sonny died he would marry her mother and they would have a good life together. On the night of 30 May, Catherine said that Sonny was staggering and unable to walk before he left the house. Catherine and her sisters were sent to check that the neighbours were asleep. When they confirmed that there was no light in their home, the children were sent to bed and Catherine disclosed that Joyce, Annie and Sonny left together out the back door. Catherine said she was awoken later that night by Annie and Martin crawling in the window of their house as the children had bolted the door. When the children asked where Sonny was, Annie answered that he was "out abroad there". When questioned why he had not returned with them, Annie claimed that Sonny "had his knife open going to stick Martin Joyce." There was no more said about it and the two adults went to sleep beside the children. The children found out about Sonny's death the next day and Catherine deposed that Martin Joyce did not come to their home again for a month, apart from a brief appearance at the wake. After the month had elapsed, however, he was constantly in the house, going up to the loft and hiding when he knew that the Gardaí were paying a visit. At this point Joyce had told the children then that he and their mother were going to get married and they would all go to Canada together.

Mary Kelly, Catherine's sister, corroborated much of Catherine's evidence. She stated that her mother often asked her if she wished Sonny was gone. Mary also said she often witnessed her mother giving Martin Joyce better food than Sonny and that she had once put manure in Sonny's tea. When he complained that the tea was bitter, Annie insisted that there was no taste off it. Sonny had then drunk the mixture. Mary said that her mother and Martin had gone off with Sonny on the night of the 30th and had come back some hours later. Both of their clothes were filthy. When Mary was cross-examined as to why she had not mentioned this crucial information when first questioned by the Guards she replied simply, "I made up my mind to tell the truth." She also said she had been afraid of her mother beating her and that her mother had told her to tell lies in court.

Sonny's nephew John took the stand and told the court that he had often been playing cards in Sonny's house when Martin Joyce was present. Martin did not play himself, but often stayed behind when all the rest were gone. He also deposed that on the night Sonny was last seen he had heard noises outside and looked out to see Martin and his uncle pass by, although he did not see Annie. John's father told the court that Martin Joyce stayed in Sonny's house at least three times a week in the year before the murder and was often seen leaving at around 7 a.m. and running across the fields. Since Sonny's death, he said he had seen Joyce and Annie alone together in the fields "six or seven times". He was asked by the defence team if, had Sonny remained unmarried, he would have a chance to gain his land. He denied this ulterior motive. Martin Conroy, the neighbour who had previously warned Sonny of his wife's affair, also took the stand. He swore that Martin Joyce said to him "What can they say to me when they did not see me do it?"

Martin Joyce chose to give evidence in his own defence. He admitted that he had spent some time in Sonny Walsh's house, but only to play cards. He conceded that Annie gave him presents occasionally, including a new pair of boots, but denied anything illicit between them. His account of the night of 30 May was that he and Sonny left the house together while Annie had stayed at home. Sonny was drunk. They walked together as far as the townland of Strabogue where Martin turned east and Sonny west towards Oughterard. Martin got a boat and slept on Illaunmore until morning because he was drunk. When he came around he visited several houses where he was told the news of Sonny's death. Joyce denied hiding from the guards in the loft, although he admitted he was afraid of them because of the rumours local people were spreading about him and Annie. He also emphatically denied having slept in Annie's house the night of Sonny's death. He told the court that the children had invented the story of him staying there that night and many times after Sonny's death. Annie's two daughters were recalled and cross-examined about their testimony. Neither wavered from their original testimony.

Annie Walsh also took the stand. She chose to address the court in Irish, stating that although she could understand English she did not speak it comfortably. She told the jury that any rumours about her and Martin were untrue. She said that Joyce used to work for Sonny regularly and would receive food as part of his payment, which explained why he was in the house so frequently. She said that as far as she knew Martin Joyce slept in her house only two nights. On the night of the tragedy, Annie claimed that she had given her husband 30s. and some bread and butter for the journey and gone to bed. Her husband and Martin were in the kitchen and she heard them leave some time later via the back door. The next she heard was the following day when her daughter told her that Sonny had drowned. Annie was asked why she had suggested at the inquest that Sonny had left the house on his own, but she stated that she could not remember making such a statement. She denied that she had any particular reason to protect Martin Joyce, who as far as she knew was "the last person to see (her) husband." She also said her children were speaking false when they said she slept with Martin Joyce. Although she admitted describing her husband as "queer" and "strange", she also claimed that they lived happily together. She said he was a friendly man who got on well with all his neighbours and she had no reason to want to harm him.

The defence complained that the children's evidence was inconsistent and had changed over time. Mary Kelly had at one point told the Gardaí that it was just Martin and Sonny who had left the house on the night of 30 May, but now claimed that her mother had gone with them as well. They admitted that there were questions over the nature of the relationship between Walsh and Joyce but said that this was not relevant to the case, which involved a simple accidental drowning. The prosecution quoted all the witnesses who gave damning evidence, putting special emphasis on the children who claimed that both accused had talked of it being better if Sonny was dead. They also insisted that both accused had "reason to want him dead".

The judge, in summing up, asked the jury if they thought Sonny's body had been placed in such a way as to make his death look like an accident. He asked them to carefully consider what had happened to the 30s. which he had in his possession when he left the house. The jury retired for an hour, coming back to ask the interesting question about which pocket the five-naggin bottle had been in when found on Sonny Walsh. The judge repeated the relevant statements and the jury again retired for forty-five minutes. They then returned with a guilty verdict. The two prisoners were then asked if they had anything to say. Martin Joyce stayed silent, while Annie Walsh cried "Not guilty." After what was described as a tense silence, Justice O'Byrne sentenced both to be hanged on 18 July.

Joyce and Walsh both appealed their sentences on such grounds as "they should have received separate trials", "the learned judge misdirected the jury" and "the Irish had not been accurately reproduced". Leave to appeal was granted but the Court of Criminal Appeal, represented by three judges, agreed unanimously on 24 July that the guilty verdict should stand. Martin Joyce and Annie Walsh were again sentenced to death, scheduled for 9 August 1929. A large number of local people, including priests, bishops and several TDs, petitioned the government on behalf of the condemned prisoners. Eventually, on 1 August, the two convicted murderers were reprieved and sentenced instead to penal servitude for life to be served in Mountjoy. In 1932 the sentence was further reduced to ten years penal servitude each. Annie was released from prison in January 1936. Her co-conspirator had to wait nearly twelve months longer, finally being released in December of the same year.

It is unquestionable that the evidence of Annie Walsh's children was the main reason the two accused were found guilty. Did the reprieve, like the one received by Patrick Aylward (Chapter 5), come from the profound discomfort the state felt at the thought of executing people on the evidence of children? Quite possibly. A reasonable doubt was also present in the minds of many who commentated on the case. After Annie was incarcerated, her three young children with Sonny, namely Daniel, Annie and Thomas, were adopted by their aunt, Sonny's sister Kate Walsh.

A murder in Co. Galway has not resulted in an execution since 1902. On that occasion, a "lame and deformed cripple" visited the gallows.

Thomas Keeley had fallen on hard times and was begging around the town of Athenry, twelve miles from Galway City. Keeley, who was aged about 35, told some locals that he was a painter and that he needed lodgings. He was directed to a local landlady, Mary Clasby (60). Clasby took pity on Keeley, and allowed him to stay in her home on Northgate Street in the town. Keeley repaid this kindness by beating the elderly woman to death with a hammer he carried with him and stealing her money and valuables. He was quickly traced and found to be carrying items belonging to the deceased woman. Keeley was arrested, found guilty and sentenced to death. The condemned man, who had taken ill after the sentence, was brought to the scaffold in a state of collapse. Nevertheless, the hanging was carried out as planned and a black flag was hoisted outside Galway Jail, a tradition that was discontinued shortly afterwards. Fortunately for Annie Walsh and Martin Joyce, Keeley would prove to be the last person hanged for a murder in Co. Galway.

JANE O'BRIEN

"I'm sure I must have shot him."

William Cousins was a small farmer from Killinick, not far from Rosslare in Co. Wexford. He lived in the townland of Sanctuary three hundred yards from the village. He resided with his son, John, his wife Kathleen having passed away some years before. After her death, he invited his sister, Jane O'Brien, to move in with them on their seven-acre farm. Jane, whose husband had left her to go to England and never returned, agreed. She moved into the neatly-kept farmhouse and acted as an extra pair of hands around the house, bringing along her own son, also named John. William died in December 1931. He was his mid-60s, but left no will. Nevertheless, his estate passed automatically to his son John. The comfortable life Jane O'Brien enjoyed in Sanctuary would change rapidly after her brother's funeral.

Shortly after his father's passing, John Cousins informed his aunt that he was engaged to be married to his neighbour, Annie Maguire, whom he had known all his life. She was ten years his junior and a domestic servant. The newly-engaged couple had planned to marry earlier but had postponed it due to William Cousins' illness. The nuptials were now arranged for December 1932. John told his aunt that the house would not be big enough for all of them and she would have to leave Sanctuary to make way for his new bride. Jane O'Brien pleaded her case with her nephew, reminding him of all the work she had done around the house since his mother's death. Her petitions fell on deaf ears. Jane O'Brien's days in Sanctuary were numbered.

On 26 March, Holy Saturday, John Cousins went to Treacy's public house for a couple of pints before heading to the Maguire household to spend the evening dancing and chatting. He left the Maguires for home at about 11.30 p.m. with his friend James O'Reilly. They parted ways at the bottom of Cousins' avenue. When O'Reilly was gone about fifteen yards up the road he heard a loud bang, which seemed to come from inside the Cousins' gate. He turned around and saw John Cousins in a state of collapse holding his stomach. "I'm shot, Jem," he gasped. Garda James Grimes was on the scene within minutes to examine Cousins, who had over one hundred and fifty pellets in his body. The authorities seemed to underestimate his injuries and there was a considerable delay in getting the critically-wounded man to hospital. Eventually, some time after 1 a.m., a car was found to bring Cousins to Wexford Hospital. He never made it, however, dying en route.

The State Pathologist examined Cousins and found that he had died after being shot in the abdomen. Death was due to shock and haemorrhage and there was no doubt that he had been murdered. The Gardaí wasted no time in informing Jane O'Brien of the tragedy that had befallen her nephew. She showed no emotion and asked if it was a motor accident. She was told that it was not, but surprisingly she did not make any further enquiry about the nature of the tragedy.

The Gardaí initially suspected that the IRA were involved in the ambush. The shotgun killing bore all the hallmarks of an IRA attack and Cousins had been an active campaigner for the outgoing Cumann na nGaedheal government, the arch-enemies of the republicans. Fianna Fáil, the reincarnation of the anti-Treaty side in the Civil War, had just gained power in the general election two weeks before and the stability of the country seemed balanced on a knife-edge. It was not known whether the government would be willing to peacefully hand over power to the side which had up until several years before refused to recognise the state. Tit-for-tat shootings were still occurring and election agents had been shot in the past. John Cousins looked to have been just another murder in the bloody political feud. The IRA however quickly released a statement in which they denied all culpability in the killing. This prompted the Gardaí to begin looking a little closer to home.

The Gardaí made a search of the scene of the shooting and found a hole in the hedge that appeared to have been made recently. While conducting enquiries locally, a local woman named Johanna Moran mentioned in passing to the authorities that she had seen Jane O'Brien beside this hedge the day before the murder. She appeared to be holding a tool of some sort and hammering it against the bush, although Moran could not be sure what it was. The Gardaí had already heard whispers of the recent animosity between Cousins and his aunt and began to look into the possibility that this had been a domestic crime, rather than a political one.

The day after the shooting, the Gardaí interviewed Jane O'Brien. She told them that the previous night had been a normal evening where she had prepared meals for her son and John Cousins. She denied any animosity between herself and her nephew, even claiming that she was unaware that he was planning to get married. The Gardaí were suspicious and ordered that Cousins' house be searched. When they got to Mrs O'Brien's room, one of the Gardaí noticed a cut on her hand. When she was asked about it she replied curiously, "It may have been the cat or the dog but at any rate it was not the bush." Superintendent McCarthy asked her to save them the trouble of a further search and produce the gun used to shoot John Cousins. Mrs O'Brien became excited and nervous, and initially denied knowing of a firearm in the house. Eventually, however, she pointed to the mattress and the Gardaí pulled out a single-barrel shotgun which they noted had recently been discharged. Jane O'Brien then said, "I will now tell you all about it."

O'Brien told the sergeant that the trouble began about two weeks before the shooting. She and her nephew had been arguing steadily until the night of 26 March. Cousins, while shaving, had said, "Jane, you'll have to be out of this in a week." She responded that she had worked hard in the house in her twelve years. Cousins then asked her several times "Who asked you to do it?" An angry O'Brien threatened to tell the authorities about Cousins' gun, which he held illegally. Cousins replied "If you do split (about the gun) I will give you the contents of it." O'Brien responded, "You'll never get the chance of giving me the contents of it." The argument finished with Jane O'Brien refusing to leave until she was compensated for the twelve years work she had done in the house. John would not contemplate this suggestion. After the argument, he left the house to go dancing in Killinick, as he did every Saturday.

After Jane O'Brien finished her work in the house, she took the gun from under John Cousin's bed, where it had been for the last two years. She then retrieved three cartridges from over the bedroom door, putting one in the shotgun. Afterwards, she baked two cakes of bread leaving the gun outside the kitchen door. Finally she went out to the laneway and paced up and down, waiting for her nephew's return. She recounted later that she knew he always returned around midnight and that she planned to "give him a fright tonight for what he said to me".

At around 11.50 p.m. she heard a footstep and she pointed the gun through the hedge and pulled the trigger. "I'm sure I must have shot him. I then walked down the lane in the direction of my house. I pegged the cartridge away. I walked straight up to John's room and put back the gun where I found it." The Gardaí, while searching the house, had also discovered a hand-saw with fresh sawdust on it which had been used to cut the hole in the hedge. Jane O'Brien was immediately arrested and charged with the murder of her nephew. Her trial began in the Dublin Central Criminal Court on 6 June 1932 in front of a packed gallery, the peculiar details of the case attracting huge attention nationally. Jane O'Brien, described as cool and indifferent during the trial, pleaded not guilty. She also withdrew the statement she had made earlier in which she admitted the shooting.

The prosecution put it to the jury that Jane O'Brien's motive was jealousy against Anne Maguire who would be taking her place in the home in which she had worked for so long. O'Brien's account of the threats she had suffered from John Cousins were challenged in court. It came to light that O'Brien had been sending anonymous postcards to her nephew which insulted his fiancée and made threats against him if he did not break off the engagement. Although she denied writing or sending them, a handwriting expert took the stand and vouched that they were written by the hand of Jane O'Brien. The anonymous writer had misspelled the word lovely as "lovilly" on several of the postcards, a mistake also found frequently in O'Brien's diary. Annie Maguire took the stand and produced four of the offensive postcards which all bore the stamp of Killinick post office. She told the court that O'Brien had been in the post office one day when she had walked in. O'Brien said snidely to the postmistress, "I had better run out for fear Nan would blame me for sending postcards." At this stage, Anne Maguire and her fiancé had not mentioned to anyone about the malicious correspondence, indicating that they could only have been sent by O'Brien. The prosecution counsel also reminded the jury that John Cousins was shot by someone who knew his movements and had shown their premeditation by calmly cutting the hedge. They believed that that person could only have been Jane O'Brien, who had been seen with an implement beside it the day before the murder. O'Brien had a strong motive for the killing and had admitted it in initial statements to the Gardaí.

The defence counsel, Mr Wood, did not call Jane O'Brien, telling the court that there was no necessity. He said that the statement taken from her had not been signed until twenty-four hours after it was taken and that the facts contained in it were untrue and had been bullied out of the elderly woman. He asserted that the Gardaí had come into the house and said, "Give us the gun that shot John Cousins", an unacceptable statement to make. He further said that the evidence was circumstantial and did not incriminate his client. She had been seen cutting the hedge in the middle of the day, hardly cast-iron proof that she was trying to carefully plan a murder. He asserted that nothing linked O'Brien to the murder and that it was more likely to be associated with the election in which Cousins had actively campaigned. He also insinuated that Jane O'Brien could be shielding her son John who also had the means and the motive to commit the crime. John O'Brien had initially been arrested for the crime, but released after his mother's confession.

The jury were not convinced and only needed one hour to find Jane O'Brien guilty of murder, with a strong recommendation to mercy due to her age and sex. She did not reply when asked if she had anything to say, but stood up "stolid and ashen-faced". The judge sentenced her to death. Her leave to appeal failed and the prospect of a reprieve appeared grim. The execution of an elderly woman would have been unpalatable to the public, however. It was therefore not surprising that a week before the execution, which was scheduled for 25 July, the Governor-General James McNeill signed an order commuting Jane O'Brien's death sentence to penal servitude for life.

After her reprieve and while she was in prison, Jane O'Brien applied to be granted a portion of the estate of the nephew whose death she had planned. This was considered the first time in Irish history that a prisoner had attempted to claim property belonging to a person they had murdered. Somewhat unsurprisingly, the request was denied. Jane O'Brien went on to serve ten years in prison. She was released in July 1941.

Jane O'Brien was one of three Wexford people sentenced to death in just over ten years, and the only one reprieved. James McHugh from New Ross was hanged in 1926. He had entered the house of his elderly neighbour William Dollison demanding money. He had then viciously beaten the 75 year old to death with a shoemaker's iron last before robbing the house of any valuables. McHugh's girlfriend and her daughter had given evidence against him which eventually led to his capital punishment. John Hornick was also executed in 1937 for the robbery and murder of James Redmond in his caravan outside the village of Taghmon. Hornick was apprehended in Dublin when he used the murdered man's bank book to obtain money. This left Wexford as one of several counties to suffer two executions in the lifetime of the state, the others being Wicklow, Roscommon, Kerry, Offaly, Louth and Meath. Limerick had three executions for murders committed in the county. Unsurprisingly Co. Dublin, the home of the capital city and the population centre, leads the way with five hanged.

ELIZABETH & ROSE EDWARDS

"I am nearly gone in the head."

Infanticide, the killing of an infant under the age of twelve months, was a much more common feature of Irish life during the last century than it is today. The Catholic Church, which largely dictated the social policy of the country in the 1930s, considered children born outside of wedlock to be illegitimate. As well as this, there was a stigma attached to single motherhood which often led to young women's institutionalisation in Magdalene Laundries and the forced adoption of their children. Cases of infanticide rocketed after the foundation of the new state. Between 1922 and 1949, twelve women and one man would face the death penalty for the crime. In almost all cases, the killing was done by the unmarried mother. Young women's conduct was watched closely in those days and it was well known, especially in rural areas, when a single woman was heavily pregnant. When no baby appeared, the Gardaí were informed. They paid a visit to the house, and if no satisfactory explanation was forthcoming then the woman in question was questioned at length. In most cases, the woman would break down from the sustained questioning and admit to the whereabouts of her baby. Unfortunately, the baby had often been left to die or even killed by the desperate mother. Faced with the numerous social obstacles, as well as grinding poverty, some women chose to do the unthinkable. Unlike in Britain, the Irish state made no distinction between infanticide and murder in the 1930s, a fact that would lead women like Elizabeth and Rose Edwards to a condemned cell.

On 2 October 1934, a heavily-pregnant Elizabeth Edwards booked in to the Roscommon County Home maternity ward under the name of Mannion. Edwards would claim to the staff at the home that she was newly married and that the child's father was Thomas Mannion from the townland of Ballyglass. She also showed a ring to several people in the institution, which she said had been given to her by her new husband. Elizabeth soon gave birth to a healthy baby girl which she named Mary Teresa. Mother and baby stayed in the home for two weeks until 16 October. Nurse O'Gorman later described the infant as strong and healthy and stated that Elizabeth "appeared to be fond of her baby". The staff noticed, however, that her husband or family did not come to visit her in the home and doubtlessly figured out that she was in fact an unmarried mother. For this reason, two members of staff saw fit to warn Elizabeth before she left the home about her conduct towards Mary Teresa. One nurse told her not to abandon the baby or "the guards will be after you". A doctor, C.J. Kelly also said that he advised the new mother that if the baby was not taken care of she would get into trouble.

At about 4 p.m. on 16 October, Elizabeth's sister Rose (20) came to collect the new mother and bring her and her new-born home. Rose had hired a car from a local man, John Keegan, to chauffeur them. There was one problem, however. Elizabeth and Rose lived at home with their parents, who had no idea that their unmarried daughter had become pregnant and given birth to a child out of wedlock. Elizabeth had told them that she was going to hospital due to appendicitis, whereas other people had been told she had been admitted due to a case of swollen feet, having struck her foot against a pot. Nevertheless, the girls directed the driver to bring them from the hospital to their home in Castlestrange, a small townland on the River Suck situated eighteen miles from Roscommon Town.

Ordinarily, the girls would have driven home through their local village of Fuerty, where both their father and brother happened to be working that day. On this occasion, however, they directed a surprised John Keegan to go through Athleague instead, adding about three miles to their journey. Elizabeth held the new-born baby in her arms, although Keegan said he did not hear it cry. At one point, Rose stopped the car at Keane's shop and left briefly, returning with a parcel which was "the size of two loaves". At around 4 p.m., the taxi reached a place called White's Gate, the ruins of an old mansion. The two women asked Keegan to turn off the main road and drive them some distance up the avenue. They instructed him to stop when they got to an orchard which lay on the banks of the River Suck. It was about a mile from the Edwards' house but the two women told Keegan that they would walk the remainder of the journey. They got out of the car, taking Mary Teresa with them and walking off. About an hour later, at 5 p.m., Rose and Elizabeth Edwards were walking near their home when they met a road-worker, James Keegan. Keegan saluted the sisters and shook Elizabeth's hand to welcome her home. Elizabeth was not holding anything that Keegan could see. There seemed to be no baby present.

Two weeks later, on the night of 29 October, the Gardaí paid a visit to the Edwards home. They had been tipped off about the possibility of a child having been born in the household. Sergeant Tobin asked Elizabeth about the whereabouts of the infant, which had not been seen since the day she left the county home. Elizabeth divulged that it had died the morning after returning from the hospital and that Rose had buried it in their field. Rose confirmed that this was the case and was asked to show the sergeant the grave. She initially hesitated but eventually led the Gardaí to a field two hundred and fifty yards from the house. The Gardaí conducted a forty-five minutes search but could find no trace of a grave in the spot Rose indicated. They promised to return the following morning to search in the daylight. The next day they found a small hole which had fresh clay around it as well as several used matches scattered nearby. There was no body, although there were pieces of white cloth protruding from the hole. Rose said, "Dogs or something must have got at it." The sergeant remarked that the hole had not been there the night before to which Rose responded, "That is where I buried the baby anyhow."

Elizabeth elaborated on her original statement, telling the Gardaí that when she arrived home on 16 October she hid her baby in a grove of trees before going into the house. After about ten minutes, her mother went out feeding turkeys. She then retrieved Mary Teresa and brought her to her own room. Every few minutes either she or her sister would check the baby's progress. They stated that they had tried to give Mary Teresa milk and sugar but she would not take it. At 9 a.m. the next morning they checked the baby, who was not breathing. Elizabeth told the Gardaí that she cried and called Rose who came in and confirmed that the child had died of natural causes. Only she and her sister knew about the baby's death. At 2 p.m. she asked her sister to bury the body. Rose replied that she was afraid to go to the churchyard, to which Elizabeth replied that there was no need to bury a baby in the churchyard. Elizabeth said she had then given the body to Rose who had buried it on the farmyard. They could not explain the body's absence from the grave, except to say that animals may have taken it.

Elizabeth, when asked to sign the statement she had dictated to the Guard, refused. She told the Gardaí, "I do not know what I'm saying, I am nearly gone in the head." All the local Gardaí were mobilised and a month-long search for the body was inaugurated in the area around the girls' home. They also dredged the fast-flowing River Suck but they could find no trace of the missing baby. Despite this, Elizabeth and Rose Edwards were arrested and charged with the murder of Mary Teresa Edwards. The body of the victim was never discovered, making this an extremely unusual case. Notwithstanding the lack of a corpse, the Gardaí were confident there was enough evidence to suggest the Edwards sisters were complicit in the infant's death. The women appeared together in the Central Criminal Court in Dublin on 26 March 1935. Both women pleaded not guilty.

It was the Edwards sisters second time to appear together in court in just over a year. They had been summoned to Roscommon District Court on 9 December 1933, to answer charges on the relatively minor offence of stealing three turkeys valued at 18s. On this occasion, the stakes were far higher. The crime was murder and the sanction if found guilty was the death penalty.

The parents of the two girls both took the stand and admitted that they were unaware of Elizabeth's pregnancy. The first that they had heard about her giving birth was when the Gardaí had come to the house and interviewed them. When Sergeant Tobin addressed the court he told of a conversation he and Garda Connolly alleged they had heard as they stood on a ladder underneath the girls' bedroom.

Rose: *I wonder what is bringing them out tomorrow?*
Elizabeth: *I do not give a damn.*
Rose: *Jesus, I do. I will not sleep a wink tonight.*
Elizabeth: *What do you care about them anyway? Sure they cannot find it now.*

Rose took the stand and told the court that she was fond of Mary Teresa. She said that when they had left the County Home, they had initially intended to bring her to the house of their cousin, John Conboy, which explained why they stopped the car a mile from their own home. She admitted that they had not discussed the matter with Conboy but they thought he would not object. They had noticed that the baby was ill on the journey, however, and had then chosen to go back to their own house instead "irrespective of who would see it". Rose, who described herself as "anxious that the child should live", had checked Mary Teresa's condition every few minutes but the infant had died the next morning. The sisters had told no one but Rose had buried the body in the field. She admitted that nobody else but herself and Elizabeth had known where the baby had been buried but could not explain why her body was missing when the sergeant was brought there.

Elizabeth also told the court that she was not surprised when the baby died as several people had told her in the county home that she was weak and would not live. Miss Rose O'Beirne, a maternity nurse from the maternity ward was called to the stand. She directly contradicted

Elizabeth's evidence, telling the court that the child was in a "normal, healthy condition" when she was taken the home with the two women and that Elizabeth was warned about her conduct towards her new-born daughter as she left.

Defending, Mr Hogan, told the jury that no body had been found and the authorities had not proven that anyone had been murdered or even that violence had taken place. The murder of the baby was only a theory and the prosecution was "vaguely guessing" what happened to Mary Teresa Edwards. Since they could not prove that she had even been killed, they certainly couldn't convict the accused for it. Mr, Haugh, prosecuting, disagreed and said that both of the accused had admitted that the baby had died and if she had died a natural death then the body would not need to be hidden. They maintained that the girls got out of the taxi at White's Gate, a location described as "sheltered and secluded…near a deep river and with everything conducive to the disposal of a body". They surmised that the two women had come out of their way to go this route so that they could bury the baby, or throw her into the river. This is why Elizabeth carried no child when she met James Keegan shortly afterwards.

The girls had managed to stick steadfastly to their story and had not buckled under the enormous pressure put on them at any stage. It was not enough to convince the court of their innocence, however. The jury considered the evidence for an hour before returning with a verdict of guilty, but with a strong recommendation to mercy. Justice O'Byrne said that he agreed with the verdict and donned the black cap before sentencing both women to death for murder. The women showed no outward sign of emotion in response to the verdict.

Since the state had been established several women had been sentenced to death for infanticide, but on every occasion this had been commuted. The defence counsel appealed on the grounds that there was no evidence whatsoever to suggest that the baby had been murdered. The appeal was unanimously rejected, however, and the Edwards' death sentences were fixed for 31 May 1935. There had only been one woman executed in the history of the state and the government was always unlikely to triple the number after this case. On 18 May, the government of the Free State commuted the death sentences to penal servitude for life. Women guilty of infanticide always received shorter sentences than those found guilty of murder and the Edwards sisters were no exception. Rose served just two years in prison, her sister being released a short time later. Mary Teresa Edwards' body was never discovered.

Two Roscommon denizens had been executed by the Free State in the years before the Edwards' trial. 42-year-old Thomas McDonagh was the third individual hanged since independence. He shot Ellen Rogers in Loughglynn over a financial argument and was executed on 12 December 1923. Patrick McDermott, of Rosmoylan near Castlecoote, killed his elder brother in 1931. John had inherited the farm leaving Patrick with bleak prospects and no land. He had also started showing interest in a girl Patrick had previously been courting. Patrick lay in wait for him coming home and shot him dead. He was found guilty and executed on 29 December 1932. Roscommon has a population of just 64,000 and a low crime-rate. Notwithstanding this, in the space of ten years they would have two people put to death as well as four death sentences commuted, including the two Edwards sisters. This is in stark contrast to neighbouring County Galway, which has a population of a quarter of a million but has not experienced an execution for murder since 1902. The dawn of the new state proved a bloody period in Roscommon's history.

THOMAS KELLY

"I will do in that old bastard yet."

Thomas Kelly found himself in the unusual position of being tried three times for the same crime, also undergoing the trauma of having the death sentence imposed on him by the state twice. Despite having numerous witnesses who seemed to provide him with a solid alibi, the court chose to disbelieve them and convict Kelly of the vicious murder of his elderly housemate, Patrick Henry.

Patrick Henry was 67 years of age in 1935. As a young man, he had worked in England as a labourer for five years before setting sail for America. Unlike most emigrants, however, he had the financial means and the desire to return to Ireland, arriving back in 1922. He had amassed over £2,000 in his time abroad, an extremely large sum at the time. Henry initially returned to live in his native Ballymote in Co. Sligo but then used his earnings to buy two farms in the Boyle area of Co. Roscommon. Eventually he would sell both and invest in six tobacconist shops in Dublin instead. His business venture failed in 1932 and Henry sought the protection of the bankruptcy court. He claimed in court that he had no money or valuables left whatsoever. The court did not believe him, however, and a warrant for his arrest was issued. Instead of handing himself in, Patrick Henry fled to the north. He returned soon afterwards, however, and rented a rundown two-room cottage in Great Meadow, just outside Boyle. He still claimed to be bankrupt, listing his assets as "nil". It was thought locally that Henry had money, however, and that he was afraid to put it in the bank. The elderly man was believed to be concealing at least £650 in his home.

By April 1935, Henry was drawing unemployment assistance and eking out a living sowing potatoes. He maintained to locals that he was penniless, although he had been seen carrying a bundle of notes on several occasions. Eventually he decided to get a lodger to help him pay his rent. He met Thomas Kelly at the unemployment exchange. Kelly, who had left his wife and moved without her knowledge to Boyle, was looking for a place to live and Henry invited him to join him in the small cottage.

Thomas J. Kelly was 55 years of age and a powerful man of six feet. He was described as "tall, sandy-haired and athletic", and unusually possessed several gold teeth. He was quiet and rarely talked about himself. When he did speak, he had a slight foreign accent, despite being a native of Co. Roscommon. He had left Ireland aged just 18 and lived a transient existence. He travelled much of the world as a sailor spending time in Canada, Scotland and eventually thirty years in America. He worked hard in his new homeland but eventually ran into trouble with the law when he was imprisoned for theft. After his release, Kelly returned to Ireland in 1931 with £1,300. He continued his nomadic existence, living in various locations around the country initially. In July 1933, however, Kelly married a Longford woman. The marriage was widely described as "unhappy" and the groom stayed with her for only a month before leaving and living for various spells in Leitrim, Antrim, Dublin and Sligo. He finally moved to Boyle in February and started to draw unemployment assistance of 6s. a week. In April 1935, he moved in with Henry in the small cottage, although it was rundown and did not have electricity or running water. The two men seemed to have an amicable relationship at first, and were often spotted drawing turf together. It would not be long before relations would deteriorate between them, however.

After July, the pair were no longer seen in public together. On one occasion, Kelly was talking to a neighbour in Boyle when Henry walked past. The pair did not speak to one another so the neighbour asked if they were not on good terms. Kelly replied, "Nobody could talk to that contrary old bastard." On 10 September, he remarked to another local man, "I will do in that old bastard yet." That night, Kelly invited his neighbour Peter Reynolds to a local pub, something he had never done before. Kelly seemed troubled and muttered at one point, "He's a contrary old son of a gun", but Reynolds did not know who he was talking about. Meanwhile on that day, Henry had visited a neighbour named Mary Kate Brennan at about 2 p.m. and was then seen walking towards Boyle. This was the last time Henry was seen alive. At the strange hour of 9 a.m. the next morning, a sleepy-looking Thomas Kelly entered a public house in Boyle and drank several pints of stout. He also paid for several glasses of whiskey, something he had never done before. He then left the pub and went in the direction of his home. He would not be seen again around Boyle.

By the morning of 12 September, a large padlock had appeared on the door into the cottage Henry and Kelly shared, rendering the milkman unable to deliver his usual supply of milk. Patrick Henry had left his house and travelled around the country for weeks at a time on numerous occasions before so the locals were not surprised or worried about his absence. Henry, who used to be seen every day reading the newspaper under the town clock, did not collect his dole which was due on 11 September. Neither did Thomas Kelly. As weeks turned into months, people became curious about the men's lengthy absences from the town. Several locals attempted to peer in the window of the cottage but they could not see anything in the darkness. Garda Sherlock had even checked around the house on 14 November but saw nothing that aroused his suspicion. Henry's landlady Harriett O'Callaghan, however, was concerned that she had not heard anything from her tenant. Henry paid his rent religiously on Saturdays but had not turned up since 7 September. She decided to visit the Garda station on 12 December to express her concern about Henry's whereabouts.

The next morning, Detective Officer Doyle arrived at the cottage with O'Callaghan. The door was still fastened by a padlock, which the Garda broke open. On entering the house, they were met with an overpowering smell. The decomposing corpse of Patrick Henry lay on the floor. His body had been dragged to the fire and burned beyond recognition and his head bore the signs of having been battered with a blunt instrument. His clothes had been cut off in an attempt to find valuables and his trousers were either removed or not present when the murder was committed. There was also a bloodstained hammer just inside the door and the house was in disarray. A sod of turf and a newspaper, the *Irish Press*, were found on the bed. The paper was from 10 September, indicating that Patrick Henry had lain dead for at least three months. The house had also been ransacked, a suitcase had been forced open and any money or valuables present had been taken. The £650 rumoured to have been in the house was nowhere to be seen. Thomas Kelly, the mysterious lodger, had vanished. Patrick Henry's funeral took place on 15 December 1935. There was a hailstorm at the time and unusually for rural Ireland it was poorly attended, described in one newspaper report as having "four or five people present." None of Henry's relatives were present. His brother, who had not seen him for over a year before his death, did not attend. Unsurprisingly, Thomas Kelly did not make an appearance.

Thomas Kelly had left the district on 11 September and had enquired in the town about bus times. When asked what direction, he replied, "I do not care as long as I get out of this place." He had no luggage but boarded a bus to Sligo. He withdrew £10 of his savings from the bank while in the town, leaving a further £80 in the account. He then bought a single, third-class rail ticket for Belfast. He had not been seen since. The Gardaí took the unusual step of giving a statement to the press which was placed in all national newspapers. It included a photograph and detailed description of Kelly who seemed to have dropped off the face of the earth in the weeks after Henry's brutal murder, for which he was the prime suspect. He was rumoured to have been spotted in Co. Meath in January 1936, but attempts to trace him came to nothing. Eventually it was assumed that Kelly had absconded abroad and the police forces in the UK, the USA and Northern Ireland were put on alert. Finally, the Gardaí traced the suspect to Lanarkshire, Scotland, where he had been living in a workman's hotel under the pseudonym Smith. Gardaí who were familiar with Kelly were sent to the Coatbridge area, ten miles east of Glasgow. Kelly was known to have travelled there, and the town was placed under surveillance.

Gardaí got their breakthrough when Kelly walked into Coatbridge Scottish Bank on 5 June 1936 and attempted to get a transfer of the £80 from the bank in Sligo. He was asked to call back later to collect the money and the Gardaí were notified. They identified Kelly, although he had attempted to disguise his appearance by wearing glasses and growing a moustache. He also gave his name as "John Hill", although he eventually admitted to being Thomas Kelly as he was being brought to the station. He had over £14 in his possession. As he entered the station, Kelly managed to take a razor from his pocket and draw it across his throat. Several policeman were needed to restrain the powerfully-built Kelly, who resisted violently when they attempted to dress the wound, which at this point was spouting blood. Kelly was initially in a critical condition. He was hospitalised for twelve days and required stitching to stem the blood-flow. He was arrested immediately on his discharge and charged with the murder of Patrick Henry on or about 11 September. He made no reply.

On 10 November 1936, Kelly's trial opened in the Dublin Central Criminal Court. The defence produced a witness that stated they had seen Patrick Henry alive and well the day after Kelly was proven to have left Boyle. Kathleen McPherson said she was exhibiting crochet at the Boyle Agricultural Show on 12 September when she spotted Henry walking near the exhibits. If her testimony was true, Kelly, who was in Belfast at the time, could not have been responsible for the elderly man's death. The prosecution, however, disputed the evidence. McPherson had not mentioned seeing the deceased when initially questioned by the Gardaí and had only disclosed the evidence shortly before the trial. The witness was also unable to pick out the sergeant who had interviewed her about the incident, and the prosecution implied that she was an unreliable witness. She also said that it may have been at the show the year before that she had seen Henry, although she did not think it was. Four other witnesses, including two siblings of McPherson, corroborated the evidence swearing that they had seen Henry on the day of the show. The prosecution poured scorn on these witnesses, however, noting that none of them had told the Gardaí the story of seeing Henry until they entered the witness box.

Defence counsel also attached importance to Kelly's clothes. There was no evidence that he had destroyed any items of clothing and the ones he possessed were free of bloodstains, even though Patrick Henry had been covered in blood. Kelly also had the option in the bank in Sligo of taking out the full £90 present in his account. Instead, he had only taken out £10, binding him unnecessarily to the area. They asserted that these were surely not the actions of a man attempting to abscond and escape justice. No one, not even Mary Kate Brennan who lived just yards away, had heard the crime being committed or seen Kelly committing it.

Kelly claimed that on the night of 10 September he had been playing cards and then drinking in a pub in Boyle. When he arrived home Henry was in bed. The next morning Kelly awoke feeling ill on account of the alcohol he had drank the night before. He talked to Henry about the agricultural show which was to be held the following day. He then changed into his suit and told Henry he was leaving for Scotland where he hoped to get a job. Henry, who was reading the *Irish Press* did not say much as Kelly had been talking about leaving for several weeks coming up to that day. Kelly then claimed that he bade Henry farewell before leaving to catch the bus from Boyle to Sligo and that his housemate was alive and well when he exited the cottage. He had travelled to Belfast, and subsequently Scotland, where he had first worked on a farm in Ayrshire. Kelly had read about Patrick Henry's death in the library in Coatbridge and had seen the Garda appeal for him to come forward. "I got a little worried about it, and I intended to come back, but I was afraid they would put it on me." He had not come forward but had thought about it a lot. He told the court that there was no particular reason that he had grown a moustache or started wearing glasses. He added that he had not known what he was doing when he slit his own throat. The defence told the jury that the case had not been proven and that as Henry had been seen after Kelly's departure an acquittal was an appropriate verdict.

The prosecution disagreed. They reminded the jury that Kelly, who had left Boyle hurriedly, had used several aliases after the murder, had grown a moustache and worn spectacles and had attempted to slit his own throat when approached by the Gardaí. He had disappeared at the same time as Henry had died and there was no evidence that anyone else had gone into the cottage. He had also made several threatening remarks about Henry to various locals before his housemate's untimely death.

On the fifth day of the trial the jury deliberated for an hour. The extraordinary co-incidence of Kelly disappearing at exactly the same time Henry was murdered may have swayed them because they returned with a guilty verdict. This led Justice O'Byrne to administer the mandatory death sentence. Kelly's wife, clad totally in black, wept bitterly at the pronouncement. Her husband, conversely, remained unmoved and merely remarked, "I have nothing to say." Justice O'Byrne announced his agreement with the verdict and reminded the court that the state's foremost responsibility was the protection of its citizens. Kelly's execution was thus set for 3 December. That was far from the end of the story, however.

Kelly's counsel immediately appealed and the guilty verdict was quashed by the Court of Criminal Appeal three months later. This was because additional witnesses were found who swore they saw Henry alive on 12 September. Kelly's second trial opened on 19 April 1937. The evidence was almost the same as the first trial apart from the new witnesses, all of whom testified to having seen Henry alive and well the day after Kelly had left the locality. One witness, when asked why she had not revealed the information before, answered, "I did not realise it was serious, or I would have." A second witness, when asked the same question remarked, "Nobody likes to get mixed up in a murder trial." A third witness, George Johnston, deposed to having seen Henry at the workhouse in Boyle on 12 September. When asked why he had not told the Gardaí about this vital piece of evidence before, Johnston said, "If I knew it would have been of interest to them I would have told them." Defending solicitor, Mr Brereton Barry, said that there was no greater outrage than the conviction of an innocent man by the state. The prosecution, however, called the array of new witnesses "dishonest and untruthful", saying that they would prefer the guards to be defeated than justice to be served. They urged the jury to find the defendant guilty.

The second trial took six days and after the evidence the jury was deadlocked and unable to agree a verdict. Kelly thus faced into a third gruelling trial in November 1937, two years after Patrick Henry had been murdered and almost a year after his own death sentence was supposed to have been carried out. This time another new witness, Michael Muldoon, testified that he had seen an unknown man coming out of Henry's house and padlocking the door. There were also several other witnesses who had regained their memory of having seen Henry on 12 September. Amazingly, it still wasn't enough to convince the court of the accused's man's innocence. The trial lasted eight days, exceptionally long for the era, before the jury got the chance to deliberate. After an absence of two hours, they found Thomas Kelly guilty of murder. They added a strong recommendation to mercy. Kelly, for a second time, heard the judge pronouncing his death sentence. For the first time in the history of the state, Justice Gavan Duffy dispensed with the age-old tradition of donning the black cap. Another application to appeal failed and Kelly's execution date was set for 28 December 1937.

The Labour Party and The United Farmers Association were amongst the groups who called for a reprieve for the condemned man. His local community also petitioned the government, while people wrote into the national newspapers in large numbers questioning Kelly's guilt and sanity. Finally Thomas Kelly got his reprieve on the day before Christmas 1937. He was sentenced to penal servitude for life instead. Kelly spent eleven and a half years in custody and was finally released from Mountjoy in November 1947. He was then 68 years old and described as being in very poor health. As there was no relative willing to accommodate the released prisoner, he was instead dispatched to St Kevin's Hospital.

This finally brought to an end the lengthy ordeal which began in September 1935, with the violent murder of an old man in a lonely cottage. Although it seems very likely that Kelly committed the murder, the new witnesses produced managed to cast doubt on Kelly's guilt. The discrepancy over what day Henry was killed constituted a reasonable doubt and may well have forced the government's hand into granting a commutation. Whether or not those witnesses were to be believed, many of whom had suffered severe memory lapses during the course of the trial, is another matter.

JAMES EDWARD O'NEILL (TIERNEY)

*"I had no idea of the strength
I could put behind myself."*

"I am not asking for mercy - I am asking for justice, the justice which a man with a tattered, torn, diseased brain is entitled to." So said Mr Vaughan-Buckley, defending solicitor, when discussing the case of James Edward O'Neill (alias Tierney) who was tried for murder in 1936. Unlike most men who would appear on murder charges in those days, O'Neill was raised in affluent circumstances. He was born on a ship in the Red Sea but lived in Dublin where his father was an officer in the Royal Irish Constabulary (RIC) until 1921. After the War of Independence, O'Neill Snr moved his family to Singapore where he became Chief Inspector of the Straits Settlements (South-East Asia). James himself later joined the British Army as a member of the Grenadier Guards in 1930, serving for four years. He also served in Palestine as a member of the Police Force. After his discharge from the armed services, he came to live with his father in Hampshire, England. The younger O'Neill had then returned to Ireland on 4 July 1936. It was a trip that was not destined to end happily.

The ex-soldier was aged about 30 and described as "handsome...a man of splendid physique". He had a history of fits, however, and after just three weeks in Ireland he was found unconscious on the street in Limerick. He was brought to hospital immediately. The source of the mysterious blackout was unknown but nevertheless O'Neill was

detained for nearly two weeks. After being discharged, he had gone to
Cork. Here he decided to change his name from O'Neill to Tierney.
He worked in various locations around the county, although he had no
family there and was considered a stranger to the area. Tierney would
later claim that he had a girlfriend in Dublin to whom he sent money
from Palestine. He claimed to have heard that she had moved to West
Cork and he had travelled to the region in an effort to locate her.

Tierney worked throughout the harvest months of August and
September as a labourer at a farm belonging to the Farressy Family in
Carrigaline, ten miles south of Cork City. He was earning about 10s. a
week. He left this comfortable job abruptly, however, telling the farmer
that he had been promised a job in Dunlop's Tyre Factory in Cork City
instead. This work never materialised. Eventually in October, Tierney
returned to Carrigaline and got work with a relative and neighbour of the
Farressys. He commenced employment on 9 October for Thomas Foley,
doing some interior painting. The work was not completed satisfactorily
however and while Tierney was present £1 went missing from a drawer
in the family home. The labourer was sacked unceremoniously from his
employment after just three days. He then decided to return to Cork City.

By 6 November, however, Tierney's money had run out and he was
unable to pay for a bedroom in Carbery's Hotel in Cork City. The
landlady kindly gave him the room on subscription with Tierney telling
her that he would pay for his upkeep when he found work. He then
spent several weeks seeking ways to earn money to facilitate travel
back to England, even pawning his coat on 14 November. He was
unsuccessful in obtaining the boat fare, however, and by 23 November
he was still ensconced in Carbery's Hotel, not having given anything
towards his keep. That day, he went to see a local councillor, Mr Daly,
accosting him outside his office and saying, "I am informed that you
can give me a ticket for London." Daly refused to give him anything
towards his passage on account of Tierney being a stranger to Cork
and a foreign national. Tierney argued that he had been brought up in
Dublin and then moved abroad. Daly told him that there was nothing

he could do. Tierney then left, telling the councillor that he would come to see him again. The Englishman now found himself in the desperate situation of being penniless and friendless in an unfamiliar city.

Thomas Vickers was neither penniless nor friendless. The 46 year old was a popular native of Rathcooney, just outside Cork City, but by 1936 he was living on Glasheen Road. Vickers was a veteran of the British Army, having served unscathed in the First World War. He received no pension, however, so had purchased a taxi-cab in 1933 from which he enjoyed a comfortable livelihood. He lived with Monica, his wife of 23 years, and was described as a "quiet and inoffensive man...obliging and always willing to do a good turn". The taxi-driver was in the habit of giving his wife his earnings, save what he would need for petrol. On 23 November, he had given her £13. He worked from 10 a.m. to 4 p.m. on the day of 24 November. He returned home at this point and ate his dinner, departing again for the second half of his workday at around 5.15 p.m. He was in possession of a good sum of money by the time he got to the Patrick Street taxi rank at 7.30 p.m. that evening, at least £1.9s. At this point, a powerfully-built man of around six foot was seen by other taxi drivers approaching Vickers and engaging him in conversation. After a few seconds, the tall man got into the back of the taxi and Vickers drove away. At 9.10 p.m. on the same evening, a Carrigaline man was driving near his home when he recognised a car that belonged to a taxi man in Cork City. He could see a man reading what looked like a road map on the driver's side. The man would turn out to be Tierney. Thomas Vickers was nowhere to be seen.

Thomas Foley and his wife were preparing to go to bed at around 11.30 p.m. when Mrs Foley thought she heard something outside. Thomas agreed to investigate and left the bedroom, going into the kitchen. He listened for a couple of minutes but heard nothing. He then pulled up the blind to be met with the terrifying sight of Tierney, his former employee, standing in the dark facing his back door. He had made no effort to knock or even inform the family that he was outside. Foley asked Tierney through the window what he wanted.

The Englishman replied that he was there to explain why he had not finished the painting and needed to come in for a few minutes. Foley said no. Tierney pleaded, telling the terrified homeowner that he would not keep him long as he had a car waiting at the road. Foley replied that his baby was sick and that he was going to bed, adding that he would not let anybody in at that hour. Tierney then said thank you and goodnight. He did not leave, however, instead going around the front of the house and looking in the front window. Foley heard footsteps around the bungalow for almost an hour before Tierney finally departed. Foley, understandably petrified by this night caller, retrieved his shotgun and stayed awake all night.

The car that Tierney had mentioned was the taxi belonging to Thomas Vickers. However, it was only Tierney who was in it late that night on the drive from Carrigaline back into Cork City, arriving at the Carbery Hotel at 1.20 a.m. Tierney parked the car outside the hotel before going to bed. He rose the next day, 25 November, at 7 a.m., far earlier than usual. He immediately left the hotel and again took Vickers' taxi, driving once again in the direction of Carrigaline. Tierney was then seen parked on the road near the Foley household. The car was later spotted being driven back in the direction of Cork City but was found abandoned half way, by the Chapel Steps in Douglas village. Shortly before 9 a.m., a tall, dark-haired sallow man, later identified as Tierney, got a bus from Douglas into Anglesea Street in the city. Witnesses would later describe lower portions of the man's trousers as wet and muddy. An hour later he was seen eating in a restaurant in Cork City. He ordered rashers, eggs, tea and toast which cost one shilling. He then went again to meet Mr Daly. This time he told him, "A ticket to Fishguard will do me now." Daly said that he would have to go see the Lord Mayor about it, but kindly offered him one shilling from his own back pocket. Tierney accepted the gift. Daly also asked the man his name. "Tierney" was the reply. Tierney next went to the pawnshop where he had previously pawned his coat and retrieved it, paying the requisite price of just under 5s. He then paid for a ticket and boarded the 3.45 p.m. bus bound for Limerick City.

Meanwhile, Mr Daniel Mahony was driving cows at 9.15 a.m. on 25 November at a field in Ballinvorosig, a mile and a half from Carrigaline. He saw an object lying on the ground, and walked closer to investigate. It was the fully-clothed body of a man. He was dead. The corpse lay lengthwise two fields in from the road on the right-hand side of a cow gap, just a field away from the Foley farm. Mahony did not touch the body, instead summoning several other labourers who came and observed the grisly sight. The Gardaí were then called. The body was quickly identified as Thomas Vickers, although his money, driving licence and wallet were missing and he had only one farthing on his person. His cap and belt lay fifteen yards away and blood streamed from his left ear. The body lay in the field all that day and throughout the night covered in a sheet, awaiting the arrival of the State Pathologist and official photographers. The inquest would later conclude that Vickers' death was caused by a ligature made with his own tie, which had been pulled around his neck with great force. He also had the clear sign of a heavy blow to the chin.

A man arrived at Miss Walshe's boarding house on Davis Street in Limerick City at about 7.30 p.m. on the evening of 25 November. He had a foreign accent and was tall and smart. He asked the proprietor if she kept boarders and paid for bed and breakfast when told that she did. He told the landlady that his car had broken down and he was expecting another man to come shortly and fix it. He then left for a walk. By this stage, however, a description of the wanted man had been circulated nationwide to all Garda stations. Two Gardaí from Edward Street searched all the boarding houses and hotels in Limerick, eventually discovering that Tierney was staying in Walshe's. They left when they were told their suspect had gone for a walk, returning at 10.30 p.m.. At this point the suspect had come back. He was sitting in the dining room and told the Gardaí he was called "James Tierney". He was then asked about his business in Limerick. Tierney answered that he was a motor mechanic and was accustomed to travelling around. The Gardaí searched Tierney and found a union key, which turned out to be the front door key of Vickers' house. He also had nearly 4s., and could be proved to have spent about 14s. on the day after Vickers' death, a considerable amount of money at the time for a man who had been destitute shortly before.

Members of the Cork Gardaí drove to Limerick to identify and collect Tierney. In Limerick barracks, two statements were made by the prisoner about the night of the crime which would later be read in court and prove valuable evidence for the prosecution. Superintendent P. Doyle of Bandon then arrested Tierney on a charge of murder. Tierney responded to the charges read to him by remarking, "I have already made a statement and it is correct." The murder hearing began just over four months later on 5 April 1937, in Dublin Central Criminal Court. Tierney pleaded not guilty, although seventy-two witnesses would appear for the prosecution. The courtroom was crowded, the case involving the wealthy English ex-soldier having generated huge interest in the media and amongst the general public.

The prosecution intimated that Tierney had planned to rob the Foleys' house and left the taxi driver waiting for him at the road. Vickers, perhaps fearful of not receiving his fare, decided to accompany the accused across the field towards the house. Knowing he could not rob the house in the driver's presence, Tierney had then murdered Vickers before rifling his pockets and making his way to the Foleys' household alone. It is quite conceivable that if the Foley family had admitted the night-time caller Tierney would have claimed more than one victim. He had been identified by several witnesses as the man who got into the taxi with Vickers. As well as this, two fingerprints matching Tierney's had been found on the glass of the driver's door of the car. Vickers' money and valuables were missing from the taxi and Tierney could not explain where he had suddenly obtained all the money he had spent the day after the taxi driver's murder.

The defence relied almost exclusively on the hope that the court would find that Tierney was insane when the crime was committed. Michael O'Neill, father of the accused, took the stand in his son's defence. He told the assembled jurors about his son's chequered mental history.

He said that his son had been involved in two motorcycle accidents in Hampshire, England where O'Neill lived. His father recalled that after the second incident he had changed and become violent, at one time squaring up to his father and threatening to kill him. Several witnesses also appeared testifying about the poor state of Tierney's mental health, including one Limerick doctor who discussed photographs of X-rays of the skull of Tierney, which he said was abnormally shaped. Another man, who owned a house in England for "slightly abnormal people," told how he had employed Tierney, then known as O'Neill, as a servant until he was arrested for stealing a car. He had found him a good worker, although a little unpredictable. He admitted that Tierney had been quite well known to the police in England, however. Tierney had a probation officer, whom he had told at one time that on occasions "a cloud came over my brain and I forget what occurs". This probation officer considered him a "mentally abnormal person" and thought that he may have epilepsy. Two doctors also testified to two different occasions where Tierney had fallen unconscious for no reason for long periods of time, a possible indicator of said epilepsy.

Tierney also chose to address the court in his own defence, although he was not obliged to do so. He would not admit the killing, claiming to have forgotten most of the details of the night in question. His two statements were then read out in court. The first statement was described as "a bundle of lies". The second statement, which Tierney admitted bore his signature, said, "I had no intention of killing the man. I had no idea of the strength I could put behind myself. I am sorry for what I have done." In this statement. Tierney claimed that he and Vickers had walked across the field. When they got to the second field, he turned and saw Vickers raising something in the air which he felt sure was a spanner. "I managed to duck and got him first…We fell struggling on the ground. I do not exactly remember what happened after that." Tierney got a stiff cross-examination and stayed silent in response to several questions. He denied robbing the body and said he could not recall tightening the tie.

The accused was asked about his late-night visit to Foley's house and he told the court that he went for the sole reason of explaining the missing £1 from the house. He said he could not remember if he had returned to the scene of Vickers' body after going to Foley's house. He admitted going back to the hotel and sleeping there that night. He also admitted getting up and driving the stolen taxi back to Carrigaline, yards from the deceased man, although he said, "I do not think that I went near the body of Vickers at that time." He could not explain his objective in going back to Carrigaline that morning nor his reason for abandoning the car in Douglas. He did not know why he had chosen at this time to get his coat from the pawnbrokers nor could he remember where he had obtained the money to redeem it but he asserted that it had definitely not been stolen from Vickers. He also said that he did not know why he had chosen to travel up to Limerick that day.

Mr Roe, for the defence, reminded the jury of his client's abnormal medical history and the evidence of fits suffered by him, two of which resulted in motorcycle accidents. He added that 14 ½-stone Vickers had come voluntarily across the field and there was no evidence he had been dragged, indicating that Tierney had no intention of robbing him until he saw the spanner and defended himself. Tierney had then suffered a sort of fit, and did not remember the rest of the incident. Roe then implausibly added that the body was left in the field for twelve hours before discovery and it was likely that someone other than Tierney had robbed the dead man's pockets. Vaughan-Buckley, also for the defence, said that a man who had set out to rob and kill would hardly choose "a humble taxi man" and take him to the only place in County Cork where he was well known. He asserted that Tierney was hallucinating at the time of the killing and deserved an insanity verdict if the jury felt he was guilty of murder as he was unable to discern right from wrong.

Mr Kevin Haugh, prosecuting, reminded the jury that Tierney had served for several years in the army with a first-class regiment and could hardly have done so if he was insane. Haugh admitted that Tierney may have subnormal intelligence due to his nonsensical answering in court, but his every action had been inspired by a level of cunning. When Vickers accompanied him across the field, he seized his chance in the lonely rural area on that dark night. Vickers' empty pockets discounted the self-defence version of events and Tierney had then fled the city. When he was eventually apprehended he went to great lengths to attempt to conceal his heinous crime. He also reminded the court of Tierney's signed confession.

On the fifth and final day of the trial, the judge addressed the jury for just under three hours, telling them that it would be tragic to convict an insane person for a crime as they were not responsible for their actions. He added, however, that although the intellect of the defendant was below average, this did not in itself mean he was insane and that he had shown a certain amount of shrewdness in the commission of the crime and his attempt to cover it up. He continued that a man with epilepsy, as suggested by the defence, would not be kept for three years in the Grenadier Guards. He also said that there was no evidence of self-defence, as Tierney had no wounds on himself whatsoever and Vickers was unlikely to be the type of man to attack anyone else. "The probability of an attack by Vickers in the manner suggested by Tierney seemed to be remote." After an absence of two and a quarter hours, the jury returned with a guilty verdict, although adding a strong recommendation to mercy. Mr Justice O'Byrne announced his agreement with the verdict, sentencing Tierney to death on Thursday 29 April. When asked if he had anything to say, Tierney replied, "Nothing."

An application to appeal was put to the Court of Criminal Appeal on five grounds. These included that the defendant was insane; that the weight of evidence was not enough to convict and the signed statement made by the accused should not have been submitted in evidence. The court was unmoved and without calling counsel, permission to appeal was rejected on 11 May. The death sentence was re-fixed for 29 May.

A petition for the condemned man was then organised by the Dublin's Men's Association. A similar effort for Patrick Boylan (Chapter 14) who had been sentenced to death some weeks before, had attracted 25,000 signatures and helped in securing a reprieve. This petition may have made a vital difference. James Edward Tierney (O'Neill) was reprieved less than a week before the execution date. He served nearly twelve years in prison. His petition to be freed was rejected by the government in 1947 with the prisoner eventually securing his freedom the following year.

Tierney's insanity defence did not cut much ice, although his low level of intellect may have played a role in his reprieve. His foreign citizenship may also have had some effect on the mindset of the government. Relations between Ireland and the United Kingdom were already at an all-time low due to the Economic War between the two countries. Ireland may have been unwilling to ruffle the feathers of their powerful neighbours further by hanging the son of an important officer in the British police. Éamonn De Valera escaped the hangman's noose in 1916 for being an American citizen, after all. Not all foreign nationals would be so fortunate, however. James Herbert Lehman, a Canadian citizen and compulsive liar, moved to Ireland in the 1940s. He married but poisoned his wife after starting an affair. He would be the only foreigner ever hanged by the state, being executed in 1945.

PATRICK BOYLAN

"I know I done it. I will swing for it."

In early December 1936, many Irish people were too preoccupied with our economic depression and the adverse weather to think about Christmas. Nevertheless, Patrick Boylan decided to organise a party at 13 Coburg Place, near Sheriff Street, in north-inner city Dublin on Saturday 5 December in an attempt to kick-start the festive season early. He was a talented musician and wanted to show off his skills at a dance. Patrick was 23 years of age and had gained an apprenticeship in the dockyard aged just 17, qualifying as an electrical welder. He was described as "a sturdily built dark-haired man of rather good appearance". Boylan had found himself a good job and was keeping company with a girl named Norah Whelan for the past six months. The couple were very devoted to each other, spending most nights together. The hard-working Boylan also had a darker side, however. He had been known lately as having "a violent temper". He had been a keen footballer but had quit a couple of years before, complaining of consistent pains in his head and saying that "the game is doing me no good". Worst of all, he was insanely jealous of any attention his girlfriend received from other men.

Norah Whelan was 18 and a factory worker in Jacob's Biscuits, one of the major employers in Dublin at the time. Considered a kind and hard-working young woman, Norah had three sisters and two brothers and lived with her parents at 19 Nicholas Street, two miles south of Coburg Place. At 6 p.m. on 5 December, she bid farewell to her father Joseph and left the house. She was in high spirits and looking forward to the party being organised by her boyfriend. She met her sister Mary and Mary's husband, Patrick McNeill. The trio then walked onwards to meet Boylan, who had spent a large part of the evening socialising in pubs on nearby Burgh Quay. He had been drinking with three friends and had consumed at least six drinks. Boylan then left the pub and joined up with Norah and the McNeills, the group making their way to Coburg Place.

They arrived at the house at 8.20 p.m. Boylan and Norah were described as being on good terms at this stage. Boylan did not stay long, however, leaving the house with Patrick McNeill just minutes after they had made their entrance, the two men going for two drinks in a local pub. When they arrived back at the party it was 9.45 p.m. There were now about seventeen guests and the soirée was in full swing. Boylan played the piano for about three songs and then another man volunteered to play the accordion. At this point, Boylan spotted Norah talking to other men at that the party and this caused his mood to suddenly change. Soon after this incident, he got up and departed the house, alone. He walked towards Norah Whelan's house where he was seen pacing up and down her street alone despite the inclement weather conditions. Norah Whelan stayed at the party, unaware that her boyfriend had left.

When Boylan returned to the party he found Norah sitting between two local men, James McDermott and Charles Osborn. McDermott was an electrician and a former boyfriend of Norah. They had been seeing each other for about three weeks before Whelan started going out with Boylan and it was well known that her new boyfriend was jealous of their friendship. McDermott had not been invited to the party but had come anyway. Boylan said nothing about the seating arrangement initially but danced instead with Norah Whelan's sister, Mary McNeill. After a couple of dances, he joked to Norah that if he could not make a dancer out of her then he would make one out of her sister. Norah laughed. Boylan then noticed that McDermott and Osborn had their arms around Miss Whelan. The two men could not have anticipated the murderous rage this would inspire in Boylan. After noticing this, Boylan came over and asked Norah angrily "Would you not get up and dance?" She made no reply.

Boylan was in a violent mood by this time. At 11 p.m., McDermott began to sing a song. Boylan heard him and rushed across the room with a clenched fist, striking the singer on the side of the head. He was restrained by several revellers while McDermott was led out through the hallway to the street. Osborn was also ejected. Boylan ran around the hall in "an absolutely mad condition". He hit his uncle and another man who tried to prevent him from going after the two men. Boylan was heard asking Norah loudly if she was going to go home with McDermott, who at this point was standing outside. She replied that she was not but added to her violent boyfriend "I am finished with you". Some time after 11 p.m., Boylan seemed to have calmed down. He asked his girlfriend to accompany him into the backyard so they could talk privately. Norah's sister Mary and her husband Patrick McNeill joined the quarrelling lovers. Boylan repeatedly asked to be left on his own to discuss the argument with his girlfriend. As Norah Whelan showed no reluctance to be left with Boylan, the McNeills eventually hesitantly agreed to his request and went inside, shutting the door after them. Within seconds, they heard a bloodcurdling scream coming from outside. The McNeills hurriedly opened the door to see Norah and Boylan struggling.

Norah Whelan then freed herself and stumbled in the door of the house with her hands to her neck, which was spouting blood. McNeill asked Boylan in a panic what had happened. Boylan said coolly, "I have cut her throat." Boylan had his arm raised and looked "like a madman". He attempted to push past McNeill into the house. McNeill hit him and refused to let him in. Boylan then said chillingly to his former drinking compatriot "Leave me alone. I want to get in to kiss her before she dies." McNeill still blocked his path. Boylan next pointed to an item lying in the grass and remarked "There's the thing I done (*sic*) it with." It was his father's razor, taken from a shelf in the kitchen. McNeill asked what had caused him to commit such an atrocious act, to which Boylan responded, "Did you hear what she said? She said she is finished with me." Boylan then picked up the razor and jumped over the garden wall, shouting, "I know I done it. I will swing for it. I'll do the canal."

Norah Whelan was put sitting in a chair and an attempt was made to bandage up her neck to stem the huge amounts of blood she was losing. The ambulance arrived within minutes to pick up the fatally-wounded girl. Boylan suddenly reappeared at this time, but he showed no concern for his dying girlfriend. Instead he asked for McDermott, his perceived love rival. When he found him he attacked him, punching him in the eye. One of the ambulance men had to separate the two men. Norah Whelan was admitted to Jervis Street Hospital at 11.30 p.m. that night with six serious wounds to the face, neck and right hand. She was unconscious on arrival. She had a wound through her left ear to her mouth running about four inches. Her jugular vein had also been severed, causing the major blood loss. She briefly regained consciousness during the night but died the next morning at 7.30 a.m. due to shock and haemorrhage. Her brother, Joseph was given the onerous task of identifying the corpse of his eighteen-year-old sister.

Initially Boylan went into hiding and it would be twenty-four hours before he was found. Two Gardaí arrived at James Heeney's the next night at 12.15 a.m. and arrested Boylan. It would later be proved that he had met Heeney, his uncle, during that Sunday and eaten and drank with him. The Gardaí told Boylan they would have to take him into custody. In reply, the prisoner said "I know nothing". The prisoner was then taken to the station on Fitzgibbon Street where he made a statement at 1.10 a.m. He said he did not remember what he had done that day or the night before. "The only thing I remember I was in the room where the party was dancing and I saw two fellows - one sitting and the other standing on each side of that girl. One was a former lover and the other was in deep conversation with his arm on her shoulder." He went on to describe how her brother-in-law had asked Norah to dance but she had not answered. Boylan then asked her outside to enquire as to why she had not danced with her sister's husband. "Then she ran away and said she was finished with me. I remember nothing else."

The murder trial began three months after Norah Whelan's death on 3 March 1937, in Dublin Central Criminal Court. Boylan pleaded not guilty to the charge, claiming he had no recollection of the incident. The prosecution alleged that the case was one of "jealousy and pride". The accused man, they said, was looking for revenge. "He sought revenge not on the man, who might have defended himself, but on the girl." They declared an open and shut case of murder most foul.

The defence case was "not that the accused had done this terrible thing but that when he did it he was insane and insane to such a degree that he was not responsible for his actions…the slashing must have been done with a maniacal frenzy." His uncle, James Heeney (who had been struck by Boylan on the night of the party), deposed that he had worked with his nephew for the last fourteen months. He had always found Boylan a pleasant and amiable man but noticed in the months coming up to the incident that he had become "peculiar and quick tempered" and that he found him talking and laughing to himself on numerous occasions as well as continually complaining of a pain in his head. Heeney also said that there had been a change in the boy since he had been in an accident in 1930, a common theme in defence arguments at the time. This accident had been in the dockyard and Boylan had received injuries from a steel plate falling on his head. He was subject to headaches and nausea afterwards, and went to see a surgeon about the injury eighteen months later. The defence maintained that this incident caused him to suffer amnesia about the events leading up to Norah Whelan's death. Another co-worker deposed that ever since Boylan had finished his apprenticeship in the dockyard he had become awkward and "one could hardly speak to him, he always seemed to want to have his own way." He was also prone to forgetting things, including whether he had brought his tools to work or not. Michael Boylan, father of the accused, also took to the stand and identified the razor used as his own. He gave evidence that his son had been a good-natured boy "but changed completely in the last couple of years. He became fiery and you could not speak to him, he was very hot." He also told the court that the family had a history of insanity and that Patrick's aunt, Margaret Doyle, had died as an inmate of Grangegorman Mental Hospital.

Patrick Boylan chose to take the stand in his own defence. He gave evidence of the events of that Saturday night up until about 10.30 p.m., testifying that he remembered playing the piano and dancing. After this time, he claimed not to remember anything until he woke up on Monday morning in Brideswell Garda station. He insisted that he did not recall striking McDermott, attacking his girlfriend or where he had slept on the night of 5 December. He also denied remembering making statements to the Gardaí, although he admitted they bore his signature. He did not remember going to meet his uncle in a pub on Sunday 6 December. Boylan asserted, somewhat spuriously, that he did not know Norah Whelan had died until the Garda station on Monday night and that he had to ask the Gardaí why he was in custody in Brideswell Garda station. Boylan admitted that he told his brother to make sure that McDermott and Osborn did not come to the party that night. However, when he found them in the kitchen he drank and chatted amiably with them, initially. He did confess that he remembered McDermott and Osborn having their arm around Whelan and that he didn't like it. When asked why he it had bothered him, Boylan said that he had invited Norah to dance and not to sit talking all night. He said he couldn't remember getting angry or any of the subsequent events. When it was put to Boylan that someone told him pretending to remember nothing would be his best defence, he denied it vehemently.

Mr McAuley, a neurological expert, deposed that he believed that Boylan had an injury to the brain which may have influenced his behaviour on the fatal night. This did not show up in X-rays, however, and McAuley admitted that he based much of his evidence on the symptoms Boylan had described to him. The defence case relied strongly on the jury believing that the accused had sustained a serious brain injury which caused him to forget his murderous actions.

Justice O'Byrne summed up for two hours, telling the jury that, in a way, every crime of this magnitude was committed by a madman as "it was such a departure from the normal standards of life". He said that the best way to ascertain the mind of a man is to judge what he says and does immediately after the crime. In Boylan's case he had said, "I cut her throat. I know I done it. I'll swing for it." The judge opined that this showed not only that he knew what he had done, but also that he knew it was a capital offence. He had then disappeared with the murder weapon, only to return to attack his love rival. Finally, he had absconded from the scene and had not returned to his home. O'Byrne reminded the jury that in 1930 Boylan had had an accident after which he had only missed a couple of days of work. He strongly implied that the accused was exaggerating the effects of this event.

The jury had listened to much evidence regarding a possible mental disorder caused by an accident. They chose to either disbelieve or disregard this testimony however. On day four of the trial the jury deliberated for just fifty-five minutes. The gallery was thronged and included many of Boylan's workmates, although his father was conspicuous in his absence. Although they added a strong recommendation to mercy, a noticeably nervous jury found Boylan guilty. There was a murmur of excitement in the courtroom and Boylan was given the mandatory death sentence by Justice O'Byrne, scheduled for Good Friday, 26 March. When asked if he had anything to say regarding the sentence, the condemned man answered "I have a lot to say as regards the evidence." He then went on to dispute several pieces of evidence given against him, including the account that he had walked to Norah's house on Nicholas Street in twelve minutes, which he claimed was impossible. He also claimed to have been misrecognised by two witnesses. Neither of these pieces of evidence were crucial to the case, however. After his oratory was over, his face reddened briefly as he listened intently to the judge's words. He soon regained composure, however, leaving the dock with a large smile on his face, although his sister left the court sobbing loudly.

The defence team lodged an appeal on seven grounds, including that the judge had misdirected the jury in not telling them that Boylan may have had an inability to control his actions due to a disease of the brain. His appeal against his conviction and sentence was summarily dismissed on 20 April, almost a rite of passage in capital punishment cases at the time, the Court of Criminal Appeal almost never overturning the Central Criminal Court's Decision in that era. Boylan's death sentence was re-fixed for 7 May.

Like they would do for James Edward Tierney some weeks later, The Dublin Men's Association started a petition for the condemned man. Time ticked slowly by, as the number of names on the petition went up and up. In the end, the petition garnered an incredible 25,000 signatures. Perhaps most importantly, the signatures of several members of the late Norah Whelan's family were amongst them. This extraordinary act of forgiveness and generosity resonated powerfully throughout the country and was mentioned frequently in the media at the time. Hannah Sheehy-Skeffington, famous Irish suffragette and outspoken pacifist, also spoke strongly on the condemned man's behalf. The executive council resisted however, saying just days before the execution date on 3 May "it would not be justified in interfering with the sentence of the court and the law must take its course." Two days later, something caused them to change their mind. By the skin of his teeth, Patrick Boylan avoided the hangman's noose. He had been less than twenty-four hours from death. Patrick Boylan served eleven years in jail, and was described as being well disposed and anxious to make amends for the crime for which he was incarcerated. He was released in September 1947, whereupon he returned to live with his parents.

At the same time as Patrick Boylan was being tried, a 38-year-old farmer named John Hornick was on trial for the murder and robbery of James Redmond in Taghmon in Co. Wexford. He had gone to Redmond's caravan and clubbed him to death with a shotgun. Hornick was a stranger to Redmond but had heard rumours that the returned emigrant was well-off. Hornick then stole Redmond's bank book and fraudulently withdrew his money from a bank in Dún Laoghaire, Co. Dublin before attempting to cover his tracks. Thomas Kelly and James Edward Tierney, cases discussed earlier in this book, were also sentenced to death around this time for separate brutal robberies and murders, in Roscommon and Cork respectively. All four men committed unspeakably callous and violent murders. For a reason that shall never be known, Hornick would pay with his life, being hanged on 17 June 1937. Boylan, Kelly and Tierney, on the other hand, would be sentenced to death before receiving reprieves. Instead of execution, they each spent just over ten years in prison. We can only speculate as to whether it was pressure behind the scenes that saved the life of the latter three men or if the state felt the element of pre-meditation was absent in the other three cases. Either way, John Hornick would pay a far heavier price for his actions.

The view of Illaunmore, the island where Martin Joyce claimed to have spent the night Sonny Walsh was killed.

The scenic townland of Toureen in Co. Galway was shattered by the murderous events of a quiet summer night in 1961.

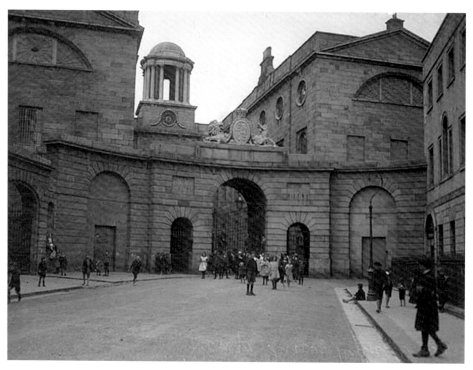

Green St Courthouse, Dublin. Many Irishmen and Irishwomen were condemned to death in this building.

Four Courts, Dublin.

FOUR COURTS. DUBLIN. 733. W.L.

*Éamon de Valera – de Valera himself had the sentence of death passed on him,
but eventually received a reprieve. Later in life, however, he chose not to exercise
mercy in several cases.*

Harcourt Street in Dublin was the scene of a truly horrific murder in 1963.

A crowd gathers outside Mountjoy prison. Most executions saw a group of people gathering outside the prison gates waiting for news of the condemned convict's death.

The Grand Canal. Joseph Bergin's bullet-ridden body was found in these quiet waters.

An aerial view of the Curragh Camp. Joseph Bergin was employed here before he was shot by Free State troops for being a spy

ABOVE LEFT: *Timothy Healy, the first Governor-General of the Irish Free State. He was responsible for signing the reprieves of a large number of condemned prisoners.* RIGHT: *One of the members of the original cabinet, Kevin O'Higgins defended the new state's use of the death penalty.*

BELOW LEFT: *W.T. Cosgrave, Ireland's first Taoiseach, who said of the death penalty "There is no other way that I know of that ordered conditions can be restored in this country".* RIGHT: *Taoiseach Seán Lemass, whose brother Noel was executed without trial by the Free State Army. James Murray was rumoured to have been involved in his abduction and murder.*

Douglas Hyde. As the first President of Ireland, Douglas Hyde was responsible for the commutation order of several condemned prisoners

The peaceful town of Ardee was shattered by the events of a summer's day in 1985.

Dan Duff (centre) at a dance with colleagues and friends in 1945.

Pallas Green Barracks pictured in the 1970s, before it was closed down. It was here that Garda Byrne and Garda Duff were stationed at the time of Byrne's shooting.

MARY SOMERVILLE

"I put the child in the hole all right.
What else can I say?"

Fianna Fáil was founded in 1926 as the republican voice of the country. When they assumed power in 1932, amongst the party's first acts was to withhold the payments to Britain that had been agreed in the Anglo-Irish Treaty. Britain responded by placing large tariffs on Irish agricultural products. "The Economic War" killed trade with our nearest neighbour but was considered a good thing by Fianna Fáil. They believed that it would allow the Irish distance themselves from our colonial oppressors and force the people to become self-sufficient. Sadly, this proved not to be the case. Irish farmers found themselves deprived of their biggest market. The price of cattle and crops tumbled. It was only a couple of years after the worldwide depression and Ireland, so reliant on agriculture, saw its small rural farmers pay the heaviest price for political decision-making. Mary Somerville in Co. Monaghan was one such farmer whose financial circumstances were dire. So dire, in fact, that they led her to commit an unspeakable crime.

Mary Latimer was born into a Church of Ireland family in Monaghan Town in the late 1880s. Although her father was a bailiff, Mary grew up in poor circumstances. As a teenager, she worked as a domestic servant until she gave birth to an illegitimate child, a major scandal at the time. Unsurprisingly, she chose not to keep the child. In 1905,

Mary married John Somerville from the townland of Knockaturley, despite the fact that he was thirty years her senior. The couple had seven children but John died in the early 1930s, leaving his wife with a young family to raise. The farm they inhabited was situated on poor land a couple of miles south of the town of Monaghan. By 1938, four of Mary's children still lived in her home, three young sons and a seventeen year-old-daughter. Another daughter was living in Northern Ireland but had also given birth outside of wedlock some years before. She had left the child in Knockaturley to be looked after by Mary, thus adding even more pressure to the already squeezed household budget.

Mary was the only adult and the sole provider in the house, barely eking out a living as a farmer from the stony soil. The small cottage they inhabited was already full to capacity and it was a struggle to fill all the hungry mouths in her care. Her daughter, Mary Anne (Annie) aged 17, then informed her mother that she had become pregnant by a local teenager, Robert Harvison. The birth of this baby would stigmatise and shame the family as well as stretch their resources to breaking point. At some point after hearing the news, Mary Somerville decided that she would commit a shocking deed in order to avoid these obstacles.

On 29 July, Sergeant Michael Cahill visited the Somerville home. Annie was rumoured locally to have given birth to a child and he was making routine enquiries about its whereabouts. Mary was interviewed first but she initially denied knowledge of the birth of a child in their home. In a second interview she eventually admitted to the sergeant that a girl had been born to Annie. She insisted, however, that she had brought the new-born baby to Belfast and left her with a Mrs Wilson of 13 Murdock Street who had promised to rear her. The Gardaí made enquiries and were informed by the RUC that there was no such house or woman. As the Gardaí were worried about the likelihood of Mary absconding over the border, which was barely ten miles away, they decided to bring her to the station. After further questioning, the grandmother confessed that the baby was not in Belfast, merely adding that she had "put it out of the house". She spent the night in the cell and the following morning she beckoned a Garda into the day room. She then revealed the shocking truth of the whereabouts of the missing baby. "I put it in a well at the house."

Mary Somerville was left in the station while three Gardaí were tasked with travelling the short distance to Knockaturley. They searched the Somerville's lands and quickly located a well, sixty yards from the house and just two feet in from the public road. It was about five foot deep. They used a hayfork and, with some difficulty, managed to raise the naked and partially decomposed body of a tiny female infant from the watery depths. She appeared to have been dead for some time. The tiny body had been wrapped in dark cloth and placed in a multi-coloured rush bag which had then been weighed down with three stones, the largest weighing 10lbs, to enable it to sink easily to the bottom of the well.

The little girl's body was immediately brought to Monaghan County Hospital where a post-mortem was performed by Dr O'Gorman. The largest stone had been leaning against her head, which left a small bruise. The post-mortem also ascertained that the child had been alive when put into the water and that death had been due to asphyxia, caused by drowning. The umbilical cord had been cut, but not tied and the child had been dead for at least a week. There were no external injuries on the body, apart from the bruise on the temple.

The Gardaí arrived back to the station at 3.30 p.m. where Mrs Somerville asked them "Did you get the child?" At this point, Mary Somerville was advised that she was under no obligation to make a statement but she replied that she would "tell them the whole truth, it is the best thing." In her statement, Mary said that on 11 July, her 17-year-old daughter Annie had given birth to a baby girl in the middle of the night. Mary's three other children and grandchild were asleep in the room at the time. Fifteen minutes after the birth, Mary took the crying infant into the kitchen and laid it on a shopping bag on a couch.

Shortly afterwards, she put the child in the bag and laid two or three heavy stones on it. She then went to the well sixty yards from the front door and dropped the bag containing the baby into the hole. Mary stated that she did not look at the child in the bag as she walked to the well. "I could not say if it was then alive. The bag containing the child's body sank in the water and I did not see it since." Mary Somerville was then arrested and charged with murder of the unnamed female infant. Shortly afterwards Robert Harvison, the father of the deceased child, was also arrested, although not for the murder. Although the native of Coragh was only 16 years old himself he was charged with "a serious offence against a girl between the ages of 15 and 17."

Mary Somerville's trial began in November 1938. She pleaded not guilty. It was her second occasion in court in that year, having unsuccessfully sued a neighbour in February for non-repayment of a loan. In this instance it was not Mary Somerville's money but her life on the line. The defendant kept her head down and wept through much of the proceedings. Annie Somerville gave evidence that she gave birth at about 3 a.m. on the morning of 11 July in the bedroom of the house. Her mother picked up the baby shortly after the birth. Annie was crying but her mother comforted her, telling her that it would be alright. Mary Somerville then brought the child into the kitchen adjoining the bedroom and Annie could hear her crying. Mary next returned with tea for the new mother before leaving the room. Afterwards, Annie heard the front door open and close. She could hear footsteps passing the window. She heard nothing else until ten minutes later when the footsteps returned around the side of the house. Her mother re-entered the room and asked her if she was sleeping all right. Neither woman mentioned the baby from that point on. The other children, who were in the same room, slept peacefully throughout the dreadful incident.

Mary Somerville was not called to the stand, and no witnesses were called to her defence. Mr Hooper, defending, said there was no need for witnesses as there had been no intention on Mrs Somerville's part to take away the life of the child. He said that she had merely been making an attempt to conceal the fact that this shameful occurrence had taken place in the house and she did not know that the child was alive. This suggestion was scoffed at by the judge who wondered what other outcome there could be after putting a living child in a market bag, weighing it down with stones and throwing it in a well five-feet deep. Mr Hooper also asked the judge to inform the jury that they could bring in a manslaughter verdict against Mrs Somerville if they so desired. The judge refused this request, telling the counsel that he did not feel it was necessary to give the jury any further instruction.

After a speedy trial, the jury needed just forty minutes deliberation to find the defendant guilty in this open-and-shut case. They gave the standard strong recommendation to mercy. Justice O'Byrne agreed saying that "there is no foundation for any suggestion that the life of a child is not as sacred and as important as the life of any other person." He added that children deserve the same protection provided for the elderly. O'Byrne asked Mrs Somerville if there was any reason why the death penalty should not be pronounced. She did not respond but broke down and wept bitterly. The judge dispensed with the tradition of putting on the black cap, but the result did not change. On 15 November, Mary Somerville was sentenced to death for the murder of her new-born grandchild.

The defence applied for leave to appeal the case, asserting that the judge had asked the rhetorical question "what evidence is there of manslaughter?" He stated that the judge had erred in law by not allowing the jury consider this verdict, which had been given in other cases of infanticide. They added that it should not have been a "murder or nothing" verdict. The Court of Criminal Appeal was unmoved. Leave to appeal was refused on 9 December and Mary Somerville's date of execution was re-fixed for 23 December. The court stated in their verdict that there was no evidence of manslaughter when a new-born baby was placed in a bag of stones and thrown into a well. Mary Somerville was therefore placed in Mountjoy Prison in the condemned cell to await her fate.

Mary Somerville had been described as a woman of ill-repute. It had been speculated locally that several of her children had different fathers and her family had been shunned by some members of her community for this reason. Women found guilty of infanticide were almost exclusively given a speedy reprieve but perhaps the condemned grandmother's behaviour counted against her in what was then an extremely conservative country. Either way, Mary Somerville's commutation was slow in coming. Her appeal failed and a petition of mercy was sent to the Minister for Justice by her solicitor James O'Connor in which he prayed for mercy from the state for the poverty-stricken grandmother. These prayers would eventually be answered. On 13 December the good news finally came. Douglas Hyde, the first President of Ireland, commuted Mary Somerville's punishment to one of penal servitude for life. She had been ten days from the gallows.

The Infanticide Act of 1949, 11 years after Mary Somerville's death sentence, would finally mean that infanticide was treated as a separate crime than that of murder. Up to that point, anyone who pleaded not guilty to the offence but was found guilty was liable to face the death penalty. In 1948, just before the law was to change, an infanticide case was heard in Dublin. The unusual aspect of this case was the gender of the perpetrator in what was almost exclusively a crime committed by females. Edward O'Connor, a grocer's assistant and native of South Lotts in Dublin, became the father of Paul Alan Steele. Paul's mother had not wanted the child in the house as it had been born outside of wedlock and O'Connor was forced to assume responsibility for the ten-day-old infant. Unsure of what to do, he walked around with the small child for hours until he came to the Tolka River. He then placed the child in the water and walked home. The baby boy was found dead the next day and quickly traced to O'Connor who was charged with murder. He pleaded not guilty but the evidence was irrefutable and he was found guilty and sentenced to death. He was reprieved on 29 October 1948. He would be the last Irish person sentenced to death for infanticide, the century-old law finally being altered the following year. Although a huge number of people, almost exclusively women like Mary Somerville, had been sentenced to death for infanticide since famine times, the government had never gone through with an execution. The law change ensured that they never would.

MARTIN GRIFFIN

"I have only one thing to say; drink was the cause of it."

Martin Griffin placed the blame for his vicious and unprovoked crime squarely on alcohol after his trial in 1943. There is no doubting that it played a major role, contributing to his savage behaviour and once again nearly bringing a man to the gallows. In modern Ireland, almost half the perpetrators of homicide are found to be under the influence of alcohol. In the case of Martin Griffin, however, his extreme drunkenness may actually have been part of the reason he narrowly escaped the hangman's noose.

Martin Griffin was originally from a large family in the townland of Letteragh but by 1943 he had married and moved to the neighbouring village of Bushypark. Bushypark is situated on the N59, the main road between Galway City and the town of Clifden. Today it is a bustling suburb and residential area, but in those days it was a small farming village two and a half miles distant of Galway City. Griffin was a 48-year-old dairyman on a smallholding who supplied numerous customers locally with milk. He lived with his wife Brigid (53). The couple had married twenty years before in 1923 but had not been blessed with children. Brigid's mother, Ellen Connolly, did share the house with the couple, however, and she was the owner of the three-roomed thatched cottage and the nine acres alongside it. On 17 February 1943, Mrs Connolly died. In the midst of the funeral and the mourning, Ellen Connolly's last will and testament was read to the Griffins. Martin Griffin was then to find out that his mother-in-law had long ago written a will which had not left the cottage he occupied to himself and his wife. She had instead bequeathed it to her son Patrick fifteen years before. This was a hard blow for Griffin as he and his wife had been doing the work around the house while Patrick Connolly, the recipient, had lived in America since 1925 and had played no part in the day-to-day running of the farm since that time.

The wake and funeral were often hard-drinking occasions in the Ireland of 1943. Martin Griffin, who had previously been a heavy drinker, had abstained from alcohol for the twelve months leading up to the funeral. After his mother-in-law's death and the reading of the will, however, he began drinking heavily again. He admitted to his wife that he was angry at her over her mother's will. He said several times about her brother "as he is the owner, why is he not here, do the work here and pay the rent and rates here?" Griffin was still drinking on Sunday 28 February, and had been doing so for the previous ten days. He awoke early, milked the cows and went to his local pub, Kelehan's, where he drank three pints of stout. He took away six bottles of stout and left them at home. Although he was clearly under the influence of alcohol, he then commenced his milk deliveries. When he had finished his round, he travelled into Galway City and visited several other pubs, although he appears to have only drank in one of them. Meanwhile, Mrs Griffin had gone home and found the six bottles of stout. She was angry about her husband's lengthy bout of drinking and was determined to get him back on the straight and narrow. She therefore took the alcohol and returned it to Kelehan's before replacing it with empty bottles. She then put on her Sunday clothes and left the house to go visiting her neighbours, the family of Augustus Kelehan. She returned home at about 10 p.m. She would not be seen alive again.

When Martin came home he said he did not speak to his wife but went to bed. He awoke at midnight and got up to drink some stout and whiskey. Brigid objected to him continually getting out of bed to get drink. "Why don't you stay in bed and not be getting up like a lunatic?

You are like a madman going around." He replied, "Mind your own business and don't be interfering with me." At 4 a.m., Martin Griffin again woke up and rose from his bed. His statement described what happened next. "I knew there was something coming over me. I was so sick from drink. I went into the kitchen and got the trap lamp. I went out to the stable, I got the hatchet and I came back to the bedroom. My wife was between asleep and awake...I hit her with the hatchet on the left side of the head...She said something, I don't know what it was." That was the last time she spoke. Brigid Griffin rolled out of the bed and her husband continued to rain blows on her head, including long after she was dead. Martin Griffin then changed his clothes before hiding the bloodstained murder weapon in the manure heap in the garden.

Griffin had initially tried to cover up his crime but then seems to have had a change of heart. He walked into Eglinton Street Garda station at 6.30 a.m. on Monday morning, two and a half hours after the attack. He looked frightened and was sweating. His hands were also covered in blood. He said to the Garda on duty, "What about my wife? She is dead. I suppose I will be arrested and put in a cell. Oh my God, I have been drinking for the past fortnight." Witnesses said he was sober but looked like a man who had been on a "burst of drink". The Gardaí went to his house immediately to be confronted with the horrifying sight of his wife's bloodstained corpse face-down on the ground with her hands behind her head. She was lying on a bag containing a large sum of money. They also discovered the bloody axe in the manure heap. Griffin was immediately placed under arrest. His depositions were taken *in camera,* with spectators and press excluded. His trial was public, however, and opened to great interest on 1 June in the Dublin Central Court before Judge Overend. Griffin pleaded not guilty to murder.

The case took five days, delays being caused by most of the Galway Gardaí giving their evidence through Irish and requiring the services of an interpreter. It seemed like a straightforward case, however. The state had a confession and a murder weapon within hours of the killing, although Griffin was now pleading not guilty to murder due to his extreme drunkenness. Dr J. McGrath, the State Pathologist, described the wounds of the victim. She had been battered with a hatchet and had twelve wounds, the majority of them on the head. At least eight of the wounds would single-handedly have proven fatal. Her skull was extensively fractured and the base of it was completely shattered. She had been struck both on the bed and on the floor as there were copious amounts of blood in both areas. She also had injuries on her hands and legs, which may have been consistent with an attempt to defend herself against the frenzied attack.

Martin Griffin had never been convicted by the Gardaí for any crime and was known as a hard-working and industrious man who lived on good terms with his wife. He blamed alcohol for his violent attack on Brigid Griffin and several witnesses were called to discuss the extent of the accused's drinking problem leading up to the murder. Augustus Kelehan, Griffin's neighbour who had helped with his milk deliveries, remarked that during that week the accused was "never sober" on the round. He added that on the Sunday afternoon, Griffin had tried to gain access to three different pubs even though there was no drinking permitted between 2-4 p.m., the "Holy Hour". Mary Kelehan said that "three or four pints would affect (Griffin) as would twenty pints on any other person." Martin's brother, Peter Griffin, told the court that on two occasions in the days leading up to the murder he had asked his brother why he was drinking heavily, after he had abstained from it for so long. Both enquiries were answered only with laughter.

Several of Griffin's customers testified that the milkman had been highly intoxicated on the day of the murder. Others disagreed, opining that Griffin exaggerated the amount of alcohol he had consumed on the day in order to aid his defence. He claimed to have drank pints in every pub he had visited in Galway, a fact that was challenged by several people who saw him that day. One local publican, Michael Coyne, kept his information to himself on the stand. Although it was known Griffin went to his pub frequently, Coyne claimed he had never served him alcohol. He also claimed, through the medium of

Irish, that he had never seen Griffin drunk. He said he did not know if there was poitín in Galway and also denied selling Griffin whiskey to bring home. Not surprisingly, he was treated as a hostile witness.

Griffin himself was then examined on the stand. He explained that he had emigrated to America as a young man and lived there for eleven years. He was conscripted into the American Army in 1918 for nine months to serve in the First World War. He demobilised, returned to Ireland and married Brigid in 1923. He had problems with alcohol, however, which often made him aggressive. He abstained from drink for the year coming up to the murder but was drunk for a fortnight after his mother-in-law's death. The prisoner claimed to have been so drunk on the day of the murder that he did not remember being in the company of Augustus Kelehan on that afternoon at all, despite having spent several hours with him completing the milk deliveries. Griffin also said he could not remember going to the shed, only seeing his wife lying on the floor. He stated that he had hidden the weapon before going down into the kitchen and crying when he realised what he done. He then walked into Galway and turned himself in at the Garda station.

When cross-examined, it was put to him that his wife was fully dressed in her best Sunday clothes when found. Griffin agreed that she would not usually wear these clothes in bed and he could not explain why she had them on at 4 a.m., nor could he tell the court what time she had gone to bed. He was similarly unable to explain why a bag of money, containing £71, was found underneath his wife and he denied vehemently having murdered her over the money or his mother-in-law's will, although he admitted that they had been arguing frequently that week over his drinking. He disagreed with the prosecution that he had murdered her in the course of an argument and claimed he did not remember telling the guards, "I killed her; we fought." He finished by saying that he had never laid a hand on his wife all through their married life.

Martin Griffin had admitted the brutal and unprovoked murder of his wife. He had walked some distance to retrieve the deadly weapon and hidden it afterwards. His defence team's only hope was a verdict of

manslaughter due to alcoholic intoxication. The defence solicitor, Mr Ó
Briain, put it to the court that this was a case of manslaughter, not murder.
This was, he said, due to the diminished responsibility of the defendant
owing to the amount of drink he had taken before the killing. They
described him as "stark raving drunk" when he came home and said he was
"sodden" with drink. It was up to the state to prove that Griffin knew that
he was committing a crime and they had not done so. The prosecution
took the alternate view, with solicitor Mr McCarthy reminding the jury
that although the accused may have been drunk, alcohol is not a defence
unless it can be proven that the accused was incapable of knowing that he
was committing a crime. McCarthy continued "If a man left his house,
went to the stable, took a weapon, killed his wife and afterwards buried
it...he had intent to commit a crime."

On the fifth day of the trial Judge Overend summed up, remarking
that Griffin had admitted to killing his wife but had pleaded not guilty
to murder. He said that Griffin's drunkenness was only relevant to the
crime if it meant that he had no intention of committing a crime and
did not know he was doing so. He told the court that Griffin had
shown intention by going to get the lamp and then leaving the house
to search for the hatchet. This mirrored the words of the prosecution
and implied that the judge believed that Griffin was responsible for
his actions. He then invited the jury to deliberate on the evidence.

The jury spent two hours deliberating and returned with a guilty
verdict, although with a strong recommendation to mercy. The judge
commented that he agreed with the jury's verdict and excused them from
jury service for six years. He then pronounced the death sentence on
Griffin. When asked if he had anything to say, Griffin merely remarked
that drink had been the cause of his misfortune. The execution was fixed
for 29 June. Griffin's defence team, led by solicitor John O'Connell of
Mary Street, Galway, opened a widely-supported petition for his reprieve
shortly after the verdict. It received over 2,000 signatures in the Galway
area alone and may have swayed the government. Just four days before
Martin Griffin was due to be hanged, the President announced his

sentence would be commuted to one of penal servitude for life. Griffin was released from prison in April 1955, having served twelve years.

In the same year as Griffin killed his wife, 24-year-old Waterford labourer William O'Shea hatched a plan with his friend to murder his wife. Tommy White shot her dead on the roadside but was found insane and unfit to plead. O'Shea was found guilty and hanged for being a party to the murder. The contradiction between the two punishments is stark, although the two crimes were similar. O'Shea was executed while Griffin received a prison term. Strictly speaking, alcohol should only be a defence if the person committing the crime was unaware of the action they were committing. We shall never know if this was the case with Martin Griffin.

STEPHEN MURPHY

"Would they want much evidence before they would arrest a fellow?"

The Second World War was a conflict that had ended nearly 40 million European lives. By June 1945, it was almost at an end and the Irish could look forward to better times. Although the country had been officially neutral, the effect of the war did not stop at our borders. Instead, the people of Ireland endured ration books and a lack of coal, paraffin, wheat, tea, sugar and other necessities which had added comfort to their lives. Most Irish people were willing to accept "The Emergency" as a compromise to keep themselves safe and their sons out of the armies fighting their way through Europe. In sharp contrast to the unimaginable bloodshed and violence which was devastating Europe, however, was the crime rate in Ireland at the time. Since the Civil War it had fallen sharply and we could proudly consider ourselves one of the safest countries in Europe, if not the world. Murder was not something people in the country had to contend with, particularly in rural north Mayo where children were free to roam around without their parents having to worry. This innocence was challenged however on a summer's day in 1945 after what was described by one source as "the most horrible atrocity ever perpetrated within the memory of the oldest members of the district."

Michael Joseph Loftus was eight years old and the only child of a farming family described as well-to-do. He lived in a comfortable two-storey farmhouse in Ballinlaban, just outside the town of Crossmolina.

The healthy and stockily-built youngster had spent an unexceptional morning on 17 June. It was a Sunday and Michael had gone to 9.30 a.m. Mass with Peter Gilroy, a servant boy employed by his family. He returned home to a breakfast made by his mother. Michael was the only child in the townland so he played by himself outside for a time. At 11.30 a.m., he was seen by his mother standing barefoot at the top of the avenue leading into their house. He was due back home for dinner at 1 p.m., having told his parents that he was going into Crossmolina to compete in the boys' sports which were organised for that afternoon. His mother had the meal for her husband and son on the table at 1 p.m., as she did every Sunday. Her husband ate it but he was alone at the dinner table. Michael had still not returned and his mother waited in mild annoyance for his appearance.

By 1.30 p.m., however, the annoyance had turned to worry. His mother, unsure of his whereabouts, went to search for him around the farmyard. She could not find him anywhere. Within hours the Gardaí had been informed and a local search party was organised. Some locals dived into the fast-flowing River Deel, located just behind the Loftus farm, thinking he might have fallen in. Others searched the lonely bogland just north of his home. Neither venture was successful. There was no sign of the young boy and with each passing hour the fear and worry in the close-knit community grew. On Tuesday morning a local man claimed that he saw Michael Loftus crossing the road a mile from his home. Over a hundred locals quickly gathered to search the surrounding area. Unfortunately, there was no trace of the young boy. Tragically, this sighting was to prove to have been a case of mistaken identity for Michael Loftus had been long dead at that time.

The searches proceeded non-stop for nine days with no success. Search parties, consisting of scores of Gardaí and up to six hundred local people, combed every inch of the countryside around Crossmolina. Eventually at 11 a.m. on 25 June, the search yielded a tragic outcome, discovered just four hundred yards from the Loftus homestead in an adjoining field. Gardaí, searching in the area, saw what looked like blood on the ground. On closer inspection, the soil around it looked like it had been recently disturbed. One Garda dug with his hands and discovered the leg of a boy's trousers. The shallow grave was dug up and found to contain the body of a young boy. It was Michael Loftus. He had been buried in a grave well hidden between several clumps of furze. The grave was just two feet deep and four feet wide and the body bore signs of having been severely beaten around the back of the head. He had been murdered violently. His body was exhumed that night in the pouring rain and the State Pathologist confirmed that the victim had been hit several times from behind with a blunt instrument. He had died instantly.

The rural area was profoundly shocked at the vicious crime. Michael Loftus's funeral cortège was over a mile long, while hundreds of other mourners lined the road all the way from the church in Crossmolina to Kilmurray Cemetery at the foot of the majestic Nephin Mountain. Sadness quickly turned to anger after the ceremony as locals clamoured for the suspect to be apprehended, while Gardaí stated confidently to the media that they expected to make an early arrest. It was rumoured that the murderer was a local man. It would not be long before the suspect was identified.

After the body had been uncovered, the Gardaí discovered a pair of boots hidden in a bush nearby. Instead of removing them, however, they left them there and placed officers to watch them at night in the hope they were connected to the killer. Sure enough, in the dead of night a shadowy figure was seen walking towards the spot. It was local man, Stephen Murphy. Murphy claimed to be looking for a lost calf. The Gardaí were sceptical that he would be doing so at the time of night but released him, vowing to look into his movements further. Michael's mother had also mentioned Murphy. Nellie Loftus, who was confined to bed for a long period after the tragedy, told Gardaí she had seen 29-year-old Murphy shortly after her son had gone missing. Murphy, from the neighbouring townland of Ballycarroon, had walked past her house at 2.30 p.m. from the direction of Kelly's farm. Nellie revealed that her son, the only boy in the immediate area, was a regular visitor to Murphy's house, despite the large age difference. They spent a lot of time together and Murphy would often bring the young boy ferreting.

Gardaí had been informed by other locals that Murphy had been acting strangely in the aftermath of the murder. He was met by Garda William O'Connell on 27 June, two days after the murdered boy had been found. "Would they want much evidence before they would arrest a fellow?" enquired Murphy. When being told that it would depend, he replied, "But sure no one can say he came along this way. His mother saw him last and he was then at the gate, she does not know where he went then." He then remarked "A fellow could easily be pulled into this and be convicted in the wrong." Gardaí were also aware that Murphy, considered strange and a loner in the locality, was known to have previously attacked a fourteen-year-old boy and injured him when the boy sang a rhyme ridiculing him.

Murphy had also told a neighbour, "I am going to be arrested tonight for the killing of that child. Somebody gave away on me." When the neighbour asked him if he had murdered Michael Loftus, Murphy replied that he hadn't but if he "could get a bicycle (he'd) clear away on them." Later that evening Garda O'Connell saw Murphy walking towards McGuinness's farm, near where the body was discovered, and followed discreetly. When Murphy saw the guard he began to run. The guard gave chase and grabbed him by the sleeve. When asked why he had run, Murphy remarked "I can't stick it any longer. They have me. I don't know why I done it." The guard advised Murphy, for his own sake, to show him the articles concerned with the murder. Murphy refused as if he did "he was finished". After some persuasion he agreed, if the Garda promised not to disclose it to anyone else. He brought the policeman along to a local ringfort and asked him to wait outside. Some minutes later, he emerged with bloodstained trousers and other articles of clothing which he gave to the officer. The Gardaí took a statement from Murphy in his own house that night, lasting over six hours. Despite these incriminating articles, the suspect refused to admit any involvement in the murder.

Nevertheless, Stephen Murphy was arrested and brought to Ballina Garda barracks. The streets leading up to the building were cordoned off due to a huge number of people gathering around them. Some were curious to catch a glimpse of the curly-headed 5' 7" farmer's son accused of the brutal murder of his young neighbour. Others shouted abuse and attempted to physically attack him as he passed. Murphy, in the station, continued to vehemently deny the murder of the boy. He explained that there was blood on the trousers as he had cut his hand and wiped them on them. When asked why they were hidden in the fort, he said he was afraid people would try to connect them with the boy's murder. He told the Gardaí that on the morning of the murder he had been with the cattle until just before 12 p.m. and then he had stayed in a barn for a while. He had not seen Michael Loftus. He also denied asking the young boy to go ferreting with him previous to that day, merely admitting that the boy had followed him twice.

The state's case against Murphy began in the Central Criminal Court in November 1945. He pleaded not guilty. Sixty witnesses were to be called by the prosecution to try to link Murphy with the heinous crime. Mr Humphries, prosecuting, said that it was not up to the State to provide a motive but stated that from the State Pathologist's report "a certain association" could be drawn between the dead boy and the accused, implying a sexual motive. The press was advised by Justice Guy not to publish particulars pertaining to the sexual incidents in the case, a common practice at the time, but it was widely known that the boy had been sexually assaulted over a long period of time. The defence's case was based around the defence of insanity and coercion. Murphy's father was called to testify about the particulars of cases of insanity in the family. He revealed that many of Stephen Murphy's family, on his mother's side, had spent time in mental institutions. He told the court that his son "had been peculiar since leaving school". He could only do the farm work when repeatedly shown how. He "lived on his own" and never went to dances or races with the other boys. On top of insanity, the defence team argued that Murphy had been questioned for over six hours when he made his initial statement, rendering it inadmissible. Murphy himself had described this interrogation as most gruelling. It had begun at 4.42 a.m. in the morning and lasted until after 11 a.m.

Dr Dunne, of Grangegorman Mental Hospital, appeared in court and told the court that he had examined Murphy and found him a strange individual. His facial expressions were apathetic and he had a "remarkable lack of spontaneity in his speech". Dunne opined that Murphy would not have known that he was doing something wrong if he committed a criminal act. He believed that Murphy was suffering from dementia praecox, a condition where one does not understand the realities of life. Another doctor who examined the prisoner told the court that Murphy told him that he had never been to the pictures or to a concert and he did not play with other children at school as he preferred to be alone. The prosecution disagreed, pointing out that if Michael Loftus had threatened to tell someone about the sexual abuse it would have constituted a rational motive for Murphy to murder the young boy. They also reminded the jury that Murphy had murdered the boy in private, quickly and quietly concealed the body and covered his tracks by hiding several incriminating articles. He had repeatedly lied to the guards. The probable murder weapon, a spade linked to Murphy, had also been thrown into the River Deel.

Murphy's guilt was not in question. The bloodstained clothes, location of his spade and his erratic behaviour and statements incriminated him. Along with the testimony of locals, his guilt seemed almost certain, although he refused to admit it. He had spent a lot of time with Michael Loftus, going ferreting and inviting him to his house. He was also seen by several people in the vicinity minutes before the unfortunate boy went missing. The day before Michael Loftus' murder he had been spotted on the crossbar of Murphy's bike. Added to this was the evidence from the State Pathologist that the boy had been sexually assaulted over a long period of time. The question remained; would Murphy's strange behaviour be enough to convince the jury that he was not responsible for his own actions? Although his behaviour had been described as "eccentric" locally since he was a boy, his numerous attempts to cover his tracks and the lies he had told to make his story more plausible may have suggested comprehension of the gravity of his crime.

The jury returned on 24 November. Unconvinced by the insanity of the defendant, and with the judge giving an unsympathetic summing-up, Murphy was sentenced to death by hanging. The date was set for 12 December. He was set to be the first Mayo man executed for a criminal offence in the twentieth century. However, an appeal was lodged on the grounds of the insanity of the defendant and the overly-rigorous and prolonged questioning which Murphy had undergone when first arrested. The appeal was granted and the conviction quashed.

On 1 May 1946 the re-trial opened and the evidence was resubmitted before a new jury in Dublin. The evidence was similar to the initial trial, although the prosecution brought evidence of a statement Murphy made in prison to two other inmates in Sligo Jail where he supposedly confessed to the murder. When one of the prisoners told him he was "wrong to kill the young lad", Murphy replied nonchalantly, "I did kill him but it was unpremeditated. I don't think I'll hang for it in any case." The medical professionals again appeared and Murphy's father also retold his emotive evidence of his son's strange personality and chequered family history. It was enough on this occasion. On day five of the trial, after a two-hour deliberation, the jury returned a verdict of guilty but insane. Murphy was to be detained at the pleasure of the state in the hospital for the criminally insane. Murphy's statement "I don't think I'll hang for it in any case" proved accurate.

The paedophiliac tendencies shown by Murphy were something that Irish society of the time could not understand. The Catholic Church had the final say on morals and sexuality and paedophilia was so alien to the general population that many thought that Murphy had to be insane to commit such a grotesque act. One doctor said of Murphy' "His homosexuality may have a deteriorating effect on the mind." It may have been his sexual association with the unfortunate Michael Loftus that convinced the jury Murphy was not culpable for his actions. As we have found out since, however, paedophilia was a lot more common in Irish society at the time than was suspected.

AGNES McADAM

"If I did buy that stuff, it would be given to rats."

In the early twentieth century poisoning was one of the most widespread killing methods in Ireland. Strychnine, a common household poison used as bait for rats and other pests, was used in many cases to inflict death on another individual. It was a method that was difficult to detect, easy to administer and the eventual fatality was often mistaken for typhus, or some other natural cause of death. Less than half a grain of the poison could be a lethal dose and enough to cause any person an unthinkably painful death within a couple of hours. The unfortunate victim would find themselves struggling to breathe initially. The poison would then attack the nervous system, leading to convulsions and spasms and eventually causing the spine to arch. Finally, if a sufficient amount of the deadly poison has been ingested, an agonising death by suffocation would follow. James Finnegan suffered this torturous end, although he may not have been the intended target of what became known as the "Poisoned Cakes Case".

Agnes McAdam was 52 years old and unmarried in 1945. She was from Derrylusk, four miles north of the town of Ballybay in County Monaghan. Agnes grew up in a family of seven children, who had drifted away from the area one after another. Finally, she was left living on a smallholding with just her brother, Patrick and his wife Tessie. The McAdams made their living from a small farm, where Agnes' tasks included assisting with the housekeeping and looking after the fowl. Several years before, the farm had suffered a blow when twenty-four fowl had died after coming into contact with rats. As a consequence of this, Agnes had bought strychnine. Around this time Agnes had also been involved in an accident with a threshing machine. She wore a permanent glove on her left hand as a result of the severe injuries she had suffered. It was later remarked that her nerves had been badly affected by the incident and she was considered locally to be an anxious woman ever since.

Four hundred yards away from the McAdams, in the neighbouring townland of Cornahoe, lived the Finnegan family. The Finnegans were well liked and said to be on excellent terms with all their neighbours, including the McAdams. In September 1945, Elizabeth (Lily), Finnegan (28) and her friend Kathleen Coyle were placed in charge of a function for two local priests, Fr Markey and Fr Kelly, who were leaving the district to go abroad to the missions. An attendance of five hundred was expected at what would be a major social event in the rural community. Lily and Kathleen were asking locally for contributions of food and they went to see Agnes McAdam on 13 September wondering if she would like to bake a cake for the celebration. Tessie answered the door and told the women that Agnes was in bed. They returned four days later and this time Patrick McAdam and his wife donated £1. There was no sign of Agnes again, however, and no word on whether she was willing to contribute to the celebration.

Tessie had remembered to tell her sister-in-law that there was a request for her to make a cake to the social but Agnes had answered that it was very hard to get the ingredients and that she didn't think she would be up to the task. On the morning of 22 September, however, Agnes appeared to have a change of heart. She decided to go into Willie Smith's bakery in the town of Ballybay where she asked to look at some fancy cakes. She was shown two jam sandwich cakes. She agreed to buy both and requested that the proprietor wrap both items in brown paper. She then left saying that she would collect her purchases later, which she duly did. She cycled home afterwards passing the Finnegan household, but did not drop the cakes in at this point. She would tell Gardaí later that she brought them home to her bedroom instead, hanging them in a bag on a nail.

It was six days later that Agnes McAdam finally delivered the cakes. The Finnegans were somewhat surprised when she arrived to their house two days before the party, assuming from her lack of communication that she would not be making a donation. She had a brown paper parcel which contained the two Scribona jam sandwich cakes. When Mrs Mary Finnegan commented on how warm they were, Agnes replied, "They are only out of the oven", implying falsely that she had baked them. The Finnegans recommended to Agnes that she write her name on the package that she had kindly donated, so that people would know of her generosity. Agnes "protested violently" against this.

McAdam stayed for a short time in the house. At around 3.30 p.m. Lily's father James Finnegan (65) returned from Ballybay. McAdam left as the dinner of herring, potatoes and milk was being served. After dinner, James Finnegan suggested that since there were so many cakes in the house for the social they should have one with their tea. The two women agreed and James Finnegan took down the smaller of the two jam sandwich cakes that Agnes had just delivered. He then cut it into slices. He ate the largest slice and gave smaller portions to his wife and daughter. Elizabeth took the smallest piece. She spat it out almost immediately, however, complaining of a bitter taste. Mrs Finnegan had a bigger slice, but she only ate a small part of it, agreeing that it had a peculiar taste. Mr Finnegan finished most of his portion, however. The family dog also entered the kitchen and ingested the part of the cake that had been spat onto the kitchen floor.

After tea, Mr Finnegan said "Thank God for a good dinner", before harnessing his donkey to a cart and setting off for the bog. A few minutes after he left, the dog, who was sitting beside the fire, began to shiver and froth at the mouth. It lay down on the ground and was dead within minutes. Meanwhile, Mary Finnegan had also started feeling ill and was violently sick, temporarily losing her eyesight. She was also unable to control her limbs. She was in agonising pain for about two hours. Her condition had somewhat improved from this sudden attack by 6 p.m. when her husband came back early from the bog. He staggered in the gate with his teeth gritted. He was described as "dottery", telling his wife and daughter "my legs are not able to carry me". He could not walk as far as the house and collapsed in the yard, where a chair was taken to him. He had several convulsions and his face appeared blue. His daughter made him a concoction of salt and water which he was unable to swallow, despite several attempts. Two nurses, who were in the area on a holiday from England, entered the yard and attended to the sick man. When his condition deteriorated, one was dispatched to fetch a doctor. It was too late, however, and James Finnegan died shortly after 7.15 p.m. His Last Rites were then administered to him by one of the priests whose party the community had been planning.

The family immediately suspected that they had been poisoned and the remnants of the food they had eaten that afternoon were given to Sergeant Donoghue. The organs of James Finnegan and the family dog were both examined and found to contain significant amounts of the deadly poison strychnine. James' post-mortem confirmed that he had died due to cardiac failure. He was also found to have consumed more than one grain of strychnine, four times the minimum fatal dose. McAdam's donation, the "Jam Sandwich" cake, as it was known, was also tested and found to contain a small dose of the poison. The Gardaí called to the McAdam household on 3 October. Agnes showed them around the house and said "It is terrible sad about poor Jim."

The Gardaí asked the question "Did you examine the contents of the parcel you left at Finnegan's house yesterday?" McAdam responded, "I did not. I gave it as I got it in the shop." Agnes denied vehemently ever buying or owning any strychnine. Gardaí then produced a poison register with her signature. The entry stated that she had bought sixteen grains of strychnine from Manley's Chemist, Ballybay, in June 1942 for rats. McAdam initially denied all knowledge of the purchase and asserted' "I can read and write…I never put my name in that book". Later, when pressed about the signature and the similarity with her writing, she stared at the entry for six minutes without uttering a word. Eventually she admitted that she may have bought it but that "If I did buy that stuff…it would be given to rats."

Agnes McAdam did agree readily to make a statement. She smoked several cigarettes throughout and was "completely at her ease"according to the Gardaí. She told the Gardaí that she had cycled into Ballybay and purchased the two cakes for about 3s. after hearing that anyone who presented something for the social would get an invitation. She had hung them on a nail in her room and had not looked at them or interfered with them in any way. She had then delivered them to the Finnegans on 28 September. Her statement did not convince the authorities. She was arrested on 13 November and charged with murder.

Agnes McAdam's trial began on 11 February 1946, in the Dublin Central Criminal Court. When arraigned, she pleaded not guilty. The trial would last five days and call forty-six witnesses. The prosecuting solicitor, Seán Hooper, opened his case by stating that the court "will come to the conclusion that the accused woman certainly intended to injure somebody – if not to kill somebody – by placing the poison in these cakes." Casey, for the defence, told the court that if McAdam had committed the crime against her friendly neighbours, with no motive whatsoever, she must have been a lunatic for only a mad woman would wantonly kills another human for no reason.

State Pathologist Dr John McGrath spoke about James Finnegan's death, which he stated was consistent with convulsive poisoning of which strychnine is one of the most common forms. This strychnine certainly came from McAdam's cake. Agnes McAdam took the stand and told the court that she had purchased the strychnine years before in order to kill the rats, mixing it up in mash. The rats had eaten it all. She stated that she had told the Gardaí she had never bought poison as she had forgotten the purchase as it was so long ago. She only remembered when she was shown the poisons' register. She told the court that she had "no enmity towards the Finnegans" and as far as she knew they had none towards her.

The prosecution asserted that two of the Finnegans and their dog ate the cake donated by Agnes McAdam. One of them had fallen ill and two of them were dead. She had also purchased the lethal poison three years before and had plenty of opportunity to insert it into the cakes. They also dwelt on the fact that McAdam, on her way home from purchasing the cakes, passed the Finnegan household. She had not dropped the cakes in, however, choosing to bring them home instead and keep them for six days. The defence disagreed, arguing that Miss McAdam had no motive as she had no quarrel with her neighbours. The poison had been purchased many years before and they contended that she could not have been saving it up for three years waiting for a party for two priests she did not know. They also mentioned that there was also a bottle of poison found in the cupboard of the Finnegan house (although this was unopened) which could have caused death. Finally they stated that if the court believed that Miss McAdam had knowingly put the poison into the cake then she had done so in the expectation that it would be shared around at the social. She had no intention of killing James Finnegan. The judge, in his summing, told the jury that "if a person prepared poison with an intent to kill or injure any human being, such a person is guilty of murder of anyone killed thereby."

After the five-day trial, the jury needed two hours and ten minutes to find the accused guilty of murder, with a strong recommendation to mercy. The judge asked her if she had anything to say to which she replied quietly "Not guilty" and adjusted her spectacles. Justice Duffy then pronounced the death sentence on the woman. At this point, Agnes McAdam went pale. She grabbed the arms of two warders tightly who helped her down towards the cells. An appeal was launched but was refused. Agnes McAdam's date of execution was set for 15 April 1946. On 9 April, however, the government had a change of heart and the sentence was commuted to life imprisonment. She ended up spending a little over three years in jail, ultimately being released in September 1949.

It appears likely that Agnes McAdam did poison the cake that she gave to the Finnegans, although she pleaded not guilty to the charge. Her defence counsel argued that if she had poisoned the cake, she had only meant it to be eaten in small portions, not enough to kill or cause grievous bodily harm. The baffling question remains: Who at the social was the target of Agnes McAdam's hatred that she would be willing to endanger multiple lives to settle her score? We may never know, but it appears that her reckless act led to James Finnegan's excruciating death.

DANIEL DUFF

"Will I be hanged or get five years in jail?"

The Irish Police Force (An Garda Síochána) was founded in 1922 in the midst of the bloody Civil War. The RIC, the forerunner to the Gardaí, were armed but the Free State government surprisingly decided not to issue rank and file Gardaí with handguns. This was despite the violence that was rampant in the state in those days. This decision has been somewhat vindicated as Ireland is one the safest western democracies and the Gardaí enjoy a relatively high satisfaction rate. Unlike in other countries, instances of criminals getting shot by police are rare. Unfortunately, however, this can leave Gardaí vulnerable to criminals and numerous policemen have been murdered in the line of duty. Garda James Byrne became the nineteenth member of An Garda Síochána to die while serving the community. He is also, arguably, the Garda killed in the strangest circumstances. Garda Byrne was himself armed, but was shot dead while protecting a rural Co. Limerick farm. Incredibly, Byrne's killer was a colleague and fellow Garda.

Garda James Byrne was born in December 1907, in Askanagap, near Aughrim, Co. Wicklow. He joined the Gardaí in 1928 and had been stationed in Counties Wexford, Cork and Kerry before being transferred to Pallasgreen, Co. Limerick. Byrne worked the dayshift in the village until November 1944, when Superintendent John Dunning rostered him for night patrol. Byrne, a 39-year-old single man, was content to work these unsociable hours. The patrol was for disputed land belonging to the O'Kennedy family. In 1936, Mr Richard O'Kennedy had purchased a farm, Mount Catherine, three quarters of a mile from the village. He bought the land from the Land Commission, which had been set up to compulsorily buy and break up the large estates of landlords. This land was then redistributed amongst local families. The redistribution was not always fair or popular however and this particular farm was subject to a serious dispute. After several threats from disgruntled locals, O'Kennedy applied to the Gardaí for overnight protection. The Gardaí granted his request and two members of the force were stationed nightly at the property.

In November 1944, Daniel Joseph Duff, a 22-year-old native of Suncroft, Co. Kildare, also arrived at Pallasgreen Garda station. Duff was the third eldest of seven sons and at school was considered a brilliant student. After leaving Newbridge College he joined the Defence Forces for a year and a half where his conduct was described as excellent. On leaving the army, Duff enlisted in An Garda Síochána in June 1944. Pallasgreen was his first assignment, and after a year's service he was sent out to O'Kennedy's farm to join Garda Byrne on night duty.

The two guards worked from 11 p.m.-6 a.m. each night, with longer hours in the summer. Both guards were armed with a Webley .45 calibre revolver on this particular duty, due to its isolated location and potential for confrontation. The two men initially got on well but the huge amount of time spent in each other's company meant that relations between them were occasionally strained. The only visitor they ever had to the farm was their superintendent, who sporadically came to inspect his charges. When he was asked about the relationship between Duff and Byrne he said, "They seemed all right. I did not notice anything wrong." Other Gardaí would say that the two men were very friendly sometimes but in early September 1946, had not been on speaking terms at all. When pressed by another Garda as to what caused the argument, Duff replied that it was "over duty". On another occasion, Duff took Byrne's bicycle without permission, which resulted in the two men not speaking for several days.

Duff spent nine months on night duty out in Mount Catherine, most of them in the company of James Byrne. Duff later described the long period of nocturnal labour leaving him "tired, depressed and irritable". He did seven days a week for ten continuous months, including Sundays and Christmas Day, only requesting one day off in that period. He had to sleep during the day in the busy Garda station and found himself constantly being woken up while he tried to rest. The night duty itself was uneventful and repetitive, with no major incident occurring while the two men were stationed there. To relieve the tedium of the long nights, Duff and Byrne did not always adhere strictly to the job's conditions. Sometimes both men would leave the premises. Duff would occasionally desert his duty and visit a local family in the townland of Nicker. Byrne too would depart the estate and go off on his own. Duff said afterwards that Byrne's attitude was that "he wanted me to be at the farm when he wasn't but he wanted me to stay with him when he was there." It all culminated in August 1946, with the two men having a serious argument. Byrne insulted his colleague, after which Duff threatened him that if he called him names again he would hit him. Byrne allegedly took out his gun and replied that if anyone ever hit him, he would "blow his brains out". Duff would later say that he believed Byrne would carry out this threat because during a previous row Byrne had also drawn his revolver and waved it under Duff's nose. Duff described his colleague as "hot-tempered (and) reckless with a gun".

The superintendent visited the two men on the night-duty on 23 September. All seemed normal and neither man mentioned their recent dispute. Two days later, on 25 September, Byrne was supposed to be at work at 10 p.m. He decided instead to drive out to Limerick Junction, a nearby village, and only turned up at O'Kennedy's at 11 p.m. He, and his colleague, had both consumed several pints of stout during the day. The night was dark and dry, with a slight breeze. When Byrne arrived, he and Duff patrolled the farm. As they walked up towards the pear tree they talked of Duff's impending transfer. He was finally being moved off night duty to the daytime shift in the station in Murroe, a village twelve miles to the north. Byrne was discussing a sergeant he had in Farranfore, Co. Kerry who had made his night duty difficult. Duff responded that he wouldn't mind doing night duty again as it was alright once you got used to it. Byrne replied "You seem to be a very long time getting used to doing it here." Duff retorted that he could say the same about Byrne, except he had "the superintendent on (his) side".

Garda Byrne said to his colleague that he seemed to expect the same treatment as men longer on the job. Duff responded by accusing his fellow garda of having told the superintendent about rows between the two men and times he had "dodged". The argument escalated to the point that both men were cursing and swearing at each other loudly, only lowering their voice when they walked past the farmhouse to avoid being heard. Byrne was grinding his teeth. He said he was going to go up to the loft to sleep and that Duff could f**k off for all he cared. Duff told Byrne that he was thirsty and was going to get a pear from a tree in the orchard. He walked in that direction, but instead of going to the loft as he had said, Byrne followed his colleague.

When they got to the pear tree, Duff testified that Byrne called him a string of names and roared into his face, "You young pup. You were only dragged up. I will give you a slap on the mouth which you are looking for for a long time." Duff laughed at his fellow Garda and answered that if there was slapping done, Byrne may not come so handy out of it. "I told you before if you ever attempted to hit me I would blow your brains out," shouted Byrne. At this point Byrne, according to Duff, made a quick movement of his hand towards his right pocket. This sudden movement made Duff "panicky". "I drew quickest…I had my thumb on my gun in my pocket. I pulled out my gun and fired at him." Duff fired two shots at Byrne, both of which went through his heart. Duff later testified that his anger dispelled after the second shot. He saw Byrne jerking on the ground and he knelt down asking, "Jim, are you all right; can you hear me?" Byrne was dead within seconds. Duff whispered an Act of Contrition in his fatally-injured colleague's ear before running to the farmhouse. The O'Kennedys were woken just before midnight by frantic shouts coming from outside their window. It was Garda Duff bellowing "I shot Jim Byrne."

The two O'Kennedys accompanied Duff to the orchard where they saw Garda Byrne's body. They checked his pulse and confirmed that the Garda was dead. His walking cane, torch and cap lay a couple of yards away on the ground. The trio went back into the house where a panicky Duff asked the shaken couple if they would go with him to the station. They agreed and they arrived at 12.10 a.m. On the way Duff said, "It was either him or me", and also, "What will happen me now? Will I be hanged or get five years in jail?" Duff was arrested immediately. He gave a statement to the guard on-duty admitting shooting his colleague but insisting he had done so in self-defence and he had not planned it. The case was brought to trial in the Central Criminal Court, Dublin commencing on 19 November 1946. Daniel Duff pleaded not guilty to the charge of murder.

There were no eye-witnesses to the fatal confrontation but twenty-one witnesses did appear for the prosecution, most outlining the events of the day and discussing the turbulent relationship between Duff and Byrne. There was only one witness for the defence, Duff himself, the only man alive who could know the truth of what had really taken place on the night of Byrne's death. He outlined his version of events, reiterating that he had shot Byrne in self-defence. Duff had been extensively trained in gun use in both the Defence forces and the Gardaí and was asked several tough questions by prosecutor, Mr Murnaghan.

Murnaghan: You knew that firing at his chest was going to kill him?
Duff: I never thought of that.
Murnaghan: Was there anything to prevent you grappling with him to prevent him using his gun?
Duff: I didn't consider that, it entered my head immediately to use my gun. I just fired two shots at him. I fired at his chest alright.
Murnaghan: Were you taught only to use a revolver as a last resort?
Duff: No, I was never taught that.

When it was put to the accused that Byrne's gun was in his left pocket, despite Duff saying he had reached for his right pocket during the stand-off, Duff replied that he could not explain that. Byrne had also been holding a walking cane and a torch in his hand. When the prosecution enquired of Duff how his colleague could have quickly drawn a gun with those two items in his hand, the accused did not answer the question. Duff came across poorly in the courtroom, seeming unable to answer the simplest of questions. He did, however, assert that he had no hatred or ill will towards Byrne and that "The whole thing was a result of a savage quarrel and I only fired in self-defence."

The defence put it to the jury that the accused had been impaired by a lack of sleep for the last nine months, as had the victim. A sergeant had recommended that Duff go on sick leave shortly before the tragedy as he looked pale and gaunt. These two decent men had been irritable and had an argument. It was, according to Mr Healy, "A killing done in anger by two men equally armed." The judge summing up, rhetorically asked the jury, "Would a reasonable man, faced with precisely the same position as the accused, have taken the step of firing a deadly weapon twice with the range not more than six or seven feet?"

The jury clearly thought not. They had the option of acquittal for self-defence or manslaughter. They picked neither, however. The three-day trial ended with ninety minutes of deliberation which was enough for the jury to find Guard Daniel Duff guilty of murder, with a unanimous recommendation to mercy. Judge Overend announced that he agreed with the verdict. He asked Duff if he had anything to say in response to the verdict. Duff, who had been listening carefully with no emotion, answered "I have nothing further to say now my Lord." Overend then donned the black cap, sentencing Duff to be executed on 11 December. Five days before that date, however, the government announced that the sentence would be commuted to one of penal servitude for life.

Duff's version of events seemed unlikely and he proved to be a poor witness in his own defence. Still, there may have been a certain amount of sympathy for the talented young guard who seemed to have been under great strain at work. On top of this, there is little doubt that it would have been a national scandal to put to death a so-called guardian of the peace working for the government. Perhaps for this reason, Duff avoided becoming the only member of An Garda Síochána to be executed for murder. He would go on to serve five years and four months in custody, being granted early release in November 1951.

Daniel Duff may have narrowly escaped the hangman's noose but the state showed itself willing to execute other individuals who killed Gardaí in the same decade. Patrick McGrath, Tommy Harte, Charlie Kerins and Maurice O'Neill were all IRA members who were executed by the state during the Second World War. They were all condemned for their parts in the killings of Gardaí, although the evidence against Kerins was inconclusive and O'Neill did not fire the shot that ended the Garda's life. The case of IRA member Richard Goss was the strangest of all, however. Louth native Goss was involved in a shootout when Gardaí raided an IRA safe house in Co. Longford in 1941. A Garda was shot and injured during the confrontation but no one was killed. Despite this, Goss was arrested and found guilty of attempted murder. He was subsequently sentenced to death. Despite many believing that the state would not execute someone when a life had not been taken, Goss was not reprieved. He went before the firing squad on 9 August 1941. He would hold the unenviable record of being the only individual since the Civil War executed by the state for a crime other than murder.

JOHN FANNING

"I put my hands around her throat…
I could not take my hands away."

Kathleen Boyne found herself a widow at a young age. Her husband, to whom she had been married for eleven years, had died in 1946. She was then aged just 33 and left with two young boys to rear, Peter and Frederick. She had made the best of her situation, however, and had gone to live with her brother James Flanagan and his wife Elizabeth, on Geraldine Street in Dublin. The boys were temporarily placed in an orphanage but came on regular visits to see their mother. Kathleen also returned to work in her old cleaning and dying firm, Prescott's in Drumcondra, after her husband's untimely death.

It was through Kathleen's work that she became friendly with John Fanning, who worked as a chemist's assistant next door. Fanning was 28 years old and lived in Shandon Park in Phibsboro with his father and their housekeeper. He began keeping company with Kathleen in November 1946, and from then on they met each other three times a week or so, even after his employment was moved to the Southside of the city. They enjoyed going to the pictures and visiting the scenic seaside town of Howth. Fanning got on so well with Mrs Boyne that by June 1947, she saw fit to introduce him to her brother, James. Fanning was also friendly with Kathleen's two boys, having met them on several occasions.

James' wife would later remark, however, that she thought Kathleen was friendly with John Fanning, while he was somewhat obsessed with her. Fanning may have understated his interest in his girlfriend when he told a work colleague at one point "people have told me I should have nothing to do with her but she suits me." He also confided in another friend that he and Kathleen were to be married at the end of the year. Despite his best-laid plans, the meetings between the pair became less frequent over the following weeks and months. Fanning was studying for a chemist's examination in April, which he subsequently failed, and at this point they were only seeing each other once a week. Elizabeth Flanagan noted that around that time she noticed that "there was a change in relations between them." James, Kathleen's brother, would later say that he had not seen Fanning with his sister since the previous St Patrick's Day, 17 March 1948.

Notwithstanding this, Kathleen Boyne agreed to meet Fanning on 27 May and go to the pictures with him. She came home from work at 6 p.m. and had her tea with her two sons who were staying in the house at the time. She left again at 7.30 p.m. on that evening, going into the city centre and meeting Fanning there at 7.45 p.m. as arranged. They walked to the Carlton Cinema but found the queue to be too long so they instead decided to get a bus out to Howth, about ten miles north of the city. They got two eight-penny tickets for the 8 p.m. bus, which was full to capacity. They arrived into the Royal Hotel in Howth just after 8.45 p.m. The pair drank heavily in the hotel bar with Fanning consuming two whiskies and four stouts. Boyne, for her part, drank three sherries and two whiskies. A waiter would later remark that the couple "did not appear to have much to say and seemed unhappy." Darkness had set in when they left the hotel again at around 9.50 p.m., making their way to Brackenhurst Park, a popular spot with courting couples. Kathleen Boyne was never seen alive again.

The next morning, a message came to the Flanagan household from Prescott's. Kathleen, uncharacteristically, had not turned up for work that morning. James was worried and contacted the Gardaí immediately to report his sister missing. Later that evening an Inspector Hennon came to the house and informed James that he had found his sister's handbag out on Howth Head. As the two men were talking, John Fanning knocked at the door of the house and came in shaking James' hand and saying "This is terrible about Kathleen." He had been informed that Kathleen was missing earlier that afternoon and he was acting excitedly while seeming unsteady on his feet. He said at one point, "Why did I let Kathleen go home in the car?" The Garda asked Fanning if he knew what had happened to Kathleen. "I met Kay last night outside the Carlton." The inspector asked no further questions but took Fanning with him when he departed the house, asking him to accompany a patrol car to Howth.

The Gardaí had not, at that point, told James Flanagan or John Fanning of a terrible find in Howth that afternoon. At 12.15 p.m. Joseph Rickard, a dairyman from the town, was crossing Brackenhurst Field, on Howth Head. Suddenly, he spotted what looked like the figure of a woman partially concealed in furze. When he went closer he saw the woman was dead. Her body was in a crouching position and she had dried blood around her nostrils and mouth. Her handbag was sixty-three feet away and several of her possessions, including her face cream, tweezers and tablets were found underneath the corpse. The body was found to be that of Kay Boyne. She had been strangled and battered to death. A fountain pen belonging to John Fanning's place of work lay close to the corpse, as well as a love letter signed by him.

The Gardaí neglected to tell Fanning about the discovery, first questioning him about his movements on the night of 27 May. Fanning told them that after departing the hotel, the pair had sat at the bank of the roadside. They walked towards the bus-stop afterwards, arriving at 11.10 p.m. While they were there a car had come by with people that Kathleen knew, Fanning thought their name was something like "Howlett". He said they were all "jarred". They had only one space so Kathleen got in and the car drove off. He claimed that the car was squeezed and he could not see it properly, although it looked like a small Austin. He could not remember any other details of the occupants of the vehicle. Fanning stated that at that stage he had gone into Cassidy's pub and bought another drink, only emerging after 11.50 p.m. when the last bus and train back to the city were gone. He had hitched a lift back into Dublin instead and had not seen or heard from Kathleen since. Fanning then showed the Gardaí two walls and the grass margin where he and Kay had been sitting. He showed them another patch of ground one hundred and fifty yards from Brackenhurst Field's entrance where they had also rested for fifteen minutes. It was put to him that the ground showed no appearance of having been recently disturbed but Fanning insisted that it had been that spot. He then brought the party to the East Pier where he maintained the car had picked Kathleen up.

Fanning concluded his tour by going to Cassidy's pub, where he had allegedly drank alone after parting from his girlfriend. The Gardaí asked him to show them where exactly he had stood and to point out who had served him. Fanning indicated the spot he had occupied and claimed that the dark-haired barman who had attended him was not there that evening. The proprietor informed the Gardaí that he had not employed any dark-haired barmen for some time. He added that the pub had been quiet the previous night and Fanning had not been amongst the drinkers. Fanning was not probed about these discrepancies yet. His manner during the walkabout was described as normal, although he chain-smoked. He betrayed emotion at only one point when he was at the East Pier, saying to the Gardaí, "Oh God, why did I let her go with them?"

When Fanning went to Howth Garda station he changed his story, however. He said that he and Kay were in a park in the town, sitting on newspapers and drinking. They were courting and talking pleasantly but when they began to walk back Kathleen tore her coat on a wire. She became angry and said, "My coat is ruined." He replied, "I will buy you another one." She had answered, "I can get plenty to buy for me." Fanning said he tried to put his arms around her but she would not let him. When they reached the gate she said, "This is where we part." Fanning said that he answered, "O.K., enjoy yourself", before walking away. He said he last saw her at 11 p.m. beside the gate. The Gardaí were sceptical about this new version of events and Fanning was detained pending results of the post-mortem. He was also asked about four red stains on his trousers and fresh scratches on his leg. He refused to comment on these matters until he saw a solicitor. Some time after the interview, the Gardaí took Fanning into the superintendent's office to inform him that Kathleen Boyne was dead. He burst into tears, replying "this is terrible".

Dr McGrath, State Pathologist, concluded after the post-mortem that Kathleen Boyne's cause of death had been shock and asphyxia, caused by manual strangulation. She had also received five heavy blows to the face, two of which caused bones to be broken. Her false teeth were smashed and the State Pathologist opined that these injuries had been caused by a blunt instrument which was never found. She had died at about 11 p.m. the previous night. He also said that he thought Mrs Boyne was strangled into unconsciousness before the other blows were rained on her. Her body was then dragged a short distance into the hollow to partially conceal it.

When Gardaí interviewed Fanning's co-worker Miss Kathleen Noonan, she told them a story of a phone call Fanning had received on 28 May. Kathleen Boyne's niece rang him to ask him when he had last seen his girlfriend. He told her that Kay had taken a lift home with some friends and then asked her to ring him if she found out any more news. He hung up the phone, trembling, and said, "Oh God! Oh God!" When Noonan enquired as to what was wrong, he told her that his fiancée had not come home the night before. Miss Noonan then asked when he saw her last to which Fanning replied, "That is the point, I was with her last night." He further told his colleague about the overcrowded car and that he planned to marry Mrs Boyne. Cryptically, he then remarked, "Thank God I am in a chemist, I can always fix myself up a nice dose." Miss Mary Fanning, John's aunt, was also questioned. She told the Guards that he had told her that Kathleen Boyne had not come home after they had a row. She described Fanning as being "excited" and said this was his usual demeanour when it came to matters concerning Mrs Boyne.

The Gardaí arrested Fanning and he was brought for trial on 18 October 1948. Forty-seven witnesses were called, but it was John

Fanning's own evidence that was the most eagerly anticipated. The accused had decided to change his story once again and he was now accepting that he had killed his girlfriend. He pleaded not guilty to the murder charge, however, his counsel claiming the killing warranted a manslaughter verdict. Fanning claimed to have been in "a kind of frenzy". He described himself as being very much in love with Kathleen. He gave her lots of presents and was good to her children. On the night of 28 May they had left the hotel and went to "the usual spot" which was up in Brackenhurst Field. Fanning said they courted briefly but then she decided she wanted to go home. He stood up to put his arms around her and they both tumbled down the slope. Fanning then described how he snapped, "I put my hands around her throat…I could not take my hands away…then she fell limp. I remember feeling her heart. I did not know what I was doing. I remember trying to lift her body but I could not. I dragged her by the hand down toward the fence. I remember kicking the body several times. I was trying to light a cigarette…I scattered her bag around." Fanning was asked if at any point he had any intention of harming Kathleen Boyne to which he replied, "Not the slightest, I loved her too much."

The court was also told of the stormy relationship the two lovers shared. Fanning said they had fought hundreds of times, and described his girlfriend as "very touchy at times", often suggesting that the couple should break up, although they never did. Extracts from a letter he had written to her were also read out in court. In the note he begged her forgiveness for having failed his exam in April, "I know you are fed up of me but please give me the chance and I will make up for everything…" She responded coldly to his letter by saying that she was not in the mood to answer "such a long epistle". Fanning asserted that she had also frequently taunted him during their relationship about leaving him to get someone richer. When pressed about the argument on the fatal night, Fanning said Kathleen had said she was going on holiday. He replied that he would get someone else when she was gone and she said that they "better call the whole thing off."

It was then that Kathleen Boyne resisted kissing him goodnight and he attacked her in an inexplicably murderous rage.

The defence's case centred on the frenzy Fanning had gone into during the argument and his uncontrollable anger. They also called a Dr O'Sullivan, who told the court that the accused had an incredibly rare abnormality where his heart was on his right side of his body and his liver on his left. The doctor opined that this may have contributed to a mental deficiency on the part of the accused. The prosecution's case was that Kathleen Boyne had turned down Fanning's advances and he had knocked her, kicked her around the head and strangled her out of rage, before concealing her body in the undergrowth and making good his escape. He had then made up outlandish stories to try and exonerate himself from the brutal crime he had committed.

Judge Davitt was tasked with summing up. Davitt, son of the legendary founder of the Land League, Michael Davitt, was unsympathetic. He described Fanning as "obsessed with love" for the dead woman. He rebuffed the insanity defence, however, saying that Fanning had strangled the woman to death, felt her heart to ensure she was no longer alive and then dragged her body for the purpose of hiding it. He also said he found it "utterly impossible that any jury could accept the evidence" that Fanning had not meant to harm his betrothed.

The jury must have agreed. They deliberated for one hour and forty minutes and found Fanning guilty of murder, with a strong recommendation to mercy. Judge Davitt sentenced him to death, with the execution fixed for 10 November. Fanning trembled and grasped the dock rail before saying, "I have nothing to say, my Lord." He then hurried from the dock and ran downstairs to the cells. Fanning, like all condemned prisoners, occupied the condemned cell in Mountjoy. The prison was less than a mile from Shandon Park and overlooked Fanning's home. It must have seemed like a world away.

On 29 October, however, the Irish President Seán T. Ó Ceallaigh announced the commutation of two death sentences. One was for Edward O'Connor who had thrown his infant son into the Tolka

River some months before. The other was for John Fanning for the murder of the woman he "loved too much". Both men received life imprisonment instead. Another Dubliner, William Gambon, would not be so lucky in the year of 1948. He attacked his friend, John Long, in his digs after they had a row over money. Long had been sending him some of his earnings from abroad and there had been a drunken argument about it when Long returned to Dublin. Gambon also claimed Long had insulted his wife. Either way, he killed his friend with an iron bar before leaving the house and locking the door after him. He eventually handed himself in to the Gardaí and was arrested. He was swiftly found guilty and sentenced to death. Unlike Fanning and O'Connor, the sentence stood and Gambon was hanged. He would be the second last man in the state to suffer this fate.

MARY AGNES DALY

"She is murdering me."

On 10 August, 1948, Miss Maura O'Rourke went to pray in the Church of the Seven Dolours in Glasnevin, Co. Dublin. It was about 4.10 p.m. when she attempted to push open the door. She was surprised to find that she could not open it as it felt like someone was holding it closed from the inside. She then heard through the door what she thought was a woman's voice calling for help. O'Rourke enlisted the help of some children who were playing nearby. One of them managed to push the door open a few inches and saw the figures of two women inside. They seemed to be grappling. At this stage all present could hear loud pleas for help and someone calling, "She is murdering me." A butcher from across the road and three men from a nearby lorry had been notified by now and they attempted to open the door. It seemed to be stuck so one of the men crashed his full force against it. The door flew open. The crowd gathered outside peered in. Two women lay on the ground having been knocked by the force of the heavy door. The older of the two, Mrs Mary Gibbons (83) was covered in blood. The elegantly dressed and well-built woman handed a hammer to one of the men, Thomas Mitchell, saying, "Thank God you have come, she tried to kill me." The other woman, Mary Agnes Daly (27), had a small amount of blood on her face and clothes. She denied Mrs Gibbons' accusation, excitedly telling the crowd that the other woman had tried to take her bag.

Mrs Gibbons was brought outside in a weak condition and put sitting on a step. She was bleeding from the head. The Gardaí arrived quickly and took a statement from her, in which she told them that she had been kneeling in prayer near the front of the church. She was a devout woman who came to pray in the church almost every day. As she was finishing her prayers, she heard a noise in the aisle behind her. Without warning she then received a crack in the head. She managed to clamber to her feet to be met with a young woman wielding a hammer. Mary Gibbons took off running down the aisle, making for the door to escape her attacker. The lady followed her as she ran down the church, hitting her all the time. She added, "I got a good many blows. I could not count them." She told the Gardaí that she had never seen this woman before.

After talking to Mrs Gibbons outside, the Gardaí turned their attention to a very distressed Mrs Daly. Daly, a small and rather weak-looking woman, was clinging onto one of the men who had forced open the door and was heard saying to him several times "stay with me, please don't go away". She also repeatedly asked for her husband. When Gardaí asked her about the incident in the church, Daly said she had been doing the Holy Hour while a tall woman (Mrs Gibbons) had been doing the Stations of the Cross. As Daly was kneeling, she claimed she heard fumbling noises behind her. She turned around to see Mrs Gibbons making for the door with Daly's two bags. Daly claimed she followed her and said "My handbag." She got no answer so she grabbed at her bags. Mrs Gibbons was "very strong" and held onto them. As the women struggled over the bags, a hammer, which Daly had bought from Woolworth's the week previously, came out the top of the bag. According to Daly, the 83-year-old-woman snatched it and raised it over her head. She spat at Daly and then said something like "I will smash your face". Mrs Daly stated that she managed to take the weapon from the elderly woman before she could hit her. In her statement Mrs Daly called Mrs Gibbons "daft…a madwoman", and said that she was afraid she was going to kill her so she "gave her a wallop of it, I must have hit her on the head." They struggled for some minutes until the witnesses entered the church. Daly asserted that she was trying to protect herself when she struck the woman, who she said was bigger and stronger than she was.

Mrs Gibbons was removed to hospital after giving her statement outside the church. Mary Gibbons, a widowed mother of three, was a tall and feisty woman for her age. She had somehow managed to survive the barrage of blows she had received from the hammer. In total, she had fifteen wounds on her scalp. She had also sustained injuries to her face and arm. Her condition deteriorated rapidly, however, and it was ascertained that the 83 year old had no realistic prospect of recovery. Her next statement, therefore, would amount to a dying declaration. The judge, both solicitors and Mrs Daly were brought to the hospital where the dying woman outlined the horrific events of the day. Mrs Daly stayed silent throughout this surreal process. Her solicitor was invited to cross-examine the dying woman, but mercifully he declined. Mary Daly was initially arraigned on a charge of attempted murder which was downgraded to malicious wounding. When Mrs Gibbons died at the Mater Hospital on the evening of 17 August, however, she was faced with a charge of murder. Gibbons' death was due to coma caused by brain injuries, consistent with being hit repeatedly with a hammer. Mary Daly denied vehemently the charge, reiterating that Gibbons had been attempting to steal her bag.

Mary Agnes Daly was a native of Ballina, Co. Mayo but lived in a two-roomed flat on the Botanic Road in Glasnevin, about five hundred yards from the church. She had resided there for about a year with her husband, a civil servant, and their young child. Her husband had a salary of £280 a year as well as an army pension. Despite this, the family had been in arrears with their rent for most of 1948. On 26 July that year they were brought to court for non-payment of rent. A payment plan had been agreed whereby the couple would pay £3. 10s. each week, a large sum at the time. This would encompass the current rent and the amount she and her husband owed in arrears. Daly managed to scrape together the first instalment on 4 August, borrowing it from a priest in the church in Glasnevin. The second payment was due on 11 August, the day after the incident involving

Mrs Gibbons. Gardaí felt that Mrs Daly had been in dire straits and had decided to try her luck in procuring the money at the church again, although this time she brought a hammer in her handbag. Mrs Gibbons had been in the wrong place at the wrong time.

The murder trial opened on 8 November 1948, in front of Justice Davitt. The prosecution asserted that the motive for the brutal attack was Mrs Daly's financial troubles. She had only paid her last instalment by borrowing it and now she needed to find a way to pay the next one or face imminent eviction. She had, therefore, deliberately brought the hammer in her bag, either for the purpose of robbing someone she found inside or for breaking open the money boxes. She had then spotted the well-dressed elderly lady, kneeling vulnerably in front of her and decided to steal her handbag by force. When an emotional Mrs Daly took the stand she repeated her earlier story of being attacked by Mrs Gibbons. When asked why she had brought a hammer to the church, Daly replied that it was because she had picked it up at home and "wanted to get it out of the way". It was also put to the accused that it seemed odd that she had only one slight scratch while the victim had fifteen serious wounds, especially in light of Mrs Daly claiming that Mrs Gibbons had been far stronger than her and the instigator of the attack. When asked if she would like to explain this aspect of her story, the accused bluntly replied, "No." Mrs Daly, who left the witness box on two occasions when overcome with emotion, admitted hitting the deceased three times. She made no effort to explain the fifteen injuries Mrs Gibbons sustained, however. She finished her testimony with the words, "I did not mean to kill her. It all happened when I tried to escape from her."

The defence, in summing up, reminded the jury that Daly had been in a state of great distress when the first witnesses had entered the church and had been seeking their protection from Mrs Gibbons. They added that it had been the older woman who was holding the hammer when the men entered the church. Their case centred on the notion that the 83-year-old pensioner had attacked the 27-year-old defendant and that any woman finding themselves in the same situation would do what Daly had done.

An unusual feature of the trial was the sworn statement of the murder victim, who had managed to cling on to life long enough to tell her side of the story. Mrs Gibbon's statement proved crucial and after a five-day trial, the jury spent one hour and fifteen minutes deliberating before returning with a guilty verdict. They added a very strong recommendation to mercy. Mr Justice Davitt described it as a "painful duty" but said the law only prescribed one punishment for those found guilty of murder. Mary Agnes Daly was sentenced to death. After hearing the sentence Mrs Daly's "lips seemed to move, but no words were audible." Her husband, who was in court, put his hands to his bowed head on hearing the verdict. The young wife and mother had her death sentence fixed for 1 December.

Mrs Daly appealed to the Court of Criminal Appeal. The appeal was delayed due to an injury to the State Pathologist, leading Daly's solicitor to beg the judge for bail for his client "who had been eleven weeks in the condemned cell". The bail was refused and the appeal, when it finally came in front of the court, also failed. The Supreme Court, however, quashed the murder conviction and ordered a new trial on the grounds that Mrs Gibbons' dying declaration was inadmissible. The retrial began on 25 April 1949. Once again it lasted five days, featuring identical evidence to the original trial. The result was the same, although this time the jury needed just over two hours to come to a decision. Mary Agnes Daly was again found guilty of murder and heard her death sentence pronounced a second time, this time being fixed for 18 May.

One newspaper had noted sagely after the first trial, "Public opinion would scarcely stand for the hanging of a woman, no matter how grave the crime." They reminded their readers of the macabre ritual of a hangman cutting the woman's hair so they could have easier access for the noose to go around her neck. They were proven correct. On 4 May, the Irish President, Seán T. Ó Ceallaigh, announced that Daly's death sentence was to be commuted to one of penal servitude for life. After independence, the only woman hanged by the Irish state was Limerick woman Annie Walsh, executed in 1925. Our nearest neighbours were less concerned about public outrage. Britain hanged eleven women in the same time frame. One of these executions was as late as July 1955, when Ruth Ellis was executed for shooting her lover, David Blakeley, on Easter Sunday of that year. Mary Agnes Daly was not destined to suffer the same fate, serving a prison term instead for her brutal attack. She was released in January 1954.

There is little doubt that Mary Agnes Daly's gender worked in her favour as regards the punishment she received for her brutal crime. Only one woman other than Annie Walsh had been executed on the island of Ireland in the twentieth century. By an incredible coincidence, that woman's name was also Mary Daly. This Mary Daly lived in Crettyard, Co. Laois. She was married to John Daly and they had two children. Their marriage was far from harmonious, however, and they were known to be at loggerheads constantly. Mary Daly was even said to have attacked her husband with a hatchet on one occasion. Mary began having an affair with their neighbour, Joseph Taylor, although he was about fifteen years younger than she was. The two lovers conspired and decided killing John would be to their advantage. Mary seemed to have been the instigator, giving money to the young man to complete the grim task. Taylor, after drinking alcohol all day, arrived at Daly's house on the night of 16 June 1902. He beckoned John Daly over, before beating him to the ground. He then kicked the older man several times before finally getting a pitchfork and using it to brutally finish him off. Mary Daly's two children witnessed the attack and gave evidence against their mother and Taylor. This was enough for the jury and both defendants were found guilty and hanged in January 1903. This Mary Daly's pleas for mercy on account of her gender would go unheeded.

FRANCES COX

"I know nothing about it. That is definite and genuine."

Back in 1940s Ireland, an Irish woman being implicated in a murder case was rare indeed. However, one Laois woman was convicted in 1949 of having murdered two members of her family: her new-born son and her brother. On 20 March, Detective Garda Maguire went to the Cox household near Mountmellick and interviewed Frances regarding the reported birth of a child to her two days previously. Rumours had gone around the area that she had been pregnant, but no child had materialised. After a short interview, Cox brought the Garda up to her room and opened a tin trunk, removing a sack. In the sack lay the body of a male infant weighing just nine pounds. The infant was later ascertained to have been born alive but had severe pressure applied to its mouth and nose, causing death by suffocation. Frances Cox was charged with infanticide and brought to trial in July 1949. She claimed she had put the baby in a basin of water shortly after he was born and had then fainted, waking up to find the child dead. The prosecution refuted this evidence, mentioning "the definite signs of violence" against the infant. The legislation was about to change at this stage whereby the killing of an infant was no longer to be classified as murder and Frances Cox eventually pleaded guilty to the lesser charge of manslaughter. She was released on probation after being found guilty. Sensationally, however, she was re-arrested outside the court almost immediately and charged again. This time, it was for the murder of her brother Richard.

The Cox family lived in a two-storey house in Roskeen, a townland four miles from the Laois town of Mountmellick and nestled on the Offaly border. Richard was 35 years of age and a farmer on one hundred and twenty-five acres of good-quality land. He was renowned as a hard worker with no interest in local football matches, dances or entertainments of any kind. He shared the house with his elderly widowed mother Jemima and Frances, their father having died ten years previously. The family were close, with all three sleeping in the same bedroom in the farmhouse, the mother and daughter sharing the same bed. The two Cox children did not hire any outside help, doing all the work on the farm themselves. The family were also members of the Church of Ireland. Like the rest of his generation of Irish Protestants, Richard had seen a formerly sizable midlands community decimated by emigration and inter-marriage after the foundation of the state. The Catholic Church had decreed that any mixed marriages between Catholics and Protestants which wanted recognition must raise their children as Catholics. This had led to an ever-dwindling pool of rural Irish Protestants and Richard wanted to ensure that his family would marry into their own tradition. His sister had other ideas.

Frances was 31 years of age and known as a hard-working farm girl, described inelegantly in one report as being "as good as a man". She was secretly engaged to a local man named William Weston despite the fact that he was a member of the Catholic Church and owned just six acres. Love had crossed numerous boundaries, however, and Frances had made tentative arrangements to convert to Catholicism, even visiting the local priest. The pair had planned to marry at Christmas 1948, but this had been postponed. Unusually, it was twice more postponed, ultimately being arranged for June 1949. Frances's mother had not been informed about her daughter's impending wedding and later said she would not have allowed it on account of her hope that Frances would "get her own equals". She said she did not know or care what religion Weston was but she "would like to see (Frances) marry a Protestant." It is unknown how much Richard knew about the lovers' plans. However, he must have been aware of Frances's appearance in court on the charge of murdering her baby and in the small rural community it is unlikely that he hadn't been made aware of her liaisons with Weston. It can only be surmised that Richard could not have been happy about Frances seemingly marrying beneath herself. Weston, it seemed, had been getting cold feet about the obstacles the newly-weds might face and had talked about ending the engagement. Frances decided she needed to remove one of these obstacles, namely her older brother Richard.

On Thursday 26 May, Richard Cox spent the morning sowing turnips. He joined his mother and sister for dinner in the afternoon, eating a hearty meal of steak, sausages and tea. After 5 p.m., Richard asked Frances to prepare him a drink of orange squash before he left to visit the Kelly family, who lived in nearby Killeigh, to pay them for the use of a stallion. As Richard was cycling to the Kelly's house, he got a pain in his stomach so severe that it caused him to fall off his bicycle into a field. He told several passers-by that he was in agonising pain and a neighbour were needed to help him to his destination. He spat blood five or six times on the journey. Richard, who was shaking violently, was given a cup of tea at the Kelly's house, which he spilled on the floor. He stayed until 11 p.m. when he finally felt well enough to attempt the journey home. Frances was still awake when he returned and he told of the sudden attack. He then retired to bed and suffered a sleepless and uncomfortable night.

Richard awoke later than usual on Friday morning and refused his normal breakfast of eggs. He instead went to the bog at 11 a.m. to help his neighbours, the Weston brothers, one of whom was secretly engaged to his sister. Despite his weakened state, Richard worked drawing turf all day, not arriving home until after 8 p.m. He was still unwell, however, and only managed bread and tea, refusing the rashers that had been cooked for him. He stayed up until close to 11 p.m. before retiring to bed. Before he went to sleep, he again asked his sister for a glass of orange squash. Half an hour after drinking it, Richard "took bad" and a doctor was summoned. The patient complained of a headache and a pain in his heart. Frances told the doctor that Richard was suffering one of his fits, implying that it was a regular occurrence for her otherwise healthy brother. She was also heard commenting pessimistically to a neighbour that "the doctor has very little hope for him". She insisted on staying up all night to attend to the needs of her stricken brother.

On Saturday morning, Richard felt slightly better and took some medicine which had been prescribed for him by the doctor the previous day. He also drank a mixture prepared for him by Frances. Frances left to go shopping in Mountmellick shortly afterwards. Just after her departure, her brother again took ill. He decided to return to bed but while there he suffered an even more severe attack. He was flushed in the face and shivering and said he "felt his heart missing". He also told his mother he was "losing the power of his limbs". Richard was raving deliriously for much of the afternoon but managed to ask for his sister numerous times. "He was more in love with Francie than I was, to tell you the truth", his mother would later remark. He had three more attacks during the day but seemed to recover reasonably well later on. He even managed to sleep through most of Saturday night.

Richard did not awaken until between 11 a.m. and 12 p.m. on Sunday 29 May. He could not eat that day, but drank several beverages, some of which were prepared for him by his sister. A number of locals, having heard about Cox's illness, called to the house to visit their neighbour. They arrived around 2.30 p.m., when Richard seemed in reasonable health, although weak. The last drink he would ever have was prepared by Frances in front of these neighbours, a mixture of milk and water. Richard drank it as he lay in bed, describing it as "bitter". Within half an hour he suffered another incredibly violent attack. A doctor was sent for but Richard Cox was dead within minutes.

The circumstances of Richard Cox's death aroused suspicion in the locality and the Gardaí were informed. He had been a healthy and hard-working man whose health had always been reasonable until his inexplicable and agonising death at such a young age. His funeral, fixed for 2 p.m. on Tuesday 31 May, was well attended by both Catholic and Protestant members of the community. As it was proceeding, however, the Gardaí flagged down the hearse. The stunned attendees watched as the authorities took Richard Cox's body from the vehicle before removing his vital organs. The congregation had to wait almost six hours for the funeral to continue. After they had been extracted from the body, a post-mortem examination was conducted by the State Pathologist, Dr J. McGrath. He examined several of the organs and discovered that they contained large quantities of strychnine, more than enough to cause death. Who had the means, and the motive, to administer the deadly poison?

The Gardaí searched the Cox home, which was described as very untidy, for any clues that might lead them to the poisoner. They had examined the lumber room on the day before the funeral but found nothing incriminating. However, when searching the same room again the next day they found a bottle of strychnine lying in the middle of the floor. It had a red label saying "Tullamore, 1936" on it and lay close to where Richard kept his work-clothes. There were also several other suspicious-looking bottles dotted around the Cox's home which had not been present during the first search. Frances admitted she had been in the lumber room that morning but denied placing the bottle there. She told the Gardaí she had gone in to water the flowers. When it was pointed out to her that the dry-looking flowers had not been watered recently, Frances hastily added that she had forgotten to do it. "It was in to open a window I came." Gardaí were immediately suspicious that she had placed the bottles around the house in an attempt to make Richard's death look like a suicide. When asked about the strychnine bottle she told replied curiously, "I know nothing about it. That is definite and genuine. If I bought it, I would have to sign for it. It is beside his clothes."

The Gardaí discovered that, thirteen years before Richard Cox's death, his father had purchased strychnine in Shiel's Chemist, Tullamore, Co. Offaly. He had done this because the farm had been plagued with rats at the time. Frances told the Gardaí that they had last used the poison about three years before Richard's death. A small quantity of this poison was found on 6 June in a bottle in a tin out in the shed. Frances Cox admitted she had known it was there but had never personally used it. The Gardaí then discovered a register in a chemist in Mountmellick which Frances herself had signed for thirty grains of strychnine in December 1947. When confronted with this evidence, Frances claimed that she could not remember this purchase. She also said that if she had bought it then it must have all been used on the rats. She could not explain why she had felt the need to buy thirty more grains, when she had known there was still poison left in the shed. She was also at a loss to explain how she had used such a large amount of the deadly poison in such a short space of time.

On 31 May, the Gardaí asked Frances for Richard's clothes. She claimed she could not find his vest but gave them his waistcoat. In its pocket, they found traces of a white powder, later identified as strychnine. At this stage, she casually remarked to the Gardaí that Richard "used to be very depressed at times. He could have taken something." She eventually gave them his vest on 5 June, nearly a week later, explaining that it had been stuffed behind a press. A neighbour named Mrs Dunne would later say that Frances had asked her to lie to the Gardaí and tell them she had found the vest while cleaning and stuffed it behind the press. Mrs Dunne refused, telling the Gardaí that she had never before seen the vest. The Gardaí were convinced that Richard Cox had been poisoned and that Frances Cox had the means to do so. Her suspicious behaviour after Richard's death led to her being arrested and charged with his murder.

The trial began on 15 November 1949. Frances Cox, who wore a heavy black coat and a wide-brimmed hat, pleaded not guilty in a strong clear voice. She showed precious little emotion on the first day, but in the days following it appeared depressed and cried frequently. The case was widely followed and crowded with spectators each day, many making the long trip up from Co. Laois. The prosecution described the case as a "malevolent, malicious and callous" murder. The State Pathologist appeared, surmising that Richard Cox must have been given at least four drinks containing strychnine to account for the fits he had on the different days. Numerous witnesses also appeared, describing in detail Richard's agonising final few days.

Frances Cox entered the witness box on the fifth day, spending over four hours being questioned. In her cross-examination, she was asked whether William Weston had told her he would not marry her unless she became a Catholic. "He may have; I don't know." She admitted she had not told her own family about the arrangement as she supposed they would not have approved. She also conceded that she would have had to move out of her large home and move in with the Westons after the nuptials. She did not deny that their engagement had since been ended, but refused to say who had brought it to an end, or when. Her answers were frequently non-committal, and she responded with "I don't know" to several pertinent questions. Frances did reveal to the court that her brother had occasionally suffered from stomach trouble before the tragedy, although this could not be corroborated by anyone else.

She made numerous denials of statements attributed to her in the aftermath of the murder. She denied having made up orange squash on the Thursday before Richard left for Kelly's, stating that he must have prepared it himself. She did admit to preparing water for her brother's orange squash on Friday night but repudiated telling the doctor that Richard had been suffering from epileptic fits every day for the past two months, a clear untruth. She also denied having asked Mrs Dunne to lie about placing the vest behind the press. It was put to Frances that her brother, who had lain in bed from Saturday morning until his death over twenty-four hours later, would have had to have obtained strychnine on Sunday to account for the final fit he suffered. This implied that the poison was either in the bedroom all that time or that somebody else had brought it in. Frances Cox had said previously she had not seen poison in the room and did not know who would have left it there. She had also sworn that Richard had not left the room at any point on the Sunday. She changed her story at this point, however, mentioning for the first time that she had heard a noise which may have been Richard fetching it for himself as she had heard a noise on Sunday afternoon. "He could have been out of (the bedroom) in my absence."

The prosecution put it to the jury that strychnine as a method of suicide was illogical. "Would any man, having failed in such an attempt the first time, submit himself to the excruciating, tearing and writhing agony on four successive occasions?" They added that hard-working Richard's demeanour was not conducive to that of a man contemplating killing himself. Once accident and suicide were ruled out, murder was the only likely cause of death. The accused had administered several cups of orange squash while her mother was absent and had plenty of time to wash the cups afterwards. Frances, who claimed to love her brother, had said that she had been suspicious he was poisoning himself but had said and done nothing about it. Were these the actions of a loving sibling?

The defence disagreed, naturally. Mr J.E. Lynch reminded the jury that no one had seen the accused administer any type of poison, even if they believed that Richard had been suffering from strychnine poisoning from Thursday until Sunday. Frances' inconsistent answers stemmed from the mental strain she was undergoing after the death of her beloved brother. They claimed that she had been short and evasive in her answering in order to avoid the rigorous questions from the Gardaí which were compounding the strain of her beloved brother's untimely passing. The defence told the court that it was possible that Richard had a quantity of strychnine which he may have bought himself before his death. The court could not rule out that Richard had taken the poison himself in a suicide attempt. They argued that the circumstantial evidence in the trial could equally implicate other witnesses, including Richard's mother, and therefore they urged the jury to acquit the woman in the dock.

In his charge to the jury, the judge stated that as long as they believed the evidence of the esteemed State Pathologist then Richard's death had clearly been due to strychnine poisoning. He added that Frances Cox had equal opportunity with her mother on Saturday and

Sunday to administer the poison, but was the only person with an opportunity on Thursday and Friday. Her evidence throughout the trial had been inconsistent and evasive. The judge also said that a motive need not be proven but had clearly been present in this case.

Over one thousand people waited outside the courtroom to hear the outcome of the case that had gripped the nation. On the sixth day of the trial, the jury deliberated for one hour and twenty-five minutes. The accused cried before the sentence was returned. When she heard the jury's unanimous guilty verdict, she sobbed more audibly. Mr Justice Dixon then sentenced the young woman to death and she was led from the dock. The defence applied for leave to appeal on sixteen grounds, including that the motive for the crime was unsupported by evidence and was irrelevant to the case. They also submitted that the jury had not given consideration to the possibility that Richard took the strychnine poisoning of his own volition in a suicide attempt. The appeal was dismissed on 21 December and Frances Cox was sentenced to death for 5 January.

Just two woman had been hanged in Ireland in the previous fifty years and Mary Agnes Daly, just months before, had been reprieved for a vicious attack on an elderly woman with a hammer in a Dublin church. Frances Cox could therefore hold out realistic hope for a commutation, and so it proved. Just one day after her leave to appeal was rejected, Frances Cox's death sentence was commuted to one of penal servitude for life. She would spend over seven years behind bars, being released in 1956. Frances Cox thus escaped the noose for inflicting an unspeakably agonising death on a brother who was clearly very fond of her. The story of her child, killed at birth, was never introduced as evidence, however. The question remains: if this second death, attributable to the supposedly religiously devout young woman, had been admitted into evidence, would the judiciary have been so merciful?

PATRICK HEFFERNAN

"Why should I do anything to her when she is my second cousin?"

The death penalty started to wane in popularity in the late 1930s, and by the beginning of the 1950s its abolishment had become a major talking point in the Irish media, even being discussed in the Dáil on several occasions. After the Second World War the tide had turned in several European countries against the punishment and Ireland would be no different. Between 1945 and 1964, the year execution was finally taken off the Irish statute books for murder, there were just three hangings. In this same time frame, fifteen men and women were reprieved. In the years between 1923 and 1926, however, there had been twelve murderers executed. Some of this can be explained by a heightened crime rate in the immediate aftermath of the brutal Civil War period. It may also have been an attempt by the newly-formed Irish Government to rule with an iron fist and restore law and order in what had become a violent state. In the more peaceful 1950s, when Ireland's murder rate was at a record low however, more leniency would be shown to violent offenders. Many criminals who were deemed to deserve the ultimate penalty in the early 1920s were instead punished by imprisonment later on in the century. Patrick Heffernan could count himself amongst that number after his senseless killing of his young neighbour and cousin in 1950.

Kilcormac, Co. Offaly, is a typical Irish midland town of about 1,200 inhabitants. It lies half way between the larger settlements of Birr and

Tullamore and is surrounded by large tracts of bogland. Bord na Móna, the Irish Turf Board, has had a long association with the area and much of the turf used for heating Irish homes comes from the surrounding vicinity. Rose Hand was from a well-respected family in the area and like many in the locality was employed by the company. Despite being just 16 years old, Rose worked long hours as a typist in the Boora Scheme and was considered a hard-working and friendly young woman. She lived with her parents on Birr Street in the town and was the second oldest of nine children. Following her normal routine, Rose left for work just after 8 a.m. on Friday 12 May 1950, dressed in a blue summer frock. It was a lengthy eight and a half-mile cycle through isolated bogland, but Rose had been doing it five days a week since January that year and had grown accustomed to the journey. She was seen passing the Garda station outside the town at 8.25 a.m. The teenager was due in work shortly before 9 a.m. but did not show up. This was unusual but her colleagues felt no cause for alarm, assuming that she had taken ill suddenly. Her family were the first to suspect that something was amiss. Rose always left work and came straight home but on this evening she did not appear at her usual hour. Her father Frederick, accompanied by his son, visited the scheme to enquire when Rose would be arriving home. To his horror, he found out that she had not shown up for work and had not been seen by anyone throughout that day.

Rose Hand was immediately reported missing and a frantic search was organised involving huge numbers of the local community. Despite a thorough combing of the area, Friday night yielded no sight of the missing teenager. The search was postponed as darkness fell but recommenced at first light. Finally, on Saturday evening, everyone's worst fears were realised. The body of a young woman was discovered by the Parish Priest of Kilcormac, Fr J. O'Connor. He had been searching with Rose's own 13-year-old brother, who ran away in horror at the awful sight. The body was partly hidden underneath furze bushes in a field twelve feet from the road where she had last been seen. Fr O'Connor reported the grisly find to Sergeant J. Skeahan. The sergeant preserved the scene, and the Hand family tearfully identified the body as that of Rose. The right side of her head had been blown away by a gunshot wound. Her bicycle, also partly concealed, lay fifty feet distant. Her clothing had been interfered with, and some of her undergarments lay some distance away from the body. Footprints were clearly visible in the boggy undergrowth.

Attention immediately turned to people known to have been on the road at the time that Rose was last seen. Patrick Heffernan was identified as one man whose path crossed with the teenager's most mornings. He was a single 27-year-old night-watchman from the nearby village of Cloghan. Heffernan also worked for Bórd na Mona, being employed on the Brosna Drainage Scheme. His place of work at the time was about half a mile outside the town of Kilcormac in a hut at Barnaboy Bridge over the Silver River. This hut, as well as Heffernan's home which he shared with his father and sister, were on Rose Hand's way to work and he would have often seen her on her travels. He had begun work on the evening of 11 May at around 7.30 p.m. and finished the next morning at 6.55 a.m. He set off home at that point, wearing working clothes and wellingtons. Like many of his generation, Heffernan was an ex-Irish Army soldier and was known to own a licensed single-barrel shotgun. He often had it in his possession, even bringing it to work. He was considered a good shot locally and frequently shot rabbits for his family's dinner. It was noted by the Gardaí that Heffernan knew Rose Hand to see, but that they were not well acquainted, even though they were second cousins. Joseph Hand, Rose's uncle, had met Heffernan the day Rose had gone missing and asked him if he had seen his niece that day. Heffernan answered that he had not.

Gardaí came to see Heffernan on the night of 13 May and he was again asked about his movements on the morning of the previous day. He claimed that although he sometimes met Rose Hand on her way to the scheme, he had not seen her that morning because he had left work earlier than usual. The guards' suspicions must have been aroused, however, because the ex-soldier's clothes, wellingtons and shotgun were taken in as evidence. The clothing was subsequently found to be covered in small specks of blood. Later Heffernan was visited at the hut where he worked. While being asked some more routine questions about the morning of Rose's disappearance, Heffernan was visibly shaking, although he replied "no", when asked if he was feeling cold. The Gardaí were suspicious and decided to detain him. He was taken to Kilcormac Garda station and onwards to Mountjoy Prison. On the journey to the prison, Heffernan asked the Gardaí to tell his father to collect his bicycle and his wages. He then abruptly revealed, "I was ten yards or more from the girl when the shot went off accidentally and knocked her off her bicycle." Heffernan was cautioned before a statement was taken. "As I came up to her the gun, which I had in my hand resting on the handlebars, went off and struck her around the head and face. She fell off the bicycle on the left hand side of the road...I picked her up and went through the hedge into the field...I told no one about the shooting. I didn't know what to do." He was arrested the following day and charged with murder. When asked if he had anything to say to the charge Heffernan replied, "No, sir, only what I said last night, sir."

The trial opened on 6 November 1950, to extraordinary public interest manifested by a packed gallery every day. Heffernan maintained that the shooting was an accident and pleaded not guilty to murder. The prosecution opened with the testimony of several local witnesses. Bridie Carroll, a friend of Rose Hand's, stated that the night before the murder Heffernan had been sitting behind Rose and giving her "terrible looks" at the cinema. A local man, Bernard Guinan, also appeared on the stand and told the court that he was cycling at 8.40 a.m. on the morning of 12 May when he spotted a bicycle lying beside a bush on the left-hand side of the road in the townland of Lumcloon. A little further on, he saw Heffernan emerging from behind a wattle fence on the other side of the road. Heffernan said to him as he passed, "Hello Barney. It's great weather." Guinan agreed and continued on. He noted that Heffernan's face appeared to be stained red.

The parish priest subsequently gave evidence of finding the body. He had seen small fragments of bone, which he had thought to be from a rabbit. He had searched the surrounding area and shortly afterwards had discovered a body lying underneath the furze bush, with a shotgun cartridge nearby. It was afterwards identified as Rose Hand by the victim's 13-year-old brother. Dr J. McGrath, State Pathologist, was called on the third day of the trial and he concluded that Rose Hand had been shot from behind and from below. He said the ballistic evidence suggested that Rose had been standing beside the hedge when shot, not riding her bicycle on the road. This contradicted Heffernan's claims of an accidental shooting. Another witness, John Daly, recounted how he had seen a bicycle, beside the place where the body would be found, on the morning of 13 May. He had not seen anyone near it but had cycled on only for Patrick Heffernan to catch up with him on the same bicycle some distance on. Heffernan engaged Daly in conversation, telling him that he had seen a strange man earlier in the day on that road. The man had allegedly been holding a gun and hiding behind a furze bush.

Evidence was also given of some of the remarks made by the accused following the incident in the area. John Horan stated that he was standing in a group with Heffernan when someone suggested that they would all be questioned in relation to the killing. Heffernan replied tersely, "Why should I do anything to her when she is my second cousin?" Evidence was given that Heffernan had purchased shotgun cartridges the week before the killing. Another witness, John Guinan, told of how he had seen Rose Hand cycling very fast on 8 May with Heffernan several hundred yards behind her. Heffernan stopped Guinan and asked him who the girl was. A surprised Guinan told him it was Rose Hand and the accused cycled on after a brief conversation.

Heffernan himself took the stand as one of only two witnesses for the defence. He took part in a rather bizarre re-enactment in the courtroom where he sat on a bike with a gun and showed the jury how the gun had accidentally discharged. He said that he had been cycling, and he could see a figure in front of him who he could not recognise. He thought that he went over a stone in the road and the gun went off, killing Rose Hand in a tragic accident. He had then panicked and placed the girl's body in the bog, concealing it under some furze. Heffernan denied having interfered with her or her clothing in any way and could not explain why her undergarments had been removed and placed some distance from the body. The prosecution asserted that the State Pathologist's evidence proved that Rose had been standing when shot and could not have been riding her bicycle, rendering Heffernan's story an elaborate lie. They said that she was inches from the hedge when shot and that blood appeared on the verge and not on the road, which proved that she could not have been cycling at the time of impact. They also dwelt on the fact that she was partially undressed when her body was discovered.

The defence's case rested on accidental death. Heffernan's gun was an old farmer's shotgun, described by gun expert, Edmund White, as being in "very bad condition". White opined that it could have been discharged accidentally and that Heffernan's re-enactment on the bicycle was plausible. The defence assured the jury that Heffernan had accidentally shot his cousin and then, in a blind panic, had carried the body over the ditch. They stated that he had no motive whatsoever to deliberately kill Rose Hand, perhaps ignoring the obvious sexual one. The prosecution disagreed, arguing that it was physically impossible for the gun to have gone off as described by Heffernan. The judge, in his summing-up, gave the jury no option of manslaughter, forcing them to choose between accidental death and murder.

After seven days of evidence and fifty-four witnesses, the jury were given an opportunity to have their say on the contradictory evidence and the two very different versions they had been told of the tragedy. They took one and a half hours to decide the accused's fate. Patrick Heffernan was found guilty and sentenced to hang. He needed to be supported by two warders after hearing the sentence. Mr Justice Dixon asked him if he had anything to day. "Nothing, my Lord," was the reply. He was then brought to Mountjoy Prison to await his fate.

Heffernan appealed the sentence and the conviction was quashed by the Court of Criminal Appeal. The jury had mingled with members of the public during the trial, grounds for a mistrial. The evidence the second time around was almost identical and the result did not change. Heffernan was again found guilty and sentenced to death for a second time. His execution date was fixed for 17 May 1951. His second leave to appeal was refused and the date was fast approaching. Just two days before the sentence was to be carried out, however, Heffernan was reprieved and sentenced to life imprisonment. Heffernan came within days of suffering the ignominious fate of being the first person to be executed by the Republic of Ireland, which had come into being in 1949, replacing the Irish Free State. He certainly benefitted from a more lenient country, whose attitude against the death penalty had hardened considerably over the previous decades.

Heffernan would have been the third Offaly man to face the executioner since the state's foundation if the punishment had been carried out, a large number for the rural county with just 75,000 residents. Thomas Delaney was one of the first men executed in the new state. He attacked and murdered an elderly shopkeeper, Patrick Hogan, when attempting to rob his shop. Delaney entered the premises on the Main Street in Banagher in June 1922, and beat the elderly man to death with tongs and a slasher while looking for valuables. He was disturbed by neighbours who heard the commotion and found him standing over his lifeless victim. The trial began a year later, the delay being due to the Civil War. After less than a day of evidence, Delaney was found guilty and executed on 12 December 1923. Bernard Kirwan was also hanged, in June 1943, for the murder of his brother whose dismembered body was found in a bog outside Tullamore. Bernard had been released from prison and returned to find himself an unwelcome guest on his brother's farm. The circumstances of Laurence Kirwan's death were unknown as there were no witnesses and Bernard Kirwan never confessed. He was found guilty and hanged regardless. Kirwan's execution is possibly the most famous Irish hanging ever, due to a play written about it afterwards. Brendan Behan had been in prison at the same time as Kirwan and based his renowned drama, *The Quare Fella*, on the condemned Offaly man.

WILLIAM HOPKINS

"Someone take care of that girl."

15 November 1952 was a busy Saturday night in the pubs around Crookstown in the south of Co. Kildare. Several patrons were standing outside Byrne's pub in the village at 8.30 p.m. when a Ford 8 pulled up. The young male driver beckoned a local reveller, Patrick Keogh, over to the car. Keogh walked over to the window and the man asked him where the police station was. As Keogh was talking to him, he noticed a woman in the backseat with her hands collapsed over her chest. She asked in a weak voice for a glass of water. The driver ignored her and asked Keogh to get into the car and bring them directly to the Garda station. He agreed but first went to get the water for the young woman. As he was doing so, the other onlookers were shocked to see the woman open the back door of the car and stumble out. She collapsed to the ground immediately and began crawling on her hands and knees towards the pub. She had no shoes on and was weak and moaning. Her clothes were saturated in blood. She managed to reach the door of the pub but fainted. The concerned locals quickly placed her on some cushions in the back of a van and rushed her the thirteen miles to Kildare Hospital with a local sergeant and a priest. She was semi-conscious on the journey, muttering "Mrs O'Connor, Mrs O'Connor" several times. She drifted into unconsciousness soon after arriving at the hospital. Theola Susan Curran died before 10 p.m. She had been stabbed fifteen times in the abdomen, chest and neck. The attack had been so ferocious that the knife had bent in her body.

194

Theola Curran was 23 years of age. She lived on Larkfield Avenue in the Dublin suburb of Kimmage with her brother Paddy and his wife. Miss Curran was a quiet but popular and hardworking machinist in Harcourt Street in the capital and was known to her friends as "Lola". Lola's father had died some time before and in October 1952, her mother also passed away after a long illness. After the funeral, Lola's sister Maureen, who had a disability, has been residing with the O'Connor family in Co. Kildare. The family lived in Kilgowan, five miles north of Crookstown. Lola, too, spent a lot of time with the O'Connors, often visiting on her holidays. She had also stayed many weekends with the family since the funeral. On the weekend of 15 November she called on them with the intention of bringing Maureen back with her the following day. Back in Dublin, she was engaged to be married to a man named William Hopkins. She had not informed her fiancé of her plans to go down the country.

Hopkins was 25 and from Rathfarnham, Co. Dublin. He was the second oldest of ten children and was employed as a dairy yardman at Hazelbrook Dairy. Hopkins, like his fiancée, was described as quiet and hardworking and was said to "always be in good form". He was known to get dizzy spells and regular severe nose bleeds however, after which he would be in a world of his own. He was very devoted to Miss Curran since they had met at age 15, even spending many nights nursing her sick mother before her death. The pair spent a lot of time together, meeting three or four times a week. Eventually, they decided to get engaged in March 1951. Since that date, they had discussed getting married regularly. They had finally decided upon April 1953, as the perfect month for their ceremony. The young couple were also discussing getting a house in which the two of them could live after their nuptials. Two days before Lola's murder, Hopkins found a house which he thought would be suitable for the couple. He had sent Lola a letter asking her to meet him there. She turned up at the appointed time, but after this meeting the couple were observed coming back to the Curran house arguing fiercely.

On the afternoon of 15 November Hopkins went to the pub and

had several drinks with his work colleague, Hugh Thomas. The two men spent forty-five minutes discussing the major news story of the day, the unsolved stabbing of a judge's daughter Patricia Curran (no relation) in Whiteabbey, Co. Antrim which had happened three days before. Hopkins, seemingly furious about the brutal murder of a young woman, told his friend that if he could he would "put a rope around the neck of the man that did it and drag him around the streets behind my car." In an unrelated conversation, he told another colleague that he had not been out with his girlfriend the night before as they had a row about the house they were looking at. Hopkins, who seemed agitated, also told those present that he was sick and had a splitting headache and that he would not drink alcohol again.

After the pub, Hopkins travelled to the house of his brother, John. He and Lola had arranged the week before that they would babysit John's children on that day, allowing John and his wife to go to the pictures. When he arrived however, he was surprised to find that his fiancée had not turned up. He waited ten minutes and then left to find out where Lola was and why she had not kept their appointment. He went to her home in Kimmage, arriving at 5 p.m. The door was answered by Lola's sister-in-law who told Hopkins that Lola had travelled down the country to Co. Kildare that afternoon. Hopkins, who she described as normal and cheerful, asked when she would be returning and was told the following night. He left without passing comment. Hopkins had, however, already decided to make the thirty-mile journey to Kilgowan to find out for himself why she had not kept their rendezvous.

Hopkins arrived in Kilgowan at 7 p.m. Lola, who had only been at the house ten minutes herself, agreed to speak to him when he knocked at the door but asked him to come into another room so they could talk privately. When he asked her what had brought her down to Kildare instead of keeping their babysitting appointment, she replied by saying "we are finished". Hopkins seemed upset but understanding and he calmly asked Lola to come out to the car with him to sign a form. She agreed and got her coat. The pair then left the house together.

Hopkins did not produce a form but drove away as soon as Lola got into the vehicle. When he reached a bend in the road, Lola asked her fiancé to stop the car. He did so and they both got out. A blazing argument erupted between Hopkins and his fiancée. He held her tightly and asked her not to break up with him but she struggled and again told him that they were finished. At this point, Hopkins produced a knife which he kept in the car for cleaning points in the engine. He used it to stab Lola in the stomach, neck and chest fifteen times. Her shoes came off during the frenzied attack and were later found at the side of the country road. He then placed the mortally-wounded woman in the back of the car before spending an hour driving around the unfamiliar countryside looking for Ballitore Garda station. All the while, Lola Curran was haemorrhaging blood in the back seat. Hopkins could not find the station so he finally stopped at Crookstown to ask for directions. It was at this point that the dying girl managed to escape and stagger out towards the stunned villagers.

A local man, James Archibald, went over to Hopkins after Miss Curran had been carried into the pub asking him if there had been an accident. Hopkins, whose hands and overcoat were covered in blood, did not answer, instead asking Archiblad where the nearest police station was and if he would accompany him there. Archibald, certain that he had been involved in a collision, agreed and got into the car. Hopkins said loudly, "Someone take care of that girl" to the other bystanders before getting behind the wheel and driving off. Archibald asked Hopkins several times on the way to the station if there had been an accident. He received no reply. At one point in the journey, an anxious Archibald put his hand on the door handle. Hopkins told him, "You need not be afraid. I am not going to touch you." They finally reached Ballitore Barracks at around 8.20 p.m., and Hopkins said to Guard Lyons, who was on-duty, "I have come to give myself up, I am after murdering a girl down the road." He handed the knife to the startled officer saying, "Let me in, I will show you." He then made a statement about the crime, telling the whole story, although implying that he had only stabbed his fiancée once. It would later transpire that she had been stabbed multiple times in the ferocious and sustained attack. Hopkins did not enquire about Lola's condition until around 11.30 p.m. that night. At that point he asked, "How is she?" The Garda answered, "She is dead." Hopkins' demeanour did not change and he did not respond. He was charged with murder shortly afterwards to which he responded, "I have nothing more to say."

William Hopkins appeared for trial in Dublin Central Criminal Court on 23 February 1953. He replied not guilty to the charge, in a calm, steady voice. The trial of the dark-haired and handsome young man for the murder of his beautiful young fiancée unsurprisingly garnered lots of attention in the media and the country as a whole. Each day of the trial had queues of hundreds of people, mainly women, seeking admittance to hear the evidence. Mr Bell, for the defence, put forward an insanity plea. Dr Thomas Murphy of Mountjoy disagreed. Murphy said that Hopkins had given him a clear and lucid account of the murder. He had slyly lured Lola Curran from the safety of the house to sign a form that didn't exist. He had then held her arms and asked her not to break up their relationship. When she refused he had stabbed her multiple times before driving around for an hour even though she was clearly dying in the backseat. Dr F. McLaughlin, psychiatrist, also said he "found no trace of mental disease".

Hopkin's defence claimed that he had no intention whatsoever of hurting his beloved girlfriend when he set off for Kildare that evening. They told the jury that he had suffered a total memory loss due to epilepsy after he had struck the first blow. His counsel called his mother who recounted Hopkins falling out of his cot when he was eighteen months old. She recalled that he got a large bump on his head which reappeared when he was stressed. She also spoke of her family history and told the court that one of William's aunts had taken her own life due to a love affair. Mr Bell, Hopkins' solicitor, implored of the jury to consider this and the constant nosebleeds as symptoms of a type of epilepsy linked to his childhood injury. They cited Dr John Dunne of Grangegorman Mental Hospital who agreed with this synopsis. Dunne stated that at the time of the act Hopkins "was not able to control the act he committed…once he raised his hand for the first blow he had a complete loss of memory." Dunne, a regular witness in murder trials, had also excused Stephen Murphy's murder in Crossmolina eight years before on the grounds of insanity. (See Chapter 17.)

The medical evidence was conflicting and the jury were faced with the unenviable task of deciding if Hopkins was sane at the time of the crime. After an hour and fifty minutes deliberation they found him guilty, although with a strong recommendation to mercy. Judge Maguire told the jury that he agreed with their verdict and sentenced William Hopkins to death for murder, fixed for 18 March. Women in the packed court sobbed, while William Hopkins replied calmly that he had "nothing to say".

Hopkins' parents sought a reprieve for their son on the grounds that he was insane. The Curran family, showing incredible generosity, supported the appeal. Eventually, Hopkins got a stay of execution. He was then granted leave for an appeal, which began in May 1953. After four days of evidence, the jury accepted Dr Dunne's evidence that Hopkins had a "hypersensitive" area on the right side of his forehead which may have caused epilepsy or blackouts. He was declared unfit to plead and ordered to be detained in strict custody at the pleasure of the government. It was the closest of calls. Hopkins had avoided Albert Pierrepoint, the Irish state executioner, by just days.

ROBERT STEVENSON

"She fell to the ground and was out cold."

James Edward Tierney and James Herbert Lehman were both foreigners sentenced to death by the Irish Government. Tierney (see Chapter 13) was perhaps fortunate to escape the noose, being well connected with the British establishment. Lehman, a drifting soldier who had deserted from the Canadian army, had no such luck. A compulsive liar, Lehman claimed at different times to be both Canadian and American. He was hanged in 1945 for poisoning his wife in Dublin. A third foreign national would see the black cap being donned by the judge in 1954 and come within days of being the last person hanged in the state. Incredibly, he had spent less than twelve hours on Irish soil when the murder was committed.

Robert James Stevenson was 25 years old and described as "tall and athletic". He was a native of Port Bannatyne, a village situated on the island of Bute. Bute, just off the coast of Scotland, has a strong fishing tradition and Stevenson was himself a sailor. He left the island as a young man to travel the seas on various trawlers. He had married a couple of years later and moved to Falmouth, a fishing town on the coast of Cornwall, where he was the father of two small children. In late 1953, Stevenson was working on an oil tanker named *SS Pass of Ballater*. Like many sailors, he spent long periods of time away from his family and would be experiencing Christmas on the ship in Ireland that year. The tanker had docked in Dublin on 22 December at around 1 p.m. in the afternoon and many of the crew were looking forward to sampling the Christmas spirit in the lively city.

Stevenson departed the ship at 4 p.m. that day wearing a blue pin-striped suit. It was only the Scotsman's second time visiting Dublin and he got a taxi as far as O'Connell Street. He had arranged to meet the boatswain of the tanker there. He could not find him, however, and drank in a pub on his own for a period before making his way to the cinema to watch the film *Jamaica Run*. The film ended at about 7 p.m. and Stevenson walked to Daly's, a nearby pub. While at the bar, he started chatting to another sailor whom he had not met previously. The man was named Hector Thomas and was a native of Co. Down. The two seamen got into conversation and got on well, despite the fact that Thomas found the gruff Scotsman's accent difficult to understand. They departed Daly's together, deciding to head to O'Brien's pub on Lower Abbey Street where Thomas had earlier been drinking. The pair went upstairs to the lounge where Thomas met Teresa Lysaght, a local girl to whom he had been talking previously. Another girl, who was with Lysaght, struck up a conversation with Stevenson. Thomas could not hear what they were saying, but after about five minutes the girl arose and left. Seconds later, Stevenson had followed her out the door. It was 7.50 p.m.

At about 8.45 p.m. on the night of 22 December an emergency call was made to 999. It was received by the Central Telephone Exchange in Dublin Castle. The mysterious male caller did not leave his name, but told the operator that he had heard a woman screaming in the Beresford Lane area, just north of the River Liffey. He then replaced the receiver before the operator could ask any further questions. Garda John Walsh was dispatched to the area, arriving fifteen minutes later. The Garda got to the end of the lane, which is a cul-de-sac, and saw in the dim light what he thought was a large piece of white paper. When he got closer, he realised it was the body of a woman lying face upwards in a coat. Walsh rushed back to Store Street Garda station and brought his colleague, Sergeant Pender, to investigate his disturbing find. The two men discovered that the woman had suffered a violent death, having sustained multiple injuries on her face. Her red handbag lay nearby and there was a bloodstained, yellow woollen scarf tied tightly around her neck. A piece of elastic was also across her mouth. A hospital card in the strangled woman's handbag indicated that her name was Mary Nolan.

Mary Nolan was 24 years old and originally from Cashel Road in the Dublin suburb of Crumlin. She was fair-haired and about 5' 6". For about a month coming up to Christmas 1953, Nolan had not been living in Crumlin but residing with a man named James Little in a restaurant in Bachelor's Walk called "The Altona Café". She had introduced herself to her landlord and several other people as "Mrs Little" as unmarried couples at the time were not permitted to share a house. Nolan was described in one contemporary newspaper report as "a girl of the unfortunate class", a common euphemism for a prostitute in those days. She had been a regular visitor to both Daly's and O'Brien's public houses for the six months previous to the murder and was well known to both sets of bar staff. On the evening of 22 December she had left her lodgings at 6.30 p.m., planning to meet her friend Teresa Lysaght and visit the local pubs. She would not return.

Just after 9 p.m., Robert Stevenson bypassed O'Brien's and instead re-entered Daly's Public House. He asked the barman if there was anywhere he could wash his hands, which appeared to be bloodstained. Luke Roche was working that night and he directed Stevenson downstairs. He also asked the Scotsman about his injuries. A pale-looking Stevenson told Roche he had had a "scrap" with another sailor from his ship. He then walked downstairs and cleaned himself up. Later Stevenson met some other men from his boat, repeating to them the story of the fight with the unnamed seaman. He was also spotted by Teresa Lysaght and they had a brief conversation. Lysaght asked where Nolan had gone but Stevenson replied that he had not seen her after he had left the lounge because she had gone without him. Stevenson stayed for some hours in the pub, before leaving by himself. He arrived back at the boat the next morning. When asked where he'd been, he said he had stayed with a girl in her room on Gardiner Street. The *Pass of Ballater* departed Dublin on 23

December, just twenty-four hours after it had arrived. It was making its way to Limerick and bringing Robert Stevenson with it.

The State Pathologist, Maurice Hickey, examined Mary Nolan at 1 a.m. on the morning of 23 December. She had been struck a number of severe blows in the face, on both eyes and on the chin. These came about ten minutes before death. She had a serious scalp injury, which may have been caused by her head coming into contact with the concrete surface after being hit and falling. Hickey suggested that Mary Nolan had been strangled while still alive but the position of her arms had been changed some time after death. Blood was oozing from her nose and mouth. Tragically, it was also discovered that Mary Nolan had been ten weeks pregnant when she was callously murdered.

On the morning of St Stephen's Day, a party of Gardaí drove to Limerick and boarded the *Pass of Ballater* asking to speak with the captain. They had heard from several witnesses that Mary Nolan had been speaking to travelling seamen in O'Brien's pub and this tanker's crew had been mentioned. The captain was asked to parade all fifteen of his crewmen. Four of them were identified as being in the vicinity when Mary Nolan's murder occurred and were brought swiftly to Limerick Garda station. Stevenson was amongst them. He gave a statement, stating that he had gone to Dublin alone at 4 p.m. in a taxi before going to a cinema and watching a film, again alone. He then went to Daly's and afterwards O'Brien's pub. He had seen two girls matching the descriptions but had not spoken to them. After leaving O'Brien's, he had gone to O'Connell Street where he met another girl. He stayed with her in Gardiner Street, leaving for the ship at 7.30 a.m. the next morning. He denied vehemently having met Mary Nolan or having washed blood from his hands in Daly's.

Several other Gardaí were meanwhile sent back to the boat. They searched the rooms of the men who were being questioned. In Robert Stevenson's quarters they found a jacket with two bloodstains on the lapel, as well as a bloodied shirt. When confronted with these articles Stevenson explained that this was his own blood, shed when he had fallen against a sharp piece of wire outside the sailors' quarters. When asked about a cut on his knuckle, Stevenson claimed he got it when he was screwing down butterfly nuts on the ship. None of the other crewman admitted being able to remember these injuries occurring on the boat.

The Gardaí were suspicious of Stevenson's evasive answers and asked him to appear in an identity parade. He agreed and barman Luke Roche immediately identified him in the line-up as the man who had washed his bloodstained hands in Daly's. When confronted with this identification, Stevenson quickly changed his story, offering a third statement. He said that after the cinema he had gone to O'Brien's with Hector Thomas. As Thomas was talking to Teresa Lysaght, Mary Nolan approached Stevenson and asked him if he wanted a woman. He replied that he did and she told him she knew a place where they could go. They agreed to go outside together. Nolan then left the premises but Stevenson stayed a minute, greeting two of his fellow crewmen who had entered the pub. Next, he finished his drink before excusing himself and following Nolan outside.

Nolan and Stevenson walked the six hundred yards towards the quiet and dimly-lit Beresford Lane. They conversed on the way about where Stevenson was from and if he had been to Dublin before. In the laneway, Stevenson said he made a bargain with her for one pound. He gave her the pound note, which she held in her hand. Stevenson continued, "When I was kissing her, I felt her hand in my pocket. I drew back from her and hit her. She fell to the ground and was out cold." Stevenson stated that he then laid her against the wall and took the pound back from her, placing it in his pocket. Stevenson admitted skinning his knuckle when he struck Mary Nolan saying he had "caught a bone or a tooth". He said her scarf fell off her head and landed around her shoulders. Stevenson denied vehemently, however, having strangled the woman with the scarf. "That is all I did to her in the lane." Stevenson claimed that Mary Nolan was very much alive when he left to walk back the way he had come. He admitted bypassing O'Brien's and going to Daly's where he asked the barman if he could wash his bloodied hands, telling him the story of the scrap.

In light of his statement, Stevenson was arrested and charged with murder. Stevenson's trial was initially adjourned after he was hospitalised with a case of bronchitis. It finally began on 10 May 1954. Stevenson pleaded not guilty to the charge of murder. The trial of the exotic Scotsman caused a sensation and was crowded with onlookers every day. One source of irritation for the trial judge was the number of important witnesses not present at the trial. As many of the key witnesses were seamen and foreign nationals, the Irish courts could not compel them to appear. There were over twenty witnesses to appear, however, and plenty of twists and turns in the strange trial.

Mary Nolan had been seen talking to several men on the night she met Stevenson. One interesting example who appeared on the stand was a man named Donald Jones, an 18-year-old native of England. Jones had arrived in Dublin shortly before Christmas 1953 with £30. He was looking for work but was unsuccessful. Jones' £30 had lasted just two weeks and by 22 December he had fallen on hard times and was sleeping rough in the capital. He knew Mary Nolan, having stayed at the Altona Café for a few nights at the same time as her. He had also been in O'Brien's pub on 22 December and was seen talking to Nolan for about fifteen minutes. He claimed that he had not seen her after this encounter but was unable to produce an alibi for the night, having slept rough. He denied asking Nolan for money. The defence implied that Jones was a potential suspect in the murder case. Interestingly, Jones also stated in court that he met Nolan's boyfriend, James Little, the morning after the murder. He described the bereaved Little as "smiling all over his face". Little told him he was going "to the morgue to identify Mary Nolan". Little took the stand and denied this, saying that he had been worried and he "did not think" he was smiling. Little accepted that he was the father of Mary's unborn child and that they had planned to go to Australia together. The defence's assertion that Little may have been involved was discredited when the owner of the Altona Café, where Little and Mary Nolan were staying, gave him an alibi for the night. The café's owner told the court that the building had only one front door and he had been at home all evening. He stated that Little could not have left between 5 and 9 p.m. without being seen.

A sensation was then caused in the trial. Inspector King read a letter which had been received by Margaret Nolan, Mary's mother, two weeks after Mary's death. It began, "I am writing to let you know the truth about Mary's death. I am the man who rang up Store Street Garda station." It went on to state that the letter writer had followed Nolan and the "sailor" towards Beresford Lane. He had waited across the road under a bridge while they were up the laneway. He had been surprised to see the sailor emerge by himself so had gone up the lane. "I found her lying on her back and (she) seemed to be dazed. Her clothes were pulled up around her waist." She then allegedly came to and the letter writer said he put the scarf around her neck, "but I thought she would never die…she kept on kicking for nearly three minutes." The letter ended bizarrely stating that "I feel that if she had lived she would have suffered more in having her child than in dying." The prosecution considered this letter an elaborate hoax, insisting that it contained a lot of information which had already been in the public domain. The letter also incorrectly stated that there had been nothing in Nolan's handbag, when in fact several items had been present.

Stevenson was not obligated to take the stand in his own defence but he chose to do so. He repeated his evidence that he had brought Mary Nolan to the laneway before knocking her out when she put her hand in his pocket. She had been unconscious so he propped her up against the wall and left. He headed back to the pub where he drank some more alcohol. Some hours later he left on his own and met a girl in O'Connell Street, afterwards going back to her lodgings. He admitted that he had heard rumours of the murder of a girl in Dublin when he was on the ship to Limerick but swore that he had never connected that story with Mary Nolan as he was sure she was not dead. He told the court that he had lied to Gardaí about the marks on his body when initially questioned because he knew he had committed a crime when he assaulting Mary Nolan. He also did not want his pregnant wife to find out he had been with another woman. He stated that if he had known she was dead he would have told the truth.

The closing case for the defence was made by John Esmonde. He reminded the jury that they had seen an unsavoury and unbelievable aspect of Dublin night life. He said Dublin contained "vices, follies and rottenness" akin to other seaside towns. He said, of the prostitutes, that men "who call themselves human beings today are responsible for the fate tomorrow of these unfortunate girls." He told the jury, however immoral the Scotsman had been, that the scream heard at 8.45 p.m. would not tally with the time that Stevenson had re-entered O'Brien's pub and he would not have had time to commit the murder. Had there been someone else with her when she screamed? The letter, and the anonymous phone call, suggested that there had and this person had been the real killer. Esmonde also informed the jury that coal dust had been found on the victim's body. Stevenson worked on an oil tanker and had no contact with coal. How could this be explained? He also disclosed that Mary Nolan was known to have left the pub with unidentified men on two occasions that night. They could not be traced. Who were they? He reminded them, too, of the peculiar witness Donald Jones, who had slept rough that night and whose movements could not be verified. Might he have had something to do with the slaying? Esmonde finished by saying there was a reasonable doubt that someone other than the Scotsman had killed Mary Nolan and therefore he should be acquitted.

The prosecution scoffed at this suggestion. The letter, they said, contained numerous inaccuracies. By the time it had been received, the information in it was common knowledge, much of it having been published by the media. They also described Stevenson's numerous different accounts of his movements and his "lying statements to the police and his inch-by-inch retraction of them". Mr Justice Dixon in summing up seemed to agree. He admitted the fact that an unknown caller had contacted the Gardaí but asserted to the jury that Stevenson was with Miss Nolan for "almost all the relevant time." The jury retired at 6 p.m. on the fourth day of the trial. A crowd of over two hundred people waited expectantly for the jury to return with a verdict. When they did, Stevenson was found guilty of murder. When asked if he had any reason why the sentence of death should not be passed on him, the accused answered simply, "I did not kill Mary Nolan." Leave to appeal was refused.

Stevenson's solicitors started a petition for the condemned man, stating that the evidence was circumstantial and grave doubts existed about whether the condemned man was guilty. Perhaps the government was worried about this reasonable doubt and the many unanswered questions about the case. Either way, on 7 July, Stevenson's death sentence was commuted to one of life imprisonment. The mysterious caller and letter writer, if indeed it was the same person, was never identified.

Just weeks before the Stevenson case, the case of Michael Manning was being heard. Manning was a 25-year-old Limerick carter. On 18 November 1953, Manning had been drinking heavily throughout the day. That night, he was walking home via Castletroy, just outside Limerick City. In front of him was 65-year-old nurse, Katie Cooper. Manning caught up with her before dragging her into an adjoining field and subjecting her to a brutal beating while attempting to sexually assault her. He knocked out some of her teeth and eventually suffocated her to death by stuffing grass into her mouth. He ran off when disturbed by passers-by. He was detected within hours by his unusual hat which he left at the scene. Although his case had elements in common with that of Stevenson, public opinion dictated that Manning would not be reprieved. Unlike the majority of the condemned prisoners, many locals did not attempt to secure a commutation for the guilty man. His vicious and unprovoked crime had horrified Limerick and beyond. Katie Cooper's family did express a desire that Manning would be allowed to live and Manning himself wrote a letter begging for his life on account of his young wife and child. His pleas for mercy went unheeded. Michael Manning was hanged on 20 April 1954, at 8 a.m. He would be the last ever person executed in the Republic of Ireland. Robert Stevenson, sentenced to die three weeks later, would narrowly avoid this ignominious end in a foreign land.

DENIS FOY

"I told him to shut up,
it was worse he was getting."

James McGrath's short life came to an end by a river in Bagenalstown (also called Muine Bheag), Co. Carlow, less than a mile from his home. His clothes were neatly folded on his body and there were signs of trampled grass and a violent struggle. His left sandal and brown pants lay some two-hundred feet away. His body was discovered just before midnight on 20 November 1958, after he had been missing for six hours. The 6-year-old boy lived in Upper Kilree Street in the town with his parents, two brothers and a sister. He had returned from the Presentation Convent School at 3 p.m. and briefly spoken to his mother. He had then gone out to play with another boy named Whelan. This was to be the last time his mother would see him alive. James McGrath was subsequently noticed by several people playing in the town. The last sighting of the young boy was just before 5.30 p.m., when he was seen walking alone down the street.

Denis Foy was also a native of Bagenalstown, living in the Soldier's Cottages area of the town. He was 21 years old and lived at home with his mother, brother and sister. Foy was considered quiet and he rarely socialised, his main interests being children's comics and detective stories. He had at one time been a soldier in the FCA but by late 1958 he was employed in the locomotive department of the CIE. He drew his wages on the afternoon of 20 November 1958 and met with his friend,

209

Stephen Bolger. Although Foy was scheduled to work at 5 p.m., he and Bolger began drinking at midday. By that evening they had visited several public houses around the town, and both men appeared drunk. Foy, usually adjudged to be a hard-worker, decided against going to his shift. Publicans in the town testified later that he had consumed several whiskeys and pints of stout, unusual for a man known to be sober and industrious. He was described by one barman as "pale and drowsy…he had the appearance of being sick." He parted ways with Bolger shortly before 5.30 p.m. Foy was at this point leaning against the window of a pub. Market Square in the town was empty except for a few children playing. One of these children was James McGrath.

Foy was not seen by anyone in the town over the next half an hour, but shortly after 6 p.m. Bolger was staggering drunkenly home. He fell into a ditch in an area known as the "Sandpits" on his way. As he was unable to get up, he called for help. Someone walking by heard his calls and came to his aid. It was Denis Foy. Foy helped his inebriated friend the short distance back to Bolger's house in Kilcarraig, arriving at 6.45 p.m. Bolger's wife, Annie, cooked the two men a meal. She described her husband as very drunk but said Foy was relatively sober, despite all the drink he had consumed throughout the afternoon. She did notice that he had a terrible cough and his shoes and trousers to the knee were wet. He sat down in a chair as soon as he got into the house. Bolger suggested that he and Foy go for more drink but Annie objected and Foy said he was "too tired" anyway. Bolger gave him a glass of cider in the kitchen. Oddly, Bolger then left the house to go for a few bottles of stout but Foy stayed, awaiting his return. He was continually coughing in the house, leading Annie to remark to him "You are very cold." He remained in the Bolger house all that evening until Bolger returned at 10.30 p.m. Foy waited only another forty-five minutes, leaving for home after 11.15 p.m. He would later describe a shortcut he used instead of the main road to get from Bolger's house back to Bagenalstown.

By the time Foy arrived back in the town, James McGrath had been reported missing. His parents had initially sent his elder brother

Patrick to search for him, without success. They had become frantic by 7 p.m. and had afterwards enlisted members of the community to comb the area. The search was ongoing when Denis Foy entered the town. As he walked up the street he met John Gough, a member of the search party. Gough told him that the young boy was missing and Foy replied by asking, "Is there a guard around?" Gough told him there was one just up the town. Just before midnight Foy met Seán Maguire, a local FCA sergeant whom he knew from his army days. The sergeant suggested that Foy help search the railway grounds for the young boy as he was familiar with the area through his work with the CIE. Foy initially agreed but seconds later revealed to everyone's shock, "The boy has been found; over in the wood." He also told the group gathering around him that the young boy was dead and that he was naked. When questioned further, Foy divulged that he had taken James' body out of the water and laid him on a grass bank.

He led the group, which included his brother Anthony, towards the site of the body. As they went through Beecher's Wood he told them that he had found the body minutes earlier on the way back from the Bolger's house while taking a shortcut into town. Maguire mentioned that he must have got an awful fright, to which Foy replied, "Don't be talking." Maguire noted on the journey that there were specks of blood on the back of Foy's shirt and his overalls. There were also bloodstains on his earlobe and throat. Sure enough when the group reached the spot, the boy's body lay beside the stream with the clothes folded neatly on his person. Foy was brought to the Garda station where he was again asked to recount the story of finding the young boy. While he did so he "stood against the wall with his head down". He was allowed home but suspicion was already beginning to form that this was more than a tragic accident.

State Pathologist Dr Maurice Hickey examined the boy and stated that in his opinion the boy had died of strangulation and he had not been drowned. James also had four scrapes on his neck and the area looked to have been the scene of a violent struggle. The grass around the body and some of James McGrath's clothes were smeared with blood. There was no evidence that he had drowned or even that his face had been in contact with the stream while he was alive. It appeared that the child had been murdered and attention had already turned to the man who claimed to have innocently stumbled upon the body.

The Garda were aware that the shortcut Denis Foy declared he had taken would not have shortened his journey. In fact, it would have taken him fifteen minutes longer to walk compared to the main road. On top of this, local man James Cummins had seen him walking the main road some minutes after 11 p.m., indicating that Denis Foy had not gone through the wood that evening at all. This suggested that he must have known where the boy's body lay long before 11.30 p.m. The Gardaí had allowed Foy to return home as they dealt with breaking the news to James' devastated parents. Foy arrived home to the house he shared with his mother, brother and sister. Margaret Foy, sister of the accused, would later describe how Denis came home as she slept and she awoke to hear her frantic mother telling Denis that she would "bring Fr Maher tomorrow" and he would stop Foy drinking. There would be no chance to do that, however, as later that night a Garda car came to the house and arrested him on suspicion of murder.

The patrol car brought the suspect to the Garda station, arriving just before 3 a.m. Foy was examined and found to have several fresh scratches which he attributed to being scraped by briars. Inside, Detective Sergeant Hinphy was drawing attention to the blood and scratches on Foy's ears and throat. Foy denied knowing anything about the murder, telling the Gardaí that he had been drinking in the pub until 6 p.m. when he had left and found Bolger collapsed. He claimed he had not known anything about the boy's death until his way back from Bolger's. At that point he had seen James McGrath and taken him from the stream. The statement concluded at 5.45 a.m. that morning and the Gardaí told Foy to go home and sleep. Foy looked depressed and started sobbing. He then said, "I did it. I killed him. I am a free man. I would prefer to tell everything first as last."

At 6.55 a.m. the next morning, Foy signed a statement admitting that he held the boy's head under water and killed him, despite the clear evidence of strangulation. In his statement he declared, "I met Jimmy McGrath outside Cleary's...I took him for a walk over to the woods. He got his feet wet and started to cry. I told him to shut up. It was worse he was getting. I killed him by holding his head down in the water. I stripped him to make it look like he got into the water himself. After coming back from Bolger's I took him out of the water. I reported it to the Gardaí not that I did it at all." At this point, the Gardaí again offered Foy the opportunity to go home. He refused. His brother Anthony entered the Garda station at 8 a.m. and asked Denis, "What way does it stand with you?" Foy replied with his head in his hands, "It could not stand worse for me. Now, are you satisfied? I killed him." Denis then told his brother that he had committed the crime at 5.30 the previous evening.

On 16 December, James McGrath's father Patrick came into Carlow Garda station and asked to speak to the man accused of murdering his son. Somewhat surprisingly, the Gardaí granted his request. Patrick told Foy he had come to see him on behalf of his wife and Foy's brother. He asked Foy which way he had brought James to the river. Foy told him he'd led him through "Shiel's yard" and they had met no one on the way. Patrick then asked if his young son had ever done anything to him. Foy replied, "Oh Lord, no." When asked why he had then murdered the young boy, Foy answered that he did not know what he was doing. Heartbreakingly, Patrick also asked Foy what James' last words had been. Foy told him he had cried out "Tony", the name of Foy's own brother.

Depositions were taken in Carlow on 9 December and lasted three days. The defence applied for the depositions to be held *in camera* so that media reports would not be published which could prejudice the case against the defendant. This motion was declined, leading defence solicitor John Esmonde to produce a copy of the *Irish Press* newspaper in court, complaining bitterly of the report contained therein, which he said "took the most prejudicial parts and put them in black type at the top of the report." The judge sympathised, but deemed that the sitting would be held in public. The trial proper thus began in Dublin on 16 February in front of a large boisterous crowd who had to be hushed by the judge on several occasions. Denis Foy pleaded not guilty to the murder charge, claiming not to be able to remember anything. He was described as "looking unconcerned" for most of the trial.

The prosecution alleged that the accused had met James McGrath at Market Square in Bagenalstown, where the young boy was playing by himself. Foy enticed him into the woods and "as a result of what happened there", strangled him about one hundred yards from the river. He had then undressed him and placed him in the stream in a clumsy attempt to make it look like a drowning accident. One witness, Thomas Fitzgerald of Regent Street in the town, told the court that he was milking a cow just before 6 p.m. when he heard what sounded like a child's screech coming from the forest area.

Foy himself emphatically denied remembering anything of the murder, despite his earlier statements which described it in great detail. The defence put forward Dr Dunne who told the court that Foy had committed the crime without premeditation due to the "latent tendency in his unconscious mind brought on by alcohol". Dunne opined that the accused was suffering from schizophrenia or epilepsy at the time the crime was committed. Dr McGrath disagreed wholeheartedly saying Foy exhibited no schizophrenic tendencies whatsoever, although he was of dull intellect and introverted. With Foy's own incriminating signed statement, over fifty witnesses testifying for the prosecution and overwhelming circumstantial evidence against him, the outcome of the trial was not in doubt. The defence assertion that Foy was schizophrenic was rejected by the judge, who also reminded the jury that the boy's body had been moved to make it look like an accident, showing the defendant's steps to cover-up his crime. He also remarked that "drink was no excuse".

The verdict was predictable. Three days of evidence were presented before the jury, who needed two hours and forty-five minutes to find Foy guilty of murder, with a unanimous recommendation to mercy.

When asked for a comment on the verdict, Foy answered, "Nothing to say", in a low voice. Mr Justice Murnaghan sentenced Foy to hang on 11 March 1959. Only one man had been hanged in the state in the previous ten years and it was therefore unsurprising that a reprieve was announced, despite the senseless nature of the murder. On 24 February, three weeks before the execution date, President Seán T. Ó Ceallaigh announced that the government was to commute Foy's sentence to penal servitude for life. Foy's undoubtedly vicious murder of a young child may have received a different penalty in an earlier era, even a couple of years before. The commutation would ensure that he narrowly avoided becoming the last man hanged for murder in the Republic of Ireland.

THOMAS O'ROURKE

"She'll need another doctor when he's gone."

Finding the dead body of your own mother must be a horrifying experience, but that is exactly what Jimmy O'Rourke (15) had to endure on 29 December 1959. The festive season of Killmallock, Co. Limerick came to a grinding halt with the shocking discovery of the popular local hotelier. Worse still for Jimmy and his two younger sisters, Ita (8) and Marian (3), was the fact that their mother had been brutally battered to death, and at the hands of their own father.

Joan O'Rourke (originally Healy) was 39 years old and came from the Co. Kerry town of Killarney. She was described as "an attractive, small, blonde woman" and she had married her husband, Thomas, in 1943, in spite of an age gap of over twenty years. They had met in her home town when he was an army captain serving there during the Second World War. By 1959, they had owned The Central Hotel in Killmallock for twelve years and were consequently very well known in the area. Mr O'Rourke (60) had led a colourful life, working for various spells as a butcher, farmer and hotelier as well as a soldier. He had fought in Ethiopia and served in both the French Foreign Legion and the International Brigade before settling down with his wife to run the popular hotel in the small Limerick town.

The couple did not have a harmonious married life, however. Numerous local residents would later tell of the blazing rows that occurred between the pair and it was well known that O'Rourke had physically assaulted his wife on many occasions, leaving her with cuts, bruises and black eyes. Several employees of the couple had seen O'Rourke strike or beat his wife. In one instance, Margaret O'Sullivan, who had worked for the couple for two years, told Mr O'Rourke that she needed a car to bring his wife to hospital because he had "put out her shoulder". O'Rourke replied, "If I get up, I'll put out the other one." Another evening, as his wife was seeing a doctor to tend to her wounds, he was heard muttering to an employee, "She'll need another doctor when he's gone." O'Sullivan also recalled being awoken once or twice a month by Mrs O'Rourke screaming in fear, or by one of the frightened children of the household.

Coming up to Christmas 1959, Thomas O'Rourke's abusive behaviour was becoming even more brutal, leading to his wife frequently sleeping in the children's room. The local GP, Dr Hogan, also began calling regularly to attend to the battered woman who had spent numerous stints in hospital due to the amount of beatings she was subjected to. Thomas O'Rourke was regularly heard calling his wife a prostitute and accusing her of going off with other men, although there was no evidence of this. He also labelled her a disgrace due to her drinking problem, which had recently deteriorated. O'Rourke, however, was a hypocritical bully who was a heavy drinker himself. He had on one occasion banged on the door of the neighbouring Clery's Hotel in Killmallock at 4 o'clock in the morning. When the proprietor answered the door, he saw O'Rourke frothing at the mouth and waving a sword, while shouting that his wife was in the hotel. The owner allowed the sword-wielding maniac to search the premises but he did not find her. As O'Rourke was leaving he asked the owner "Are you going to hit me? You would not do it twenty years ago."

On the morning of 28 December, Mrs Brigid O'Regan, employee of the hotel, went to the bedroom the O'Rourkes shared. Mr O'Rourke was there and she gave him his tea, as she did every morning. Mrs O'Rourke was not present in the bedroom she shared with her husband. Instead she lay asleep in the children's room. Mrs O'Regan noted that Joan O'Rourke was bruised around the hips and had a mark on her nose. The unfortunate woman did not get up until 2.30

p.m., when she needed Mrs O'Regan to help her get dressed. She also had to support her employer down the stairs as her leg was stiff. Mrs O'Rourke and her husband did not converse and appeared to be avoiding each other on that busy Sunday. Mrs O'Rourke served the patrons of the bar and the lounge that night. Witnesses said she was sober, although she had one glass of gin with a customer who purchased it for her. Mr O'Rourke was not seen in the bar.

Four friends of the family arrived at around 11 p.m. that night and were shown to the kitchen. After their arrival, a pale-looking Mr O'Rourke came down from upstairs and joined them for drinks, all of which were served by his wife. She and her husband did not speak to each other much throughout the night although she did come in at one point to tell him that he ought to empty the till as it was quite full. He nodded. He was also overheard telling her to "bring in the drink, you drunken b***h", although other witnesses would testify that she did not seem drunk at all. The guests asked Joan O'Rourke to join them in the kitchen, but she replied that she had to serve customers in the bar. The party stayed drinking until about 2 a.m., when they left. However, one of them, Miss Campion, returned shortly afterwards to get a bottle of whiskey from the hotel. When she was speaking to O'Rourke at the door, his wife was behind him. He turned and spoke offensively to her, before knocking her down with a blow to the face. Miss Campion did not see her friend immediately get up. The potential customer, shocked by O'Rourke's violent treatment of his long-suffering wife, hurried off without purchasing the whiskey.

Nearly two hours after this unsavoury incident, at around 3.50 a.m., Jimmy O'Rourke was awoken by his father and told to come downstairs. His father told him that his mother was drunk. The teenager did so and was met with the sight of his mother sitting on the bottom step, unconscious and badly beaten around the face. She was breathing but making no sound. He tried to lift her up the stairs but could not do so alone and his father did not help him, merely slapping his wife forcefully on the face and pushing his leg into her stomach. Jimmy O'Rourke, in an attempt to keep his father away from his mother and protect her, spoke offensively to his father. He said, "Is that all you are good for?" and, "Is that what they teach you in the army?" An infuriated O'Rourke chased his son around the house three or four times but could not catch him, as he ran up and down the various stairs of the hotel. Each time he passed his wife, however, he grabbed her hair and banged her head against the steps. Jimmy managed to evade his enraged father by hiding in a backroom. When Jimmy did return downstairs, he found that his mother had been moved to the kitchen floor. There was a fresh pool of blood underneath her head, indicating that her husband had inflicted further violence on her in Jimmy's absence.

At 5.20 a.m., O'Rourke was still searching for his son. He even forced open the doors of one of the hotel's rooms where a permanent lodger, Michael O'Shea, was staying. He told O'Shea that his son was gone mad and he was going to kill him if he found him. Michael O'Shea told the hotelier that tomorrow was another day and that he should stop running around the hallway at the hour. A drunken O'Rourke responded with "I am going to clear out of this joint and go away. Jimmy is gone mad and out of control and she is downstairs drunk." The irony of this statement was presumably lost on O'Rourke, who was both drunk and out of control. The next time Jimmy saw his mother, her body had been moved again. His father was slapping her gently on the face in an attempt to revive her. He looked worried and told his son to get a priest. Fr Culhane and Dr Costelloe arrived shortly afterwards. Both considered that Joan O'Rourke was dead or dying. As the priest gave the Last Rites to his wife, Mr O'Rourke appeared to be crying. He was wearing no trousers, shoes or socks and had blood on his shins. The priest advised him to go upstairs. Thomas O'Rourke followed this advice, going back to bed. When awoken by the Gardaí, he did not enquire of his wife but instead lay in bed smoking. Joan O'Rourke had at this stage been pronounced dead downstairs, however, having suffered a brutal and sustained beating at the hands of her husband.

Guard Patrick D'Arcy spent most of that day with O'Rourke in his bedroom. O'Rourke did not get out of bed but continued to smoke cigarettes. He also asked the Gardaí if any arrangements had been made for his wife's funeral, before telling them that he was "going to England in January". He also self-pityingly remarked, "It was terrible misfortune. I'd be better off dead." He begged for some whiskey throughout the day, eventually receiving a half-glass. He was finally arrested at 10.30 p.m. that night and charged with the murder of his wife.

Thomas O'Rourke was sent for trial in April to the Central Criminal Court, Dublin, pleading not guilty to the charge of murder. This was another trial which aroused considerable interest, with huge crowds queuing each day to see the proceedings. Mr Seán Hooper, defending, put forward the argument that no one knew the exact happenings between 2.15 a.m. and 3.45 a.m. on the morning of 29 December, except that Mrs O'Rourke had drank a large quantity of spirits, which she could not have done involuntarily. He asserted to the jury that the instances of violence supposedly perpetrated by her husband may have been exaggerated and that when he was slapping his wife he could, in his drunkenness, have been making overly-vigorous efforts to revive her. Other injuries, he said, may have been caused when they were trying to bring Mrs O'Rourke upstairs. The State Pathologist described her injuries, which included extensive bruising around the scalp and down from her face to her leg. She also had two unexplained puncture wounds around her genitals, which the State Pathologist said may have been done by a corkscrew, although no such implement had been found.

Two of O'Rourke's children took the stand. Ita, his 8-year-old daughter, described being woken by her brother. She went downstairs and saw her mother lying on the floor. She said to her father, "Mammy looks awful white. She looks as if she (is) dead." Her father replied, "She can't be dead. I didn't do anything to her." He then turned to his wife and said, "Joan, Joan. I'm sorry. I could not have hurt you." James also addressed the court, recounting the shocking events of the night and his father's appalling treatment of his mother.

By 1 May all the evidence of over forty witnesses had been heard. The majority spoke of the abusive nature of the relationship between the accused and his wife. The defence called no one to the stand but insisted that alcohol "produced in this man at times a state of absolute insanity". The jury retired and the court waited patiently for four hours for their decision. When they returned that evening, they had found the defendant guilty, with a strong recommendation to mercy. Judge Davitt promised to present it to the appropriate quarters and without donning the black cap sentenced Thomas Tobin O'Rourke to be hanged on 27 May 1959. It had been five years since Ireland had put someone to death. The tide had turned on the death penalty since then, however. Although the crime was incredibly brutal, many were not surprised that the President announced on 12 May that O'Rourke's sentence would be commuted to penal servitude for life

Four Limerick people had not been so lucky in the lifetime of this country. Annie Walsh was the only woman executed by the state. Enlisting the help of her nephew and lover Michael Talbot, Walsh killed her husband Ned Walsh in Fedamore with a hatchet. Both were executed in 1925. John Cox was from Limerick City. He was hanged in 1929 when he attacked and robbed a German foreman, Jacob Kunz, at the Shannon Electric Scheme in Co. Clare with an iron bar. Michael Manning was to be the last man executed in Irish history. He attacked Katie Cooper at night from behind, dragging her into a field in Castletroy before raping and suffocating her. He was hanged in 1954.

JAMES KELLY

"I don't care if you took me into the yard and hung me."

Most murders involve people who know each other well. They often concern long-term enemies, although it is not unusual for the perpetrator to be a member of the same family, a spouse, a colleague or even a best friend. Random murders, however, are mercifully rare in Ireland. Attacks on people in and around their own homes by intruders are even less common. This was even truer in 1961 than it is today. In that year, there were just thirteen homicides out of an Irish population of nearly three million. Nevertheless, a quiet, rural area in Connemara was shattered in the summer of that year by the horrific robbery, rape and murder of 58-year-old widow Kate Conneely in her own home. The unspeakable brutality of this incident shocked the nation and the individual responsible became one of the last men sentenced to die for a criminal act in Ireland.

Carraroe (An Cheathrú Rua; The Red Quarter) is a picturesque village lying on the south-west coast of Connemara. It is, to this day, a strong Gaeltacht, or Irish-speaking district. The people of the area, like much of the rest of the western seaboard, have made a living through farming and fishing for generations. Throughout the years, however, many of its inhabitants have needed to emigrate to America and England to obtain work in one of the big cities. Kate Conneely's family were no exception. She had one married daughter in South Connemara, but all three of her other children had followed this well-worn path and lived and worked in London. Remittances were a common feature of Ireland at the time where the emigrants sent amounts of money to those left at home. The Conneely children did just that. Her son, Michael, would later testify that between February and June he had sent a total of £38 to support his mother, which she kept in a purse in the kitchen. Kate's daughters Bridie and Anne had done the same, contributing over £60 between them, a huge sum of money in the Ireland of 1961. Mrs Conneely was therefore in fairly comfortable circumstances and lived in an isolated but well-kept cottage in Toureen, a townland between Carraroe and Lettermore. On the evening of 11 July she visited various neighbours as she often did. She was described as hale and hearty when she left at 10 p.m. to return home. A granddaughter stayed with Kate intermittently but was not at the house on this evening, meaning she would be on her own for the night.

The next morning, Mrs Conneely was spotted by a young girl who was tending cows. She was lying on the side of the road just outside her home, badly injured. The girl immediately summoned help. Mrs Conneely, who was covered in blood and had suffered serious head injuries, was trying to sit up but could not. She was carried to her house on a shawl and spoke in Irish to those present, mentioning being cold and wanting a drink and also saying that she was "finished". When asked what had happened, she was unable to answer the question. An ambulance arrived but Kate Conneely died en route to Galway some time after 2 p.m. The Gardaí were now looking at a murder investigation. The people in Carraroe were in complete shock over the vicious killing. A 58-year-old widow living alone in the tranquil area had been subjected to a brutal and sustained assault. The bed, walls and fireplace of the house were covered in bloodstains while the bed was broken up. She had suffered severe wounds to the back of her skull and had been strangled with great force, breaking the bone at the back of her throat and fracturing her jaw. A knotted scarf lay nearby which had been used on the unfortunate victim. Kate Conneely had also been sexually assaulted. Her house had been totally emptied of

223

money. At least £30 was known to have present but only 19s.9d. was discovered. The Gardaí were on the lookout for a psychopathic killer in the Connemara wilderness. They did not need to look too far.

James Kelly (30) was also from Toureen in Carraroe but had lived in Manchester, England for a number of years where he worked as a labourer. He was a married father of three children but was not a devoted family man, his wife describing him as unreliable and an alcoholic. He had returned to Carraroe from England in May, initially living with his mother before lodging with his cousin, Thomas Ó Ceallaigh. Thomas would later say that his cousin had very little money, to the point where he had been forced to sell his own coat for 10s. He had been anxious to return to England but did not have the cost of the fare. On the evening of 11 July, James Kelly met with a woman named Chrissie O'Toole. They had spent a lot of time together since he arrived back in Carrraroe, and she was unaware that he was married. The pair spent the night together in a vacant house belonging to a man named Colman Kelly in Toureen. Kelly, who had been drinking and seemed tired, fell asleep shortly after entering the house. Miss O'Toole tried to wake him up several times but could not do so. She departed before 5 a.m. to go home. The next sighting of Kelly was the following morning at 10.30 a.m. when several locals spotted him running across the field in the direction of the main road.

When Kelly reached the road, he hitched a lift into Galway City with a local man. On the journey, he talked about fishing, turf and the weather. The driver would later testify that his passenger appeared normal despite the act he had just committed. When he arrived in the city, the formerly poverty-stricken Kelly somehow had the means to buy a pullover and shirt. He exchanged the new items for the clothes he had been wearing the night before, although he did not change his suit jacket. He left his own bloodstained clothes in a public toilet in the city.

Kelly then spent the afternoon drinking pints in Freeney's pub in Galway City before hailing a taxi back to Connemara with local driver Michael Cahill at 5.30 p.m. The fare was fixed at £4, which he paid with English notes. Cahill described Kelly as being normal and talkative. He told the driver that he was over on holiday from England and had won money on the English Football Pools, mentioning figures of both £900 and £2000. He asked the taxi driver to drop him to several public houses in the Inverin and Ballinahown areas, even buying his chauffeur a drink. He then directed the taxi west towards Toureen National School. As they drove by, they saw two Garda cars and several policemen on the road. The taxi driver remarked that something must have happened. Kelly did not reply and showed no interest. Chrissie O'Toole joined the men in the vehicle some distance down the road. They visited several pubs, including one in Rosaveel, fourteen miles away. Chrissie and Kelly spoke exclusively in Irish, which the taxi driver found difficult to understand.

O'Toole was informing Kelly *as Gaeilge* of the grim news in the area. She was upset because her neighbour and cousin Kate Conneely had been murdered and she told Kelly that the Gardaí were attempting to trace him as they were aware he had been in the area. O'Toole advised him that he should make himself known at the Garda station in the village to clear his name. Kelly appeared unconcerned but assured her he would do this later. The taxi dropped Chrissie home shortly afterwards and Kelly went with the driver back towards Galway. When they passed the Garda station the taxi driver asked Kelly if he would like to go in. Kelly told him to drive on. Michael Cahill returned to the city, with his passenger sleeping in the back. They arrived at 11.30 p.m.

The Gardaí were already on the look-out for James Kelly, being aware of his uncharacteristic spending and his presence in the area on the night of the murder. After disembarking the taxi, he was stopped while walking down Shop Street in the city and asked his name. He replied, "John Naughton". He got a brief interrogation but the Gardaí thought his description did not match that of the one they had received of the wanted man. He was thus released. James Kelly got a lift as far as the town of Loughrea where he boarded a bus to Dublin.

Meanwhile, the Gardaí had realised their mistake and had left two plain clothes officers in Dublin waiting for the Galway bus on the off-chance that Kelly would be on it. Their luck was in and Kelly was arrested on 13 July at Bus Áras. His jacket sleeves and the legs of his trousers were still smeared with blood. Kelly again gave his name as John Naughton and said that he was a native of Shantalla in Galway City. When asked what street he lived on, he said he could not remember. He was also asked to produce some identification, which he was unable to do. He agreed to go to the station with the pair of officers. When the Gardaí suggested to him that his name was James Kelly he denied it. He also claimed not to have been to Carraroe, or even to know where it was. The Gardaí mentioned the murder of Kate Conneely to him and he replied "foolish men", telling the guards that if he thought that they had wanted him for murder then he would have given his real name. He claimed to have assumed that they wanted him in connection with an incident involving a car he had hired the year before. Garda Malone from Galway Station arrived in Dublin some hours later. He was acquainted with Kelly and identified the prisoner. James Kelly was arrested, and brought to Carraroe Garda station where he made numerous statements. His trial occurred in Dublin Central Court nearly a year later on 14 May 1962.

The trial, conducted in both English and Irish, would hear from sixty witnesses. Kelly pleaded not guilty to the murder charge. His girlfriend Chrissie O'Toole took the stand. She told the court, "I regarded James Kelly as my boyfriend. I did not know he was married." On the night before the murder she went with the accused to the abandoned property close to Mrs Conneely's. Miss O'Toole said that Kelly had drink taken but seemed normal, although he appeared tired and quickly fell asleep. She woke him at 1 a.m. but he did not want to talk and went back to sleep. She left to go home across the fields at 4.45 a.m. She told the jury that she had tried to persuade Kelly to go to the Garda station the next day to clear his name as she was sure he had nothing to do with the murder. She was upset as she had known Kate Conneely well and had been related to her.

Kelly had given a statement in Carraroe Garda station after being returned from Dublin which was admitted in evidence. After asking the Gardaí that his children never be told of his crime, he described entering the house of Mrs Conneely. He told Gardaí, "I don't care if you took me out into the yard and hung (*sic*) me." He went on to say, "She started screaming. She would not stop and I hit her...I don't know what I hit her with. I didn't mean to hurt her and that is the truth...The next thing I remember I crossed the bog to Dangan." He refused to sign the statement until he saw a doctor. When he saw the doctor, he requested a solicitor. At this point, he refused to sign the statement altogether, also declining to give hair or blood samples. He told the Gardaí, "I was earning £40 a week in England but that is all finished now. You chaps want a sample of my blood. I do not want to be awkward. I do not want to hang." He then asked the sergeant, "What are my chances?" When the sergeant said he could not answer the question, Kelly said ruefully, "I have no chance at all." Judge McLaughlin in the trial allowed the unsigned statement to be admitted in evidence. The prosecution rested its case by highlighting the brutal nature of the crime, the rape and robbery, the lack of remorse and the attempted cover-up by Kelly after the murder.

The defence case rested on insanity. Dr Seán McBride was the defending solicitor. McBride was a former chief-of-staff of the IRA and an outspoken opponent of capital punishment. He told the court that he would not call Kelly to the stand in his own defence as he was insane and unfit to plead. Dr B. M. Mandelbrote, Oxford, gave evidence that he had diagnosed Kelly as an alcoholic with an abnormal personality. He had been prescribed therapy in England which he failed to attend. Another doctor, J. Dunne of St Brendan's Hospital, Dublin, said that the nature of the crime was not within the standards of human rationality and that at the time the accused was suffering from either epilepsy or schizophrenia. He believed that Kelly had "no mind or consciousness at the time of the crime".

The jury disagreed with the doctors' diagnosis. Kelly's total lack of remorse was startling and after a two-hour deliberation he was found guilty on the tenth day of the trial. The judge agreed wholeheartedly with the verdict and commended the Gardaí on their excellent work in quickly apprehending the killer. With his wife looking on, Kelly was sentenced to death. He replied in an almost inaudible voice, "I have nothing to say." He applied for leave to appeal the verdict but it failed on all grounds and the date for the gallows was fixed for 16 August 1962. Kelly was fortunate that the brutal attack had not taken place a few years earlier. No one in Ireland had been executed in eight years and the Dáil had discussed the abolition of the death penalty several times. The appetite amongst the public was not there for a state-sponsored killing, despite the diabolical nature of the crime. The President therefore, on the advice of the government, commuted Kelly's death sentence to penal servitude for life five days before the execution date arrived. Kelly thus, narrowly, avoided being the last Irishman executed by the state.

On 7 May 1927, William O'Neill had broken into the isolated cottage of Peggy Farrell in the valley of Glenmalure in Co. Wicklow. He tied her hands tightly and knotted a scarf around her mouth before giving her a vicious beating. He then sexually assaulted her. She was dead before morning due to suffocation, shock and exposure. Large amounts of money, along with other valuables, were taken from the house which was totally ransacked. 18-year-old O'Neill was apprehended in possession of a silver watch which had been taken from the house. His guilt was never in question and he was found guilty, being hanged on 29 December 1927. Kelly and O'Neill both broke in and brutally attacked elderly women they barely knew in their own home. The main purpose was greed and a desire to steal money from a vulnerable target. The era in which the crime occurred was the main difference, leading one man to the gallows and the other to the prison cell.

In the same year that Kelly was pardoned, two executions were carried out in Northern Ireland. This in itself was unusual as the six counties had not hanged anyone since 1942. They would also prove to be the final executions to take place on the island, with 26-year-old Robert McGladdery holding the ignominious record as the last man to die at the behest of the state. McGladdery propositioned his neighbour Pearl Gamble at an Orange Hall dance on 28 January 1961, but she rebuffed his advances. He lay in wait for her after the event, dragging her into a field and strangling and stabbing her to death before leaving her body to be discovered in Damolly, just outside the border town of Newry, Co. Down. The attitude against the death penalty had not hardened as much in the North as it had in the Republic and McGladdery was found guilty and hanged at Crumlin Road Gaol in Belfast on 20 December 1961, more than seven years after the last execution in the Republic. It was a particularly callous murder but if McGladdery had committed it five miles south in the jurisdiction of the Republic there is every chance that he, like James Kelly, would have escaped the hangman's noose. It appears quite likely that McGladdery may forever be destined to be the last man hanged on this island.

SHAN MOHANGI

"I took a big knife and cut the neck off."

Shan Mohangi was a rarity in the Ireland of 1963. The 23 year old was from Natal in South Africa but was of Indian descent. He had come to Dublin as a medical student in the expectation that he would return home to practice as a doctor when his studies were completed. His dark skin and foreign accent would have stood out in Irish society at the time. His situation here was far improved from that of his homeland, however. He considered the Irish to be a kind and welcoming people and found himself free to socialise amongst them, unlike in South Africa where the Apartheid system was still discriminating against non-whites. Mohangi secured a job and a girlfriend in his adopted country and seemed to be getting on well, apart from some difficulties in passing his rigorous pre-medical exams. He liked his new home so much that he did not return to South Africa at any stage after arrival. Despite the promising life he seemed to have ahead of him, he would soon find himself embroiled in one of the most notorious and gruesome Irish murder cases ever recorded.

Hazel Mullen was born in September 1947 in the South Dublin village of Shankill. Her father had died when she was a young girl, leaving her and her six siblings to be supported by their mother. Hazel was the third eldest and wasted no time in getting a job to help with the family's finances. Hazel finished school aged 14 and immediately found employment, first as a chemist's assistant and then in the printing department of the Bank of Ireland. She was a popular girl, both an accomplished Irish dancer and an aspiring model. It was not surprising, therefore, that men started to show an interest in her. Her family could not have expected, however, that it would be a 23 year old who she first brought home. The would-be suitor was Shan Mohangi. He quickly asked Hazel to go out with him, although he knew she was just 14. She told Mohangi that he would have to ask her mother. Bridget Mullen was understandably alarmed by the age gap and refused the request initially. However, she got to know Mohangi and a friendship developed between the medical student and the Mullen family. He took to visiting them every weekend and became very friendly with Hazel's older brother Desmond, with Desmond even staying in his flat on Harcourt Street sometimes when he was working nights. Mrs Mullen decided to reluctantly allow her young daughter to date the older man, on the condition that Mohangi take good care of her.

Shan Mohangi had come to Ireland in May 1961, and was studying medicine in the College of Surgeons. He was the eldest of eight children and from a wealthy background in South Africa. He had completed his primary education in India and had again been sent across the world to attend a good university, something he could not have done in South Africa. Despite the advantages he enjoyed, he was a poor student who had failed his pre-medical exam twice. His academic problems may have been due to some major distractions in his personal life. Firstly, he had gained employment as a commis chef in "The Green Tureen" restaurant on 95 Harcourt Street in the centre of Dublin City. He worked late six nights a week, excepting Sundays, starting at around 10.30 p.m. and not finishing until 2.30 a.m. He also lived on the fourth floor of the same building. His other major distraction was Hazel Mullen. He spent a huge amount of time with his young girlfriend and this caused him to neglect his studies. Their relationship, which started out as a happy whirlwind romance, soon experienced a negative turn, however. Mohangi had a far darker side than those who met him might suspect. He expected his girlfriend to be "untainted" and "pure" and had a violent jealous streak if he thought she was showing interest in anyone else.

Despite Mohangi's fixation on purity and faithfulness, Hazel was not his first girlfriend in the country. He had met a woman four months after his arrival in Ireland. She was from Mullingar but worked in a shop near Mohangi's lodgings. They had started going out and quickly became engaged in January 1962. Mohangi was extremely controlling over his fiancée, who was a trainee nurse, and even made plans that she would enter the College of Surgeons with him. After a short while, the pair began to row over his authoritarian nature. Mohangi was aggressive and his ex-fiancée would later depose that he had been violent towards her in the course of rows, hitting her on one occasion and grabbing her by the throat another time. He had also threatened to kill her. In March 1962, she moved back to Mullingar and a couple of months later she called off the engagement. Mohangi was allegedly devastated. Within one month, however, he discovered a new girl to shower his affections on. That girl was 14-year-old Hazel Mullen.

By spring 1963, Mohangi had known Hazel for nearly a year and was regularly discussing engagement and wedding plans. This is despite the fact that Hazel's mother still insisted that seventeen was the earliest her daughter could consider getting married. In the month of April, however, Mohangi again met the nurse, his ex-fiancée. He remarked to Hazel that he had bumped into his former lover, who seemed not to mind. He neglected to mention, of course, that he had been spending large amounts of time in her company. By August 1963, Mohangi was seeing the nurse up to five times a week while still going out with Hazel. The nurse even began staying in his apartment overnight. He was still seeing Hazel, although less frequently, and his treatment of her was deteriorating rapidly.

Mohangi had hit his teenage girlfriend in the face with his fist on one occasion when she told him she had kissed another boy. Another day he had burned Hazel with rice from a pan which required that she be admitted to Adelaide Hospital. The South African had pleaded with her family that it was an accident. Some weeks later, however, he had arranged a dinner in his flat with Desmond Mullen and his girlfriend Heather, as well as Hazel. Hazel did not show up. Mohangi was in a rage at her non-appearance and told his other two guests that he would have liked to have killed Hazel when he had thrown the rice on her. This gave some indication of his twisted mind. Mohangi was clearly a violent man with a deep hatred of women. As a result of these incidents, Hazel and Mohangi broke up for a short time in the summer of 1963. Mohangi would eventually persuade his young girlfriend to give him another chance, however. Unfortunately, he did not use this opportunity to change his ways. Instead he showed what a monster he really was.

On 17 August 1963, Hazel left work and did some shopping. After 1 p.m. she was seen walking in the direction of Harcourt Street. She knocked on the door of Mohangi's flat. She would not be seen again.

That evening, at 7 p.m., Desmond Mullen and his girlfriend Heather came to visit Shan Mohangi, having been invited for dinner earlier in the week. Their host seemed distracted. He left the couple on two occasions to go down to the basement of the restaurant. He was gone for twenty minutes on each occasion. Normally, Mohangi would have been full of conversation but on this day he was quiet and subdued. The couple left at about 10 p.m and Desmond brought Heather to a dance. He returned after 2 a.m. as he had arranged to stay in Mohangi's flat that night. While there, his mother telephoned the restaurant and asked to speak to him. She told him that Hazel had not returned home and she was worried. Desmond told Mohangi that he had to go home to help his mother. Shan kindly offered to accompany him.

On their way to Shankill, the men reported Hazel missing in the Garda station. When they got to the Mullen household, they discussed where Hazel had been that day and Mohangi told them that she had cancelled their appointment for lunch and he had not seen her at any stage. The worried family then went to bed, Mohangi sleeping in Hazel's bedroom. The next morning, Mohangi drove around with Desmond questioning Hazel's friends and colleagues about when they had last seen her. He again stayed in the Mullen household on Sunday night. While he was there, the Gardaí made a rudimentary search of the Green Tureen and its basement for any trace of the missing teenager. They did not discover anything in the rubbish-strewn cellar, although it would later be divulged that there was a large amount of incriminating evidence present.

The restaurant was re-opened on Monday night. The workers complained of an offensive odour around the kitchen and a large bone was discovered, which the staff assumed came from an animal. Disinfectant was used but it did not shift the smell. Mohangi was working but looked tired. During the service, a journalist entered the kitchen and asked Mohangi questions about his missing girlfriend Hazel. He also mentioned the fact that Mohangi had been seeing his ex-fiancée. Mohangi seemed to be in a panic as he was answering. At 3.30 a.m. on Tuesday morning, when service was finished, Mohangi was sitting in the kitchen with the restaurant's manager, Cecil Frew. Frew suspected something and could see that his employee looked worried, understandable for a man whose girlfriend had gone missing. Frew invited him to get into his car so they could search for her. As they drove around, Mohangi said, "I am in trouble and will you help me, Mr Frew?"

Frew, assuming that the trouble concerned Hazel, asked if she was dead. Mohangi replied that she was and that her body was in the building. They drove back to the restaurant where Frew dropped off his employee before making his way to the Garda station to tell them the disturbing news. They left the station immediately for the Green Tureen and attempted to gain access to Mohangi's room but could not, the door being locked from the inside. The Gardaí forced the door open, only to be met by a strong smell of gas. Mohangi was lying on the bed with his eyes closed. He had turned on two gas jets and taken several pills. He had written on a piece of cardboard that everything he owned would go to his ex-fiancée after his death. The Gardaí arrived in time, however, to bring him to the hospital where he soon regained consciousness. His suicide attempt had failed and Mohangi was arrested after a short stint in hospital.

The Gardaí searched the basement of the Green Tureen while Mohangi was in custody. The sight that met them was truly grotesque. Hazel's body was indeed in the room but had been cut into seventeen pieces. They were strewn around the kitchen, many of them badly burned. The head, which had been incinerated in the oven, was charred black. Some of Hazel Mullen's intestines had been cut out and placed in the bin, while pieces of her flesh were visible behind a gas fire in Mohangi's flat. State Pathologist Dr Maurice Hickey was not even able to determine a cause of a death for Hazel Mullen as a result of Mohangi's appalling mutilation of her body. Hazel had been dismembered and burned so thoroughly that her brother Desmond could only identify his sister by her teeth and the general formation of her face.

Mohangi was permitted to write to his ex-fiancée while he awaited the murder trial. In one self-pitying passage he wrote, "I know that you are thinking that I am a dirty, lousy, rotten murderer. Believe me, I am no more a murderer than you are. The thing that happened to me can happen to any man." He went on to complain, "I don't like to be in prison. I am fed up here, but there is nothing I can do. I have to pay the penalty for a minute's rashful deed." Finally he mentioned, "I am only allowed one visit. If you wish to visit me bring me a roast chicken and a packet of cigarettes."

The trial opened on 10 February, to intense public interest. Large queues of spectators jostled each day for admittance to hear the details of what had already become one of Ireland's most notorious murder cases, partially due to the treatment of the body after death. Mohangi appeared cool and pleaded not guilty to murder.

Mohangi's evidence was the most eagerly anticipated and it did not disappoint. He spent eight hours telling the court of the events leading up to Hazel's murder and the brutal aftermath. He told the court that he had arranged to meet with Hazel on 17 August and she had knocked at his apartment door about 1 p.m. when he was still wearing his pyjamas. He claimed that Hazel had requested that he bring her down to the basement kitchen of the Green Tureen as she had never been down there. Mohangi agreed. He showed her around for about five minutes before they started kissing in the cellar. They then stopped and she asked what they were planning for the day. He suggested that they would have dinner in a local Chinese restaurant before going to look at some engagement rings. Mohangi claimed that Hazel told him then that she had something to tell him, that she had "something to do with somebody else". Mohangi asked her if it was sex. She allegedly replied that it was. Mohangi said he got in a rage and held her up by her throat, asking her the identity of the other man. Hazel could not answer and collapsed when he let go of her throat. "I did not intend to hurt her…she fell and kind of sagged." Mohangi said he "was scared and ran upstairs."

He returned to the basement afterwards. At this point Hazel was lying on the ground with her eyes open. He called "Hazel, Hazel", but got no reply. Mohangi at this point decided that his girlfriend was dead, without checking her pulse or consulting a doctor. Hazel Mullen had been killed within minutes of arriving in the house. Mohangi decided "almost immediately" that he was going to dismember the body of his teenage girlfriend. The following passage from the court case may give some indication of the horrific nature of the crime.

What did you decide to do? Cut her up.
For what purpose? I thought if I cut her up I could burn her.
What did you do? I took a knife and started cutting the neck, but I realised I couldn't cut with a knife. Then I took the cleaver and gave a couple of blows but it was too blunt and would not cut so I took a big knife and cut the neck off.

He then burned his girlfriend's clothes on the gas cooker. At about 2.15 p.m., some firefighters arrived after some passers-by had reported black smoke billowing from the basement of the building. Mohangi was visibly pale and sweating when he answered the door. He barred the emergency workers way into the building, telling them that it was only some old rags burning. They insisted on coming down to check the kitchen, however, but they did not see anything incriminating so they left. Mohangi then continued his grotesque task. He put various parts of Hazel's body in the bin and then put the rubbish out to be collected. Mohangi had told the court that he had murdered Hazel in a rage as he had been prepared to "give up everything" for her, including his parents. He also described his love as an infatuation. His former fiancée had stayed in his house the night before he murdered Hazel, and up to five nights a week in the time approaching the murder, casting doubt on the sincerity of his evidence. His violent past also reflected poorly on the murderer.

Mohangi's defence insisted that Hazel's death had been an accident. He had grabbed her by the throat in a jealous rage and had not meant to kill her. His panic had caused him to dismember the body in an attempt to conceal the crime. They asserted that he had clearly not planned the murder, for if he had he would not have done it on the very day that he had invited her brother to his flat for dinner. They called medical witnesses to testify that a sudden shock to the throat can occasionally cause death. They described it as "a crime without a motive and an accidental death". The prosecution merely reminded the jury of the barbarity of the crime, the dismemberment of the innocent young woman and the appalling way Mohangi had acted in the aftermath of the crime.

After an exhausting eleven-day trial, the jury took just under four hours to announce the guilty verdict. Mr Justice Teevan pronounced the death sentence of Mohangi, who stood erect with his hands by his sides. His execution was set for 18 March 1964. The judge exempted the jury from further service for fifteen years, due to the harrowing nature of the evidence.

However, Mohangi appealed the sentence and the original verdict was quashed. The wealthy South African received free legal aid from the state for the second trial. The evidence was similar to the first case, although the public interest was somewhat subdued on this occasion. The retrial, in June 1964, returned a different verdict. This time, the jury declared that Mohangi had not murdered his girlfriend, but was in fact guilty of manslaughter. Many Irish people were stunned by the verdict considering the grotesque nature of the killing and the horrific lengths the murderer had gone to in trying to conceal it. Mohangi received a seven-year jail sentence. He served under four years, being released in April 1968. He returned immediately to South Africa, becoming a successful businessman in his home country, following in the footsteps of his wealthy father. In later life, he even ran for election to the South African parliament.

Bridget Mullen, Hazel's mother, had forgiven Mohangi for a crime many would consider unforgivable. She had found solace in her Christian faith to the point that she told the newspapers after the trial that she wished him well in the future. The jury also showed an incredible leniency to the student. Mohangi was never likely to be hanged, despite the death sentence imposed on him, as capital punishment was just months away from being suspended. However, a prison term of four years seems like an outrageous sentence for what can only be described as one of the most brutal murder in the history of the state.

NOEL CALLAN & MICHAEL McHUGH

"Why did he follow us? Didn't he know he'd be shot?"

The death penalty was abolished in the Republic of Ireland in 1964 for ordinary crimes. It was, however, retained for treason and "capital murder" i.e. the murder of an on-duty Garda or a politically-motivated killing. Eleven men and women would be convicted of this charge and receive the ultimate penalty, although all would eventually see it commuted. Each of the eleven sentences were handed down due to a killing of a Garda and all happened in the space of just ten years (1975-1985) when the troubles from the north were wreaking havoc on both sides of the border. The last such case involved the particularly callous and cold-blooded killing of Sergeant Patrick Morrissey near Ardee, Co. Louth.

Patrick Morrissey was a native of Belturbet, just south of the border in Co. Cavan. By 1985 he was 49 years of age and a happily-married father of four children. He had been in the army for several years before joining An Garda Síochána. In his twenty-five years in the force he had served in Waterford and Dublin but had for the past three years been stationed as a sergeant in the small village of Collon, Co. Louth. Morrissey was a popular and hard-working member of the force who had distinguished himself with his work in the Garda Subaqua Unit. He was also a well-known member of the Garda Choir. On 27 June, Sergeant Morrissey was appearing at the District Court sitting in Ardee

239

in what was shaping up to be a normal day. Events just up the street would, however, shatter the tranquillity of the summer's day.

Just before 10 a.m. on 27 June, Ex-Louth GAA star Sean Boyle was returning from the Bank of Ireland. He had collected £25,000 which was to be distributed throughout the day in the Ardee Labour Exchange. As he was about to open the office, two men wearing combat jackets and balaclavas pushed him and shouted, "Money, money." Boyle assumed it was a joke until he noticed that the two men were brandishing guns. He hurriedly gave them the key of his car where the money was left in a strongbox. The men took the £25,000. Instead of absconding, however, they decided to enter the exchange and demand more money from the manager. One of the men fired a shot into the air and told Boyle in a northern accent, "I'll put a bullet in you." The other man said, "I'll blow your f***ing head off." Boyle told them that they had taken all the cash he had. After some more jostling, the raiders eventually fled, taking Boyle's Datsun car with them. They then sped off north, in the direction of the village of Tallanstown.

As they were driving through the town they passed a patrol car which contained two uniformed Gardaí. The men fired shots at it before making their escape. The Gardaí in the car did a U-turn and picked up Sergeant Morrissey, who had by now been told of the events. An enterprising local threw a stone at the passing Datsun, shattering the side window. The raiders continued regardless. The three officers then proceeded to follow the robbers. The high-speed chase came to an abrupt end four miles up the road just outside Tallanstown where the Gardaí saw the stolen vehicle crashed at the side of the road. There was no sign of the two men. They immediately set up a road-block to attempt to snare the robbers, who were thought to be still in the vicinity. Minutes later, a high-powered motorbike, which had been concealed by the raiders in the area, came travelling at high speed and crashed through the road-block. It then continued on at a breakneck speed towards Rathbrist. The three Gardaí again gave chase, only to see the motorbike collide with a car at a crossroads a short distance away. The two injured raiders got off and ran away in the direction of Rathbrist House, leaving the £25,000 at the side of the road.

Two of the Gardaí present rushed to help the injured occupants of the car, a young mother with her three-year-old daughter. The third, Sergeant Patrick Morrissey, showed tremendous bravery by instead pursuing the two masked men, despite the fact that they were known to be armed and dangerous. They had ran up the gravel driveway of the stately home. Morrissey entered by a different route and met the two men face-to-face in front of the house. He called on them to give up. Instead of doing so, one of the men produced a gun and fired at Sergeant Morrissey, hitting him in the leg. The sergeant was badly wounded and fell to the ground. He managed to prop himself up, only to see the same man approaching him with his gun held aloft. He taunted the sergeant, who was dressed in his full Garda uniform, to get up. Morrissey was unable to do so. Despite the fact that the unarmed sergeant lay wounded and posed absolutely no threat to the men, the armed raider then cold-bloodedly put the gun into the wounded man's face. He shot the defenceless Morrissey from a distance of about five inches, killing him instantly in a "cold-blooded, savage and calculated act". The two men then fled into nearby fields, leaving the fatally-wounded policeman to bleed to death on the driveway.

A helicopter and a large force of armed Gardaí had by this point joined in the search. Morrissey's colleagues found him lying in a pool of blood. He was quickly dispatched to hospital but was pronounced dead on arrival. The hunt for his two killers did not last long. Both men had been badly injured in the motorbike crash and were unable to get far. The Gardaí surrounded the fields and followed trails of blood on the ground which led six hundred yards away. They found the first man concealed in a ditch, having covered himself in grass and foliage. His name was Noel Callan. He appeared dazed and asked when arrested, "Is the guard dead?" When told he was, Callan responded, "Why did he follow us? Didn't he know he'd be shot?" The second man, who had fired the fatal shots, had tried to hide himself in a barley field two hundred yards away. He was quickly apprehended and identified as Michael McHugh. Balaclavas, a pistol, a rifle and a handgun were all found in the vicinity of the two men.

Callan was taken to hospital where he appeared to be unconscious for several days. The medical team became suspicious after a time. Although he appeared non-responsive, neurological exams suggested that it was a pretence. One of the doctors placed the strong chemical ammonia under Callan's nose. He started to splutter and cough and woke up swiftly. McHugh was also taken to hospital with minor injuries. He was discharged on 1 July as he was considered to be well enough to face charges for the Garda's shooting. He refused to leave, however, shouting and resisting attempts to get him out of bed. He then had to be physically carried from the hospital against his will.

Noel Callan was just 23 years old and an unmarried car dealer. He was from Keeneraboy, a small townland just yards from the frontier that separates the Republic of Ireland from the northern six counties. Michael McHugh was 25 and a motor mechanic from just outside Crossmaglen in the republican stronghold that is south Armagh. He was known to the Gardaí and the RUC, having committed a string of offences around the border area in the months leading up to Sergeant Morrissey's murder. The two men were believed to be linked with the republican paramilitary organization, the INLA, who were active and dangerous in the border region and beyond at the time. Both men lived in the Dundalk area and the Gardaí felt certain that a third member of their gang had dropped them off in Ardee the night before the raid. This man, if he existed, was never discovered.

The two men initially showed some regret for the shooting. McHugh, at one point, cried on a Garda's shoulder. He told them he was adopted and "that's the cause of all my trouble. I didn't know my own mother and father."As he was being interviewed in hospital, he told the Gardaí ,"You know we shot him. What's the point in asking me questions?" He continued, "It's not my fault. I didn't know what I was doing. I wasn't thinking straight. I wish I was dead and the sergeant still alive. They should have shot me." The Garda who wrote down McHugh's verbal statement then asked him to sign it, to which McHugh replied, "I'm not saying anymore. Leave me alone." Callan had also shown contrition, telling the Gardaí as they drove him through Ardee, "It was a bad day we came here. If we never came to this place the sergeant would be alive."

The murder trial opened in November 1985. The men's remorse had evaporated and was replaced by flat denials of culpability in the crime. Both pleaded not guilty, despite irrefutable evidence against them. One hundred and fifty witnesses would appear for the prosecution.

Callan told the court that he was not guilty. He claimed that he had been approached the night before the shooting by a political activist named James Burnett (shot by the INLA shortly after the sergeant's murder) who asked Callan to do him a favour the next day by delivering a parcel. Callan agreed and Burnett brought him to a field in Tallanstown. He supposedly gave Callan a motorcycle and asked him to return to the field the next morning at 9.30 a.m. where he could pick up this mysterious parcel from friends of Burnett. Callan claimed that when he went back the next morning he saw two men in a panic. The men shouted at him, "The guards have seen us." One of the men took Callan's motorbike and drove off. Callan then got onto the second motorbike behind the other man, who turned out to be McHugh. The motorbike crashed and Callan hit his head on the road. He was dazed but followed the other man who had shouted "come on." He remembered leaning on the gable of a house and hearing a bang but he claimed that he did not realise a Garda had been shot at that time. Callan said that he was then arrested for a crime that he did not know anything about.

McHugh's story also placed him as an innocent bystander arrested for a crime he did not know had happened. McHugh claimed that the only reason he was in the area was that he was on his way to Navan, Co. Meath to fix a car. He stated that he had left Crossmaglen at 7 a.m. that morning and had been thumbing lifts and walking. As he was walking through Rathbrist, he had heard two bangs and saw some Garda patrol cars in the vicinity. He had rushed into a field as he did not want to be arrested by the Gardaí due to an outstanding bail issue in the north. He lay in the ditch to avoid detection but was then arrested and manhandled by the Gardaí. He claimed that he did not know anyone had been shot at this point.

Both men also complained to the court that they had been subjected to assaults by various Gardaí on several occasions after their arrest, an accusation denied flatly by the Gardaí. McHugh also claimed that the Gardaí had threatened to shoot him and they had shouted "kill him, kill him" during the arrest. Both of these allegations were rejected. When it was put to McHugh that he had not mentioned these allegations to anyone for some time after his arrest, he answered that he did not do it because "it wouldn't do any good". The court dismissed the accusations.

If the jury had any doubt about the identity of the killers, 16-year-old Seán McDermott may have put them to rest. McDermott was a secondary school student on his summer holidays in June 1985. He told the court that he had been sleeping in Rathbrist House when he was woken by a commotion outside and what sounded like a gunshot. When he went to look out the window, he saw a man in Garda uniform propping himself up with his arms on the ground. Another man, thought to have been McHugh, stood over him pointing a gun at his face. He then saw McHugh shoot the Garda full in the face at point blank range. The Garda fell back and his hat rolled away in the middle of the avenue. A second man covered in blood was also nearby and McDermott saw both men running into the fields after the shooting. The McDermott's housekeeper, Mary Kindlon, was in the house at the same time and she corroborated this version of events. McHugh's defence rejected McDermott's eyewitness account, saying that it was not enough to base a murder conviction on. Callan's counsel told the court that he had not fired a shot and was not even at the Ardee Exchange Office when it was being robbed, being just an innocent bystander.

On 3 December 1985, the jury returned to the court. Callan rose to hear the verdict, while McHugh remained seated. A guilty verdict was then announced for both men. Mr Justice Liam Hamilton sentenced the two men to death for the murder of the unarmed Garda, fixing the execution for 27 December. The judge asserted that he agreed with the jury and that he believed McHugh's statements had shown clearly that he had shot the Garda after robbing the exchange. He admitted that Callan had not fired the fatal shot. He stated, however, that Callan had fired at least one shot during the raid to the Exchange Office and had threatened to kill Seán Boyle and was therefore guilty by common design. The Gardaí had assured the jury during the trial that McHugh was not a member of any paramilitary organisation. As he was being led from the dock, however, McHugh gave a clenched fist salute, and shouted "Victory to the INLA, pro-British bastards".

McHugh, in a further show of his disdain for the courts, then became the first person sentenced to death in living memory to refuse to appeal the punishment. It did not matter. McHugh and Callan gained reprieves, McHugh in December 1985 and Callan in May 1986. Both of their death sentences were reduced to prison terms of forty years. They would go on to serve over thirty years in prison, being released in 2015. Just months before Morrissey's death, Garda Frank Hand had been shot dead by the IRA while escorting a cash delivery to Drumree Post Office, Co. Meath. Hand's killers were also sentenced to death but they too had their sentences commuted to forty years in prison instead. Patrick Morrissey died in the line of duty when he bravely attempted to uphold the law. Sadly, he was not the first Garda to die in such a manner, nor would he be the last.

AFTERWORD

The country was devastated and angry in equal measure after Patrick Morrissey's brutal and senseless killing. Morrissey was the twelfth Garda to die in fifteen years and Ireland seemed to have become a lawless and unsafe place for its citizens. The sergeant's horrific murder had led to widespread calls to provide rank and file Gardaí with guns. Many commentators also demanded that the death penalty be utilised for the first time in thirty years due to the brutality of the killing. Despite much debate about the ideas, neither of these calls would be acted upon. By this point, Irish public opinion had turned against capital punishment for once and for all. McHugh and Callan would be reprieved and would turn out to be the last people ever to receive the dreaded death penalty from the state. In 1990, the government passed the Criminal Justice Act which prohibited capital punishment for all crimes, including treason and capital murder. These offences would now receive a mandatory forty-year jail terms without parole instead. In 2001, Ireland went a step further when 62% of the Irish electorate voted to place a constitutional ban on the death penalty, even in wartime. Forty-seven years after the last execution by the state, the hangman's noose was put away forever; for better or for worse. Whether it had acted as a deterrent and a just punishment is for the reader to decide.